VFR Travel Res

ASPECTS OF TOURISM

Series Editors: **Chris Cooper** *(Oxford Brookes University, UK)*, **C. Michael Hall** *(University of Canterbury, New Zealand)* and **Dallen J. Timothy** *(Arizona State University, USA)*

Aspects of Tourism is an innovative, multifaceted series, which comprises authoritative reference handbooks on global tourism regions, research volumes, texts and monographs. It is designed to provide readers with the latest thinking on tourism worldwide and push back the frontiers of tourism knowledge. The volumes are authoritative, readable and user-friendly, providing accessible sources for further research. Books in the series are commissioned to probe the relationship between tourism and cognate subject areas such as strategy, development, retailing, sport and environmental studies.

Full details of all the books in this series and of all our other publications can be found on http://www.channelviewpublications.com, or by writing to Channel View Publications, St Nicholas House, 31-34 High Street, Bristol BS1 2AW, UK.

ASPECTS OF TOURISM: 69

VFR Travel Research

International Perspectives

Edited by
Elisa Backer and Brian King

CHANNEL VIEW PUBLICATIONS
Bristol • Buffalo • Toronto

Library of Congress Cataloging in Publication Data
A catalog record for this book is available from the Library of Congress.
VFR Travel Research: International Perspectives/Edited by Elisa Backer and Brian King.
Aspects of Tourism: 69
Includes bibliographical references and index.
1. Tourism—Research. 2. Tourism—Social aspects. 3. Families. 4. Friendship. I. Backer, Elisa, editor of compilation. II. King, Brian- editor of compilation. III. Title: Visiting friends and relatives travel research.
G155.A1V48 2015
338.4'791–dc 3 2015001851

British Library Cataloguing in Publication Data
A catalogue entry for this book is available from the British Library.

ISBN-13: 978-1-84541-518-1 (hbk)
ISBN-13: 978-1-84541-517-4 (pbk)

Channel View Publications
UK: St Nicholas House, 31-34 High Street, Bristol BS1 2AW, UK.
USA: UTP, 2250 Military Road, Tonawanda, NY 14150, USA.
Canada: UTP, 5201 Dufferin Street, North York, Ontario M3H 5T8, Canada.

Website: www.channelviewpublications.com
Twitter: Channel_View
Facebook: https://www.facebook.com/channelviewpublications
Blog: www.channelviewpublications.wordpress.com

The policy of Multilingual Matters/Channel View Publications is to use papers that are natural, renewable and recyclable products, made from wood grown in sustainable forests. In the manufacturing process of our books, and to further support our policy, preference is given to printers that have FSC and PEFC Chain of Custody certification. The FSC and/or PEFC logos will appear on those books where full certification has been granted to the printer concerned.

Typeset by Deanta Global Publishing Services Limited.
Printed and bound in Great Britain by Short Run Press Ltd.

Contents

Contributors

Elisa Backer PhD is an Associate Professor of Tourism at Federation University, Australia. She joined Federation University (previously called University of Ballarat) in 2008, after being at Southern Cross University for three years. Prior to working in academe, Elisa held management positions in industry, managing a range of destination marketing organisations. Elisa has co-edited three books and is on the editorial boards for 11 journals. In addition, she has been awarded 11 awards to recognise her outstanding contribution to tourism research and education. Her main research interest is VFR travel, but she also has research interests in destination marketing, partial industrialisation in tourism, social media and family tourism.

Jenny Cave is Senior Lecturer in Tourism and Hospitality at the University of Waikato, New Zealand. Dr Cave combines an academic background in anthropology, museology and tourism with 20 years' experience managing cultural industries in Canada and New Zealand. Her interest in 'visiting friends and relatives' emerges from 12 years of research about the relationship between migration, tourism and community development. Recent publications include 'Short-term visits and Tongan livelihoods: Enterprise and transnational exchange' *Population, Space and Place* (an A* journal), an edited book *Tourism and Souvenirs* (2013) with Lee Jolliffe and Tom Baum, and two special issues on island tourism.

Larry Dwyer PhD is Professor of Travel and Tourism Economics in the School of Marketing, Australian Business School, University of New South Wales. He publishes widely in the areas of tourism economics, management, policy and planning, with over 200 publications in international journals, books, government reports, chapters in books and monographs. Larry is a Fellow and current President of the International Academy for Study of Tourism. He is an appointed member of the International Advisory Board of the International Association for Tourism Economics and Building Excellence in Sustainable Tourism Education Network (BESTEN).

Zahed Ghaderi is a Senior Lecturer and Researcher in Tourism and Hospitality Management at Tehran universities. He has more than 17 years of both practical and teaching experience in the tourism industry. As a practical expert, he implemented several local, national and international tourism projects such as community-based ecotourism in Hewraman, Kurdistan, supported by UNDP, SGP and GEF. As an academician, he has published extensively in leading tourism and hospitality journals. His research interests include, but are not limited to, VFR travel, tourism management, ecotourism, tourism crisis management, organisational learning, sustainable tourism and destination management.

Tom Griffin is a Lecturer at Ryerson University in Toronto and a PhD candidate at the University of Waterloo. His thesis considers the experiences of immigrants who host visiting friends and relatives, and implications for integration and attachment, community development and place making, and destination marketing. Tom has an MA in Tourism and Sustainability from the University of the West of England and a BA Hons in International Development from the University of East London. Previously Tom worked in research at Tourism Toronto, the regional destination marketing organisation, and has participated in various tourism development projects with community and government organisations.

C. Michael Hall is a Professor in the Department of Management, Marketing and Entrepreneurship, University of Canterbury, New Zealand and Docent, University of Oulu, Finland. He also holds positions as a visiting professor at Linneaus University, Sweden and the University of Eastern Finland and at the University of Mauritius. Co-editor of *Current Issues in Tourism*, he has published widely in tourism, regional development, environmental history and gastronomy. Current research projects focus on climate change, sustainable mobility, green hotels in Freiburg, second homes and mobility in the Nordic countries, and World Heritage in Israel, Mauritius and Norway.

Brian Hay is an Honorary Professor at Heriot-Watt University and works as an independent tourism research consultant and freelance academic. Prior to this appointment, he worked for 20 years as Head of Research at VisitScotland/Scottish Tourist Board, where he oversaw its research programme, during which time he also held a number of visiting professorships. He has published a wide range of academic and industry-focused papers on an eclectic mix of tourism and hospitality topics and considers himself to be a generalist researcher. His qualifications range from a first degree in Town Planning from Heriot-Watt University through to a PhD from Texas A&M University.

Jung Eun Kim is an Assistant Professor in the Program of Recreation, Tourism and Hospitality Management at the University of Northern Colorado. She earned her PhD in Tourism Management from the University of Florida. She teaches Commercial Recreation, Tourism and Hospitality, Leadership in Tourism and Hospitality, and Event Programming and Management. Her research interests are in corporate social responsibility in tourism, tourism behaviours, tourism destination management strategies and event and festival management.

Brian King is Professor and Associate Dean in the School of Hotel and Tourism Management at Hong Kong Polytechnic University. He was previously at Victoria University, Australia as Head of the School of Hospitality, Tourism & Marketing and later as Pro Vice-Chancellor (Industry & Community). His research specialisation is tourism marketing with an emphasis on cultural dimensions and emerging Asia-Pacific markets. He has published books and journal articles on tourism marketing, resorts and tourism in the Asia-Pacific Region. He is co-editor-in-chief of *Tourism, Culture and Communication* and a fellow of the International Academy for the Study of Tourism. He holds a number of industry board positions and has held senior roles in the tour operations, airlines, cruise and destination management sectors. He has had a longstanding professional interest in VFR travel, having migrated from Scotland to Australia in the 1980s followed by frequent return visits involving friends and family members.

Gyehee Lee is a Professor in the Department of Tourism Sciences at Kyung Hee University, Seoul Korea. She earned her PhD in Tourism Marketing from Purdue University. She has published numerous research papers in both tourism and hospitality top journals. She actively serves several national tourism boards and committees for federal and regional government in South Korea. She teaches Destination Marketing Communication and Tourism Marketing Research for undergraduate students and Tourism Research Methods for graduate students at KHU. She is currently appointed as a visiting scholar at Colorado State University, in the Department of Human Dimension of Wildlife.

Alastair Morrison is a Distinguished Professor specialising in the area of tourism and hospitality planning, development and marketing in the School of Hospitality and Tourism Management at Purdue University, USA. He is the CEO of Belle Tourism International Consulting and the director for International Research and Communication at the International Center for Recreation and Tourism Research at Peking University. He serves as the president of the International Tourism Studies and is the co-editor of the *International Journal of Tourism Cities*. Professor Morrison is the author of five leading tourism books and was placed among the five top tourism contributors in the world.

Nandini Nadkarni is Vice President of Analytical Operations and Customer Insights at D.K. Shifflet & Associates Ltd. Her graduate degrees are from Purdue University. She has also worked at Best Buy and University of Illinois. She has an extensive background in consumer behaviour and the application of statistical techniques to model customer behaviour, assess brand effectiveness and conduct target segmentation using statistical techniques such as regression, factor and cluster analysis, and data mining.

Joseph O'Leary is a Professor in International Tourism at Colorado State University. His graduate degrees are from the University of Washington and Yale. He was a faculty member at Purdue University, served as department head at Texas A&M in Recreation, Park and Tourism Sciences and was dean at Colorado State University. His research interests are in recreation and tourism behaviour and the use of large data resources. He teaches undergraduate and graduate courses most recently in the Master of Tourism Management distance education programme.

Antonino Mario Oliveri is Associate Professor of Social Statistics at the School of Humanities and Heritage of Università degli Studi di Palermo, Italy. His main research interests in tourism focus on the analysis of tourist behaviours and attitudes, as well as on measurement issues related to attractiveness and tourism impacts. His publications cover a range of topics, including the review and use of quantitative methods for tourism and research methods for the investigation of local tourism. He is the co-editor of the McGraw-Hill book series on Tourism Sciences.

Christian M. Rogerson is Professor at the School of Tourism and Hospitality, University of Johannesburg. His research interests are focused on the tourism-development nexus and issues of small business development and local economic development. Among his recent publications are the following co-edited books: *Tourism and Development Issues in Contemporary South Africa* (2004 with G. Visser); *Urban Tourism in the Developing World: The South African Experience* (2007 with G. Visser); and *Tourism and the Millennium Development Goals* (2013 with J. Saarinen and H. Manwa).

Tony Seaton is MacAnally Professor of Tourism Behaviour at the University of Limerick, Ireland, and Emeritus Professor of Tourism Behaviour at the University of Bedfordshire. He has taught and published widely on tourism marketing, behaviour and history, with special focus on Thanatourism and literary and cultural tourism. He has consulted, researched and worked for many international organisations, including the UNWTO, EU, ETC, governments, and for academic and historical libraries in Ireland, America and the UK. His current research interests are in Thanatourism history and the iconography and representation of travel and tourism in art, graphic satire and literature.

Caroline Tie is a Senior Lecturer in Hotel and Hospitality Management at the University of Bedfordshire. She has researched and published on the functional place of travel and tourism in self-perception, the construction and maintenance of diasporic identity, and the generational differences that they produce, with special focus on travel by Sarawakian-Chinese to the People's Republic of China (PRC), their 'ancestral homeland'. She is currently engaged in an ongoing three-year research programme on the attitudes of indigenous residents to festival and event developments in Malaysia as community heritage initiatives, which has involved performance observations and interview surveys of Chinese in Sarawak.

1 VFR Travel: Progressing Towards Greater Recognition

Elisa Backer and Brian King

Introduction

As a form of tourism, Visiting Friends and Relatives (VFR) travel is global in its reach and is recognised in academe and industry as being substantial in its scope. It may also be the oldest form of travel (Backer, 2011), with the first recognised VFR traveller being Celia Fiennes, who constructed travel schedules around visits to friends and relatives between 1685 and 1712 (Leiper, 2004). Despite its size and long history, VFR has been largely overlooked by academics and practitioners. Whilst some academics have researched the field, VFR travel is considerably behind other spheres of tourism in terms of understanding and awareness.

VFR travel researchers have consistently observed the neglect of the topic (Backer, 2010, 2012; Braunlich & Nadkarni, 1995; Hay, 1996, 2008; Jackson, 1990, 2003; King, 1996; McKercher, 1995; Morrison *et al.*, 1995; Page & Connell, 2009; Seaton & Palmer, 1997; Seaton, 1994; Seaton & Tagg, 1995; Yaman, 1996). The 'forgotten' status of VFR travel is also evidenced by its absence in scholarly books and monographs. Many of the tourism books claim to offer a 'big picture' view of the subject, but focus on business dimensions such as marketing, management, economics and research. There are also research books devoted to ever narrower segments such as dark tourism, gastronomy tourism, sports tourism, events tourism and wellness tourism. The topics that have been the focus of analysis have become progressively more specific and now extend to slow tourism, battlefield tourism, horse tourism, island tourism, tea tourism, cricket tourism, spices tourism, sugar heritage tourism, marine tourism and scuba diving tourism. Despite the proliferation of coverage there has been no VFR-related book. Though VFR constitutes a large share of tourism activity, it has received less attention by academic researchers than other much smaller dimensions of the tourism phenomenon. It is therefore surprising that this book is the first on VFR travel. It assembles a collection of research from several continents. Some of the core issues that are covered in the book include measurement, migration links, the role of the host, the distinction between VRs and VFs, marketing and case studies.

History

The idea for this book originated in late 2013; the collaboration between the co-editors progressed from Brian King's examination of Elisa Backer's PhD thesis (in VFR travel) (another examiner, Brian Hay, has also contributed to this book). Following a face-to-face meeting at a Council of Australasian University Tourism & Hospitality Education (CAUTHE) conference after the PhD had been passed, discussions about research evolved and continued over subsequent CAUTHE conferences. This project represents a shared vision about the merit of championing VFR as a significant social and economic phenomenon. It also represents a commitment to quality and it is pleasing that the collaboration has been very smooth. The authors contributed to a common goal and were enthusiastic and punctual, leading to a rewarding experience.

Research on VFR travel is relatively new, with the first seminal paper in the field being published in 1990 (Jackson, 1990). VFR-related research activity intensified during the mid-1990s following the appearance of a special VFR issue of a tourism journal (*The Journal of Tourism Studies* 6 (1)). The guest editors of the special issue were Alastair Morrison and Joe O'Leary and it is pleasing that both have contributed to the present volume. Two other authors from the special issue, Nandini Nadkarni and Tony Seaton, are also contributors.

An international conference dedicated to VFR was hosted in the mid-1990s. Held at Victoria University (Australia), the 1996 conference saw a collection of research assembled in the form of proceedings that continue to be an important source for VFR researchers. Three of the contributors – Brian King, Tony Seaton and Brian Hay – have contributed to the present volume.

A trickle of research appeared over the following decade but no real momentum was generated. More recently, a new wave of researchers has entered the domain and many have contributed to the present volume. Reflecting on the past two decades of VFR research, there has been no significant boost-point since the special issue and conference during the mid-1990s. It is hoped that this book will provide academics and practitioners with a useful resource to further knowledge and application of this substantial form of tourism.

Contents

The book may be read either sequentially or as single chapters and/or sections. Following this introductory chapter, the next section is VFR Travellers: Understanding the World's Largest Travel Segment. The relevant chapters – 2 to 7 – provide the reader with an understanding about VFR Travel. Chapter 2 is co-authored by Alastair Morrison, who is now based in China, and Elisa Backer, based in Australia, and discusses the value and contributions of VFR travel to destinations. It highlights the important role of the destination marketing organisation (DMO) as a vehicle for applying and implementing VFR initiatives. The chapter discusses the findings from two rounds of empirical research to ascertain what DMOs in Australia perceive and know about VFR travel. The findings of research undertaken in 2009 reveal that most DMOs know little about VFR travel and incorrectly assume that it is a market which needs minimal dedicated attention and can be a by-product of marketing to the leisure market. At that time, DMOs expressed reluctance to engage in marketing to VFR travellers on the basis that VFR travellers are inactive, are modest in their spending and will arrive irrespective of any destination-based marketing. The research was replicated four years later (in 2013) to determine whether perceptions had changed. The findings are presented in the relevant chapter and should be of interest to both academics and practitioners.

The co-authors of Chapter 3 are Tony Seaton, who is based in Ireland, and the UK-based Caroline Ti. They write about the important distinction between those who visit friends (VFs) and those who visit their relatives (VRs). In the mid-1990s, Tony Seaton undertook research to highlight the difference between VFs and VRs (Seaton, 1994, 1996; Seaton & Tagg, 1995), arguing the case for disaggregating VFR into two subsections. Given the inadequate attention that has been devoted to the distinction between the two groups, the chapter makes an important contribution. The chapter authors draw upon findings from their primary research interviews as well as from secondary research to reveal the profiles and characteristics of the two separate groups.

The fourth chapter discusses the VFR/migration relationship and is co-authored by Brian King, based in Hong Kong, and Larry Dwyer, based in Australia. The authors have been active in the VFR/migration space in recent years and discuss the correlation between migration flows and VFR travel. VFR and migration are major forms of human mobility both domestically and internationally. Understanding how they interconnect can provide insights into future scholarly work on human mobilities that extend beyond the tourism domain. Their chapter is followed by a discussion on the true size and dimensions of VFR by Elisa Backer. The author notes that, because of a lack of measurement, VFR travel is frequently underestimated and misunderstood. Official data only provide information about the proportion of travellers who stated a VFR purpose of visit *or* stayed in the homes of friends/relatives. Neither statistic measures the size of the segment. The chapter provides information on the actual size of the segment and outlines the profiles and characteristics of VFR travellers relative to non-VFRs.

The author of Chapter 6 is Tom Griffin from Canada. His chapter discusses the important role that hosts play in accommodating VFR travellers. The author notes that the limited research that has been undertaken on VFR has focused on the visitor, whereas host experiences also merit attention. The final chapter in the section examines a range of VFR travel campaigns. Co-authored by Elisa Backer and UK-based Brian Hay, it outlines a range of successful VFR travel marketing campaigns from across the globe. Some of the highlighted campaigns relate to small regional communities, whilst others are nationwide in scope. One of the featured cases refers to a VFR initiative conducted by a transport company, the largest ever marketing campaign undertaken by this organisation. Some of the VFR marketing campaigns that are featured were recipients of substantial advertising and/or industry awards. The chapter may be of particular interest to practitioners and provide insights into implementing VFR campaigns in their own destination or for their own organisation.

The following section (Chapters 8 to 13) is VFR Travel Profiles – Perspectives on Developed and Emerging Countries. This diverse section presents the profiles and characteristics of VFR travellers from various regions of the world. As noted by Griffin (2013), VFR research authors have been predominantly based in Australia/New Zealand, Europe and North America and little research has emanated from other countries and regions. Most VFR travel publications have been destination focused (Griffin, 2013). Furthermore, while researchers based at European institutions have contributed to a substantial proportion of existing VFR research, only 7 out of the 12 articles (15.2% of the total number) focused on a European destination (Griffin, 2013). As revealed in Table 1.1, only 46 tourism articles on VFR research were published in journals (with 39 of those in tourism journals) between 1990 and 2010. It is evident that there has been some growth over time, but the sample size is modest, particularly in view of the size of VFR travel.

This section of the book provides important insights into VFR travel by comparing and contrasting the findings from different countries. Though

Table 1.1 VFR journal paper author origin over time

Location	1990–1996 (n=6)	1997–2003 (n=19)	2004–2010 (n=21)	Total (n=46)
North America	66.6%	34.2%	34.7%	38.7%
Europe	16.7%	31.6%	23.8%	26.1%
Australia/NZ	16.7%	34.2%	21.4%	26.1%
Africa	-	-	14.3%	6.5%
Asia	-	-	5.7%	2.6%
Total	100%	100%	100%	100%

Source: Griffin (2013: 790).

the section could not cover every continent it provides an important extension to the limited geographic spread of previous VFR research.

Chapter 8 by Zahed Ghaderi, based in Malaysia, examines the profiles of VFRs from Iran and draws upon the results of two separate data sources – a domestic tourism study and a household travel study. These findings have allowed the author to identify the demographic profiles and travel characteristics of VFR travellers in Iran. His chapter emphasises the importance of VFR travel for destinations of all types, highlighting that a region does not need to have major tourism attractions or natural scenery in order to benefit from VFR travel.

In Chapter 9 the focus of attention shifts to North America. Together with Gyehee Lee, Nandini Nadkarni and Jung Eun Kim, Joe O'Leary outlines the profiles and characteristics of VFR travellers in the United States. As was the case in the previous chapter, the authors deploy a large national data set involving an annual collection of 60,000 travelling households. In addition to discussing the traveller profiles, it also considers the differences before and after the economic downturn.

Chapter 10 on South Africa by Christian Rogerson highlights the importance of VFR travel for a number of expanding cities in the country. The author notes that the four destinations of Ethekwini (Durban), Johannesburg, Ekurhuleni and Tshwane (Pretoria) jointly account for almost one-quarter of all VFR travel in South Africa. He also highlights that various district level destinations are substantial beneficiaries of VFR travel.

In Chapter 11 Antonino Oliveri focuses on the VFR travel phenomenon in Sicily, Italy. The size of VFR travel in Italy is presented using an analysis of data from the official tourism surveys. This is done in three ways. Firstly the size of VFR travel is based only on purpose of visit data. The proportion of VFR travellers is revealed on the basis of accommodation type. Drawing upon the VFR Definitional Model, the author then aggregates the three types of VFR travellers to assess the real size of the segment in Italy. A range of statistical tests were undertaken, including an assessment of the profiles of Commercial VFRs (CVFRs) – i.e. VFRs staying in commercial accommodation relative to VFRs who were staying in the homes of friends/relatives.

Chapter 12 presents critical information about VFR travel in Abu Dhabi (in the United Arab Emirates or UAE). Authored by Hamed Suwaidi, Shabbar Jaffry and Alexandros Apostolakis, the chapter assesses VFR travel in light of the large expatriate community that is present in the UAE and the strength of the tourism market. The chapter offers a demand-based analysis and contributes to the field by comparing and contrasting VFR travellers with non-VFR travellers.

The section concludes with a chapter by Jenny Cave and C. Michael Hall on VFR travel in the Pacific. Their chapter stresses the importance of family to the Pacific Island people, arguing that it is the family that binds society in the Pacific over and above anything else including government. The chapter provides a valuable perspective on the history of the Asia-Pacific region from the pre-colonial period and contributes to understanding VFR travel more broadly.

The final section of the book, VFR Travel Futures, concludes with a chapter (14) by the editors. It highlights where VFR travel has been and its potential future directions from both an applied and a research perspective.

Methods

The authors of the various chapters in this book have deployed a range of research methods. As noted by Griffin (2013), previous VFR research has been strongly characterised by quantitative approaches (71.7%) with almost half having relied on secondary data. This book offers a number of typically non-empirical chapters (Chapters 4, 6 and 13 contain no empirical research). Chapter 2 is qualitative, Chapter 7 is case-study based, Chapter 3 uses mixed methods and the remainder are quantitative in their emphasis.

The authors of the various quantitative chapters have employed various approaches to conduct their analyses on large-scale national tourism databases. One limitation of using official tourism databases is, however, that the researcher is bound by the questions and the format, thereby restricting potential analysis. Some of the quantitative research chapters provided an analysis based on the VFR definitional model (i.e. an aggregation of the three VFR types), while some analysed data were based exclusively on purpose of visit.

VFR Travel: A Paradigm Shift?

The term VFR travel has been used purposefully throughout this book. The VFR literature reveals some interchangeability between the terms 'VFR tourism' and 'VFR travel'. However, Backer has noted that 'tourism and travel are not the same' (2012: 74). The seminal VFR paper (Jackson, 1990) used the term 'VFR tourism' as he asked the question in his article title 'VFR tourism: is it underestimated?'. Two decades later, the question was answered but with a change in terminology, 'VFR travel: it *is* underestimated' (Backer, 2012).

In reviewing the evolution of VFR-related scholarly papers, the editors note that a mixture in terms was used during the debates which characterised the mid-1990s. The special VFR issue of the tourism journal that was mentioned previously contained six articles, including the editorial introduction, which all applied different terms. Most of the articles used neither expression in their title and the authors chose to refer to the term VFR 'market' (Braunlich & Nadkarni, 1995; Morrison *et al.*, 1995;

Morrison & O'Leary, 1995; Yuan *et al.*, 1995) or 'visitor' (Meis *et al.*, 1995). However, one used the term 'tourism', one avoided the use of either 'tourism' or 'travel' throughout the article, while four used the term 'travel' in the body of the article (Braunlich & Nadkarni, 1995; Morrison *et al.*, 1995; Morrison & O'Leary, 1995; Yuan *et al.*, 1995).

The proceedings of the international VFR conference that was held in the following year referred to 'VFR tourism: Issues and implications' (Yaman, 1996). These proceedings contained seven papers including an introduction by the editor, although one of the publications was a collection of PowerPoint slides, not an article. Four publications used the term 'VFR tourism', while one used the term 'market' and two used the term 'VFR travel'.

Over the past two decades authors appear to have opted for their personally preferred term, with some using 'travel' (for example McKercher, 1994, 1996; Navarro & Turco, 2004) and others using the term 'tourism' (for example Bischoff & Koenig-Lewis, 2007; Boyne, 2001; Shani & Uriely, 2012). However, alternating between the terms 'VFR travel', 'VFR tourism' and 'VFR market' in the one paper has also occurred (for example McKercher, 1995). A recent 'think tank' dedicated to VFR and hosted at the University of Surrey in Guildford, UK (on 13 July 2013) adopted the term 'travel', calling the think tank 'Reconceptualising Visiting Friends and Relatives (VFR Travel)'.

Noting the inconsistency of terminology that has been prevalent since 1990, the present volume has made systematic use of the term 'VFR travel'. In adopting this approach it is acknowledged that official data may include people travelling to a destination for VFR purposes who are engaging in activities such as attending a funeral, assisting with the care of a newborn baby or visiting an ailing friend/relative (Backer, 2012). Though travelling for VFR purposes, this group may encounter no tourist-related experiences during their stay. They may spend money in the local economy, but may do so without pursuing leisure or interacting with the destination. On this basis they are not tourists and should not be considered as such; they are, however, travellers (Backer, 2012).

VFR Travel: The Importance of Disaggregation

An important point about disaggregating VFRs is made in Chapter 3, which highlights differences between VFs and VRs. It is an important reminder that much is concealed behind averages. This was exemplified by primary research that was undertaken in four local government areas in Melbourne, Australia. The combined data demonstrated a wide range of VFR and host profiles and characteristics. However, more detailed analysis at the individual local government area level revealed a different picture. This highlights the risk for practitioners of making decisions on the basis of 'big picture' data. In such cases, marketing campaigns may be misdirected because of a potential skewing of information from the data applicable to a neighbouring region. This can be particularly well demonstrated by considering the data in Table 1.2, which presents selected VFR profiles and characteristics.

The aggregated data column in Table 1.2 refers to data that has been derived from a report undertaken for local government and industry in Melbourne, Australia (Backer & Lynch, 2011). The data were drawn primarily from primary research undertaken for four local government areas, supported by Destination Melbourne, the relevant destination marketing organisation. Such data were used by Destination Melbourne and also the Victorian transport company V/Line to inform relevant VFR marketing campaigns (these are introduced briefly in the following chapter and discussed in Chapter 7).

As is evident in Table 1.2, aggregated data indicate that almost two-thirds of VFR travellers are VRs, and almost one-quarter of VFRs are from overseas. However, the data from each of the four LGAs highlight the distinctiveness of each region, with Maroondah only having 19% VFs and only 1% international VFRs. In contrast, Dandenong had a more even VR/VF composition and 57% international VFRs. Similarly, the average

Table 1.2 VFR profiles and characteristics from four LGAs within Greater Melbourne, Australia

	Aggregated data	Wyndham	Dandenong	Manningham	Maroondah
VRs/VFs	VRs (62%) VFs (38%)	VRs (59%) VFs (41%)	VRs (55%) VFs (45%)	VRs (54%) VFs (46%)	VRs (81%) VFs (19%)
Proportion of international visitors	VFRs (24%) Non-VFRs (8%)	VFRs (24%) Non-VFRs (21%)	VFRs (57%) Non-VFRs (3%)	VFRs (10%) Non-VFRs (0%)	VFRs (1%) Non-VFRs (0%)
Travel party size	3.2	3.5	3.1	3.5	3.0
Length of stay (nights)	3.7	1.21	10.15	1.33	0.75
Daily visitor expenditure	VFR ($288) Non-VFR ($140)	VFR ($171) Non-VFR ($188)	VFR ($500) Non-VFR (158)	VFR ($209) Non-VFR ($98)	VFR ($215) Non-VFR ($103)
Total expenditure (including hosts' outlays)	VFR ($398) Non-VFR ($140)	N/A	N/A	N/A	N/A

Source: Backer and Lynch (2011) and analysis of author's (Backer) data.

length of stay across the four LGAs is 3.7 nights; yet this has been heavily boosted by Dandenong's 10.15 night average. Meanwhile, the other three regions have very low average length of stays.

These findings are interesting to note from an academic perspective. However, such differences also have relevance for operators. Developing a promotional campaign on the basis of LGA level aggregated data could lead to misplaced decisions. Embarking upon an international marketing campaign on the basis of anticipated market potential could be misplaced in some regional settings.

Conclusions

The authors who have contributed the various chapters of this book are based in a wide range of countries and regions and a section has been dedicated to understanding VFR in different country settings. The interpretation of data that has been gathered in different places reveals distinct patterns of social and familial networks and interactions in destination settings. The use of evidence gathered from a variety of settings informs various VFR-related themes including migration, the role of the host, the size of the VFR phenomenon, case studies of VFR marketing campaigns, disaggregation into VF/VR and the role of DMOs in promoting VFR.

In the mid-1990s when VFR research first started to appear in tourism journals, special issue guest editors Alastair Morrison and Joe O'Leary wrote that VFR travel was 'desperately seeking respect' (Morrison & O'Leary, 1995: 2). Two decades later, the editors of this book make the same claim – that VFR travel is *still* desperately seeking respect. It is hoped that this book will provide an impetus to grant VFR the respect that it is still seeking.

References

Backer, E. (2010) Opportunities for commercial accommodation in VFR. *International Journal of Tourism Research* 12 (4), 334–354.

Backer, E. (2011) VFR travellers of the future. In I. Yeoman, C. Hsu, K. Smith and S. Watson (eds) *Tourism and Demography* (pp. 74–84). Oxford: Goodfellow Publishers.

Backer, E. (2012) VFR Travel: It *is* underestimated. *Tourism Management* 33 (1), 74–79.

Backer, E. and Lynch, D. (2011) *VFR Travel Research Project: Melbourne*. University of Ballarat: Ballarat.

Bischoff, E.E. and Koenig-Lewis, N. (2007) VFR tourism: The importance of university students as hosts. *International Journal of Tourism Research* 484 (June), 465–484.

Boyne, S. (2001) Hosts, friends and relatives in rural Scotland: VFR tourism market relationships explored. In L. Roberts and D. Hall (eds) *Rural Tourism and Recreation: Principles to Practice* (pp. 41–43). Wallingford: CABI Publishing.

Braunlich, C. and Nadkarni, N. (1995) The importance of the VFR market to the hotel industry. *The Journal of Tourism Studies* 6 (1), 38–47.

Griffin, T. (2013) Research note: A content analysis of articles on visiting friends and relatives tourism, 1990–2010. *Journal of Hospitality Marketing & Management* (June 2013), 1–22.

Hay, B. (1996) An insight into the European experience: A case study on domestic VFR tourism within the UK. In H. Yaman (ed.) *VFR Tourism: Issues and Implications. Proceedings from the Conference Held at Victoria University of Technology* (pp. 52–66).

Hay, B. (2008) An exploration of the differences in the volume and value of visiting friends and visiting relatives tourism in the UK. In S. Richardson, L. Fredline, A. Patiar and M. Ternel (eds) *CAUTHE 2008 Where the Bloody Hell Are We?: Proceedings of the CAUTHE Conference Held in Gold Coast, Australia, 11–14 February 2008* (pp. 488–497). Gold Coast: Griffith University.

Jackson, R. (1990) VFR Tourism: Is it underestimated? *The Journal of Tourism Studies* 1 (2), 10–17.

Jackson, R. (2003) VFR Tourism: Is it underestimated? *The Journal of Tourism Studies* 14 (1), 17–24. Melbourne: Victoria University of Technology.

King, B. (1996). VFR – A future research agenda. In H. Yaman (ed.) *VFR Tourism: Issues and Implications. Proceedings from the Conference Held at Victoria University Conference, Victoria, Australia.* (pp. 85–89).

Leiper, N. (2004) *Tourism Management* (3rd edn). Frenchs Forest: Pearson Education.

McKercher, B. (1994) *Report on a Study of Host Involvement in VFR Travel to Albury Wodonga.* Albury-Wodonga.

McKercher, B. (1995) An examination of host involvement in VFR travel. In R. Shaw (ed.) *Proceedings from the National Tourism and Hospitality Conference, 14–17 February 1995. Council for Australian University Tourism and Hospitality Education* (pp. 246–255). Canberra, ACT: Bureau of Tourism Research.

McKercher, B. (1996) Host involvement in VFR travel. *Annals of Tourism Research* 23 (3), 701–703. Charles Sturt University.

Meis, S., Joyal, S. and Trites, A. (1995) The U.S. repeat and VFR cisitor to Canada: Come again eh! *The Journal of Tourism Studies* 6 (1), 27–37.

Morrison, A., Hsieh, S. and O'Leary, J. (1995) Segmenting the visiting friends and relatives market by holiday activity participation. *The Journal of Tourism Studies* 6 (1), 48–63.

Morrison, A. and O'Leary, J. (1995) The VFR market: Desperately seeking respect. *The Journal of Tourism Studies* 6 (1), 1–5.

Navarro, R. and Turco, D. (2004) Segmentation of the visiting friends and relatives travel market. *Visions in Leisure and Business* 13 (1), 4–16.

Page, S. and Connell, J. (2009) *Tourism: A Modern Synthesis* (3rd edn). China: Cengage Learning.

Seaton, A. (1994) Are relatives friends? Reassessing the VFR category in segmenting tourism markets. In A. Seaton (ed.) *Tourism: The State of the Art* (pp. 316–321). Chichester: Wiley.

Seaton, A. (1996) Making (even more) sense of the AFR category in tourism analysis. In H. Yaman (ed.) *VFR Tourism: Issues and Implications.* Melbourne: Victoria University of Technology.

Seaton, A. and Palmer, C. (1997) Understanding VFR tourism behaviour: The first five years of the United Kingdom tourism survey. *Tourism Management* 18 (6), 345–355.

Seaton, A.V. and Tagg, S. (1995) Disaggregating friends and relatives in VFR tourism research: The Northern Ireland evidence 1991–1993. *The Journal of Tourism Studies* 6 (1), 6–18.

Shani, A. V. and Uriely, N. (2012) VFR tourism. *Annals of Tourism Research* 39 (1), 421–440.

Yaman, H. (1996) VFR tourism: Issues and implications. In *VFR Tourism: Issues and Implications, Proceedings from the Conference.* Melbourne: Victoria University of Technology.

Yuan, T., Fridgen, J., Hsieh, S. and O'Leary, J. (1995) Visiting friends and relatives travel market: The Dutch case. *The Journal of Tourism Studies* 6 (1), 19–26.

Part 1

VFR Travellers: Understanding the World's Largest Travel Segment

2 The Value and Contributions of VFR to Destinations and Destination Marketing

Elisa Backer and Alastair M. Morrison

Introduction

As outlined in the introductory chapter of this book, Visiting Friends and Relatives (VFR) travel is a substantially large tourism segment throughout the world. Indeed, it is surprising that, despite the size of VFR travel, Destination Marketing Organisations (DMOs) have generally failed to consider VFR travel in any major way. Given the important role that DMOs hold in terms of marketing tourism, the understanding that DMOs have concerning VFR travel is an important key to grasping how VFR is perceived by industry. It is therefore appropriate that a chapter is dedicated to discussing the value and contributions of VFR travel to destinations.

This chapter will firstly provide a background and touch briefly on the significance of VFR travel and its value. However, only a brief discussion will be held on that area, as the size of the 'market' and its value is discussed in detail through Chapter 5. This chapter will then provide a literature review focusing on the attention dedicated to examining the link between VFR and DMOs and will then provide empirical research undertaken that considered how VFR travel has been historically perceived by DMOs. This chapter will be concluded by introducing a number of successful VFR travel case studies, which are subsequently discussed in detail in Chapter 7.

Background

One of the largest and most significant forms of tourism is VFR travel, which is recognised as being a sizable form of travel worldwide. The size of this form of travel has been reported as comprising around half of the US pleasure traveller market (Braunlich & Nadkarni, 1995; Hu & Morrison, 2002) and around half of the domestic travel market in many developed countries (BBC World News, 2009). As outlined in Chapter 5, it is also around half of Australia's tourism market.

Despite the size of VFR travel, it tends to be overlooked as a market segment and rarely appears in the marketing plans of DMOs and tourism businesses. Part of the reason for this is the lack of education in the relationship of VFR travellers with industries, and as such an assumption that VFR travellers do not participate in tourism activities and inject negligible funds into local economies (Backer, 2007). In addition, the relationship that the host has in shaping VFR trips has been under-researched and has not been fully explored as a marketing opportunity. The lack of attention given to VFR travel has been bemoaned by VFR researchers for almost two decades, as discussed in the previous chapter.

Literature Review

It was over a decade ago when Morrison, Woods *et al*. (2000) considered the perceptions of VFR travel by DMOs and highlighted the importance of offering specific marketing campaigns targeting VFR travellers. By the mid-2000s, VFR travel was being recognised by researchers in the field as providing substantial benefits to many regions. However, despite those research findings, VFR tends to be grouped together with other visitors by DMOs. In research undertaken by Morrison, Woods *et al*. (2000), DMOs were surveyed to ascertain whether they specifically target VFR travellers in their marketing or whether VFR travellers are 'lumped together with other groups of visitors' (106). The researchers concluded that a majority of tourism organisations did not specifically market to VFR travellers. This was in part due to the perceived disadvantages associated with VFR travel, with one of the main perceived disadvantages being that VFR travellers have low expenditure levels (Morrison, Woods *et al*., 2000).

However, a number of studies have demonstrated that this perception does not reflect the actual levels of expenditures by VFR travellers. This is in part because a lower daily spend can be compensated by VFR length of stay, resulting in spending over a longer period (Hay, 1996; Seaton, 1994). More specifically, in some expenditure categories, VFR travellers were shown to outspend non-VFR travellers (Morrison, Verginis *et al*., 2000; Seaton & Palmer, 1997). In fact, much of the lower overall expenditure levels can be attributed to the smaller expenditures by VFR travellers on packaged tours and accommodation (Seaton & Palmer, 1997).

This notion is evident through research examining the economic contribution of French VFR overseas travellers (Lee *et al*., 2005). While the overall expenditure by VFR travellers was lower than for other categories, this was mainly driven by the lower accommodation and package tours amounts. VFR travellers spent more on shopping, meals and 'other' than the pleasure market. The perception that VFR travellers make little use of accommodation, food and beverage operations was found to be unsubstantiated in a US study conducted in Illinois (Navarro & Turco, 2004). Their study found VFR travellers to actively participate in activities and attend events, as well as being consumers of accommodation facilities and restaurants.

The 'relatively low spend' by VFR travellers (Seaton & Palmer, 1997: 347) can be viewed as being a misleading statement because the key factors accounting for their lower expenditures are the virtual absence of package trip costs and minimal accommodation expenses (Seaton & Palmer, 1997). Once these categories were removed, VFR expenditures were found to be in some cases higher than non-VFR travellers (Seaton & Palmer, 1997). Their expenditures also tend to be quite broad, spread widely throughout the community rather than confined to the narrow tourism sector (Backer, 2007, 2010; McKercher, 1994). In addition, while VFR travellers are not inclined to be large purchasers of packaged holidays (Hay, 1996; McKercher, 1994; Seaton, 1996), their expenditure on travel, shopping, and on food and beverages is at least as high as other tourists (Backer, 2007, 2010, 2012; Seaton, 1996). Jackson (1990) showed that the average per trip values for VFR travellers to Australia were only around 15% lower than other holiday travellers, being $1,305 compared to holidaymakers' $1,530 spend. Furthermore, Jackson (1990) pointed out that the real economic benefit of VFR travel may actually be as great as that of non-VFR travel since VFR expenditures tend to be more direct and localised with fewer leakages from the economy.

However, despite the research demonstrating the benefits that VFR travellers can bring to destinations, it is not understood whether these benefits are realised by industry. Certainly, the findings from Morrison, Woods et al. (2000) suggested that many DMOs had not considered VFR to be a segment worthy of directing specific campaigns to. This chapter will outline whether DMO perceptions changed, based on interviewing DMOs in Australia.

Method

Qualitative research was considered the most appropriate method for this study. This method can be useful to add depth into areas that are relatively unknown because it involves collecting and analysing information rather than numerical data (Minichiello et al., 2008). Little research has been undertaken to understand what senior managers of DMOs believe regarding VFR travel in their regions. The only research undertaken to examine this based on the literature reviewed was Morrison, Woods et al. (2000), which used quantitative analysis. Some statistical comparability of the interviews was desired for this study in order to draw some conclusions from the differences in DMO perceptions from those found in the Morrison, Woods *et al.* (2000) study. However, some flexibility was desired and there was an interest to go beyond close-ended questions. Therefore, a semi-structured to structured approach was adopted, which was in between those two approaches. It was deliberately exploratory in order to gauge perceptions and issues and probe opinions.

In order to achieve this, the general managers or chief executive officers of Regional Tourism Organisations (RTOs) in Australia were identified as the most appropriate group to interview. As the perceptions of DMOs were wanted, receiving these at an RTO level seemed appropriate, since at this level, the organisations have dealings with State Tourism Organisations (STOs) as well as Local Tourism Organisations (LTOs) and are closely associated with a wide range of tourism industries and typically operate Visitor Information Centres (VICs). As a result, these respondents would be well-positioned to address the issues pertinent to answering the questions. A database of RTOs within Australia was collected through accessing publicly available information and all heads of these organisations were invited to participate in the research.

This research reports on the key findings from two rounds of surveying, undertaken four years apart. The same questions asked in 2009 were repeated in 2013 to determine whether the perceptions had changed as new research revealed more information. The initial research was undertaken in 2009, with an overall response rate of 47 organisations (77%). Telephone interviews were undertaken, which were semi-structured in format, and each typically lasted around 40–50 minutes, with some taking around 60 minutes. Key points were written down during the interview and read back to the participants to ensure they were satisfied that this reflected their perspective accurately. The responses were then typed up and forwarded via email to each participant to enable the respondent to make alterations if they did not feel that the transcript reflected their thoughts adequately. The questions were then repeated in 2013, except the questions were asked online using an online survey instrument. The sample size was much lower, with only 22 organisations participating. Responses were exported to SPSS. Both sets of data were analysed using thematic analysis.

Results

This section will report on the key findings from the research. There were 19 questions asked each time, and some of the questions involved very detailed responses. As such, this chapter will only concentrate on discussing some of the central issues relating to DMOs. Most notably, this chapter will discuss in what ways there have been any changes in how VFR is understood and rated amongst DMOs.

Knowledge about VFRs

Almost all of the respondents were unable to provide any information about VFRs across both years of asking the question. Many respondents commented that they assumed that VFR travellers would mimic the leisure market. Therefore, they stated that VFR travellers would be likely to come from the same generating regions and have the same length of stay as the other visitors to their region.

Respondents were also asked to define VFR travel, and most of the respondents struggled to answer this question. During the telephone interview, respondents generally stated that this was a difficult question and took their time to respond. This was surprising in two respects. Firstly, the questions had been sent to all respondents in advance. Secondly, since VFR travel is well known, it was interesting that attempts to define it were challenging. The definitions offered varied considerably, in both 2009 and 2013. The assumption that VFR travellers would be staying with friends and relatives was a central theme across both data sets. One example comment was that

> they are people who come to the region on holiday and are staying with friends or relatives or they can be coming up for family reasons. They do not stay in commercial accommodation. This is the defining aspect – they are travelling on a budget; not a higher yielding market. (Queensland DMO)

Interestingly, one respondent did not see VFR travellers as tourists as 'they are visiting friends or relatives and staying in local homes so are not tourists' (New South Wales DMO). This non-tourist behaviour was also captured by a statement of a VFR traveller being 'someone who is in our region for reasons other than a holiday. The primary reason is to meet and catch up and relate with friends or relatives, not enjoy what the destination has to offer' (Tasmania DMO). Other statements also highlighted the lower status VFR travel is perceived to have, as 'their spend is lower than other visitors' (South Australia DMO). They were also assumed to stay less time since they are 'someone who stays in non-paid accommodation and is known to the individual and is invariably passing through on a short stay' (New South Wales DMO). A definition that distinguished between purpose of visit and accommodation type was provided by one respondent who claimed that VFR travellers are 'visitors to the region whose main purpose of visit is to visit a friend or relative or to stay with them' (South Australia DMO).

Use of industries by VFRs

All respondents were able to list many types of businesses that they considered would be strong beneficiaries from VFR travel. The most commonly mentioned business types were: attractions, retailers, restaurants, cafes, pubs and clubs. Petrol stations were a central theme that came through regional destinations; and wineries were a consistent theme mentioned for wine-growing regions.

When it came to ascertaining what businesses were not likely to benefit from VFRs, there were two distinct groups of respondents across each data set, and no change in perceptions across the years. One common theme was that accommodation providers were not beneficiaries. This came through from over half (55%) of the respondents in 2009 and 53% in 2013. In both years, this was often the only group mentioned as being unlikely to benefit from VFR travel. For many respondents this was considered to be obvious, with comments such as 'accommodation would be definite' (New South Wales DMO), 'accommodation of course' (New South Wales DMO) and 'accommodation obviously' (South Australia DMO). An interesting response came from one region that had recently commissioned a consultancy report into VFR travel. They stated that commercial accommodation operators were not likely to benefit from VFR travel, citing that '80% of VFRs in the region are staying with hosts, 20% are staying in commercial accommodation' (New South Wales DMO). This highlighted an interesting perception issue, that despite knowing that 20% of VFR travellers in their region utilised commercial accommodation, they still considered that commercial accommodation providers do not benefit from VFR travel.

Others were more specific about the type of accommodation providers that would not benefit. 'Accommodation in prime areas would not benefit but accommodation in regional areas would benefit' (Northern Territory DMO). For those that considered that accommodation providers may benefit, VFR travellers were assumed by some to be more of a budget traveller: 'any accommodation would be budget if not staying with friends or relatives' (South Australia DMO). Another respondent specified that 'motel accommodation, apartments and high-end accommodation' would be unlikely to benefit from VFR travel (Queensland DMO).

The other theme that came through was that VFR travel benefited all businesses at some level and when asked what businesses did not benefit from VFR travel, many respondents couldn't think of any. Comments from respondents included 'none...can't think of any' (Victoria DMO). Similarly another respondent stated, 'none – even solicitors, accountants etc. benefit' (New South Wales DMO). Another respondent stated that they 'can't think of a business type that would get nothing from VFR tourism' (Queensland DMO). In the telephone interviewing, it was apparent that some people took considerable time to think of businesses that may not benefit from VFR travel, with one respondent suggesting 'perhaps a funeral parlour' (Queensland DMO). However, this was used as an example of beneficiaries by another respondent who claimed that a 'funeral parlour even can benefit...actually a member of our organisation is a funeral parlour' (Victoria DMO). The perception of the impact of VFR travel was captured by some respondents, such as one respondent who stated, 'I'd say VFR penetrates pretty well' (Victoria DMO). Another respondent stated, 'I think all businesses benefit to some extent. But some are less likely to benefit' (South Australia DMO).

DMO marketing plans

Respondents were asked to identify whether their DMO or any tourism operation in their region had undertaken a strategy aimed at attracting VFRs. Many respondents across both years of data collection simply stated that there had not been any known strategy aimed specifically at VFR travel. In the 2009 data collection, many respondents mentioned that they 'don't know how to reach VFRs' (Queensland DMO). There was also the suggestion that 'there may have been something...in previous bad times' (Queensland DMO). This was a recurring theme, that VFR was considered to be reliable in economic downturns when the leisure market was not as strong. Similarly, another respondent indicated that a campaign was undertaken five years ago 'prior to our tourism growth when VFR was larger' (Queensland DMO).

The overall theme of 'no' had not changed between 2009 and 2013. In fact, despite the research that has been developing in the VFR area, and the growing understanding of the benefits of VFR, it was generally dismissed. One respondent stated, 'No. Why would you...repeat VFRs are not likely to spend as much as "normal" tourists and first time visitors' (South Australia DMO).

However, of those respondents who were aware of previous VFR campaigns, many acknowledged that they 'target VFRs indirectly' (Tasmania DMO) by making 'an effort to educate locals on what there is to do in their own backyard' (Tasmania DMO). This concept was highlighted by many of the respondents. 'We have just launched a campaign "know your own backyard" to get residents to become ambassadors' (Queensland DMO). Another campaign was called 'life's a dish' (Victoria DMO). They further understood that 'the local is more likely to participate in a tourism experience when VFRs are staying' (Tasmania DMO). Some campaigns involved developing a sense of pride amongst local residents, while others focused on passport programmes that 'give the local free entry if they bring a friend or relative' (Victoria DMO). One respondent mentioned that they deliberately marketed to weddings to capitalise on this area of VFR travel (Victoria DMO).

Some respondents in 2009 indicated that they were 'developing one as we speak' (Victoria DMO) and were about to launch campaigns in response to dwindling numbers of tourists due to the economic crisis. Again, this was aimed at educating locals: 'the notion is for locals to get to know their city better. We will be encouraging them to invite friends and relatives. We want to create pride amongst local residents – they should want to show off the city' (Queensland DMO). Similarly, another respondent stated that 'we identified a few years ago that we would like to market to the residents...that they could send their friends/relatives to our region' (Western Australia DMO). Another campaign that was mentioned involved linking with the international education sector: 'we work with language schools...to maximise the market of friends/relatives that come to visit them' (Western Australia DMO).

Since the 2009 data collection, some of those respondents had developed VFR campaigns. One respondent spoke of a VFR campaign run in Southern Highlands that had 'achieved some success in terms of extended stay and awareness' (New South Wales DMO). Another respondent spoke of an 'explore your own backyard' campaign that has had 'reasonable success' (New South Wales DMO). There was also discussion about working closely with 'the education sector to promote to the VFR market' (South Australia DMO), while another DMO mentioned that they were a 'regional partner of Discover Your Own Backyard...targeting VFR...to be launched early in the new year' (Victoria DMO).

VFR campaigns

Respondents were asked how they would go about convincing their board of directors to approach a VFR strategy if they wanted to undertake a VFR marketing campaign. For those respondents who previously indicated that they were either currently undertaking a VFR campaign or were planning one, boards had already passed the VFR marketing campaign. However, for those who were not planning a campaign, many reported that 'it would be extremely unlikely to get up' (Queensland DMO) and they would have 'great difficulty' (Queensland DMO) getting it passed by the board. One respondent simply stated, 'I would not do it' (Western Australia DMO). Another respondent indicated that 'it would be a tough sell' (Queensland DMO), which was similarly stated by another respondent: the 'board of directors would really question the value. It would be a tough sell' (South Australia DMO).

Similarly, another respondent felt it would be 'unlikely to be approved. We promote tourism not VFR. We focus on bums in beds' (Northern Territory DMO). The perceived issue that commercial 'accommodation would not benefit much' (Queensland DMO) was frequently raised as many felt 'the board might say they are coming anyway and accommodation operators may not like the concept' (Queensland DMO), as 'the challenge is accommodation' (South Australia DMO). Another respondent stated that it is 'better to focus on other markets. Mainstream markets are better as then the visitors stay in accommodation therefore we concentrate on it' (Western Australia DMO). Another thought there would be 'resistance because we reach these people anyway in general marketing' (Northern Territory DMO). The link with accommodation operators and the board was also captured, in that 'most of the operators on the board are accommodation providers so such a campaign would not be supported at the board level' (Queensland DMO).

Some respondents discussed the economic climate and considered that 'the economic climate at present indicates the opportunity. VFR is easier to sell than international at present' (Tasmania DMO). The issue of how well VFR was performing led another respondent to believe that 'if VFRs were decreasing in numbers we would address it; but it is level so no need to action anything at this stage' (South Australia DMO). Other respondents felt that 'it would not take a lot of convincing' (Northern Territory DMO) and they would only need to 'illustrate the size of the market and value' (Queensland DMO) and 'prove a return on investment' (South Australia DMO).

Interestingly, the general themes did not change between 2009 and 2013 responses. There remained a strong theme that VFR is not worth marketing to in 2013, with comments such as 'I wouldn't, as we have other market priorities based on visitor spend' (New South Wales DMO). Similarly, another respondent stated, 'there is very little point in doing this, as a broader marketing campaign aimed at all visitor segments also stimulates interest from those considering a VFR trip to the area' (Western Australia DMO). Those thoughts were also shared by a South Australian DMO that highlighted that the 'main component is ROI…I doubt targeting VFR would be agreed unless there was specific data that showed there was value in doing so'. However, in contrast, one Victorian DMO revealed that 'it has already been approved – our board fully appreciates the importance of the VFR market'.

DMO budgets

DMO representatives were asked what percentage of their marketing budget they thought should be allocated towards VFR travel. In 2009 this question resulted in the strong theme that, historically, 0% of their marketing budget had been assigned to VFR strategies. Only a very small number of DMOs had allocated funds towards a VFR campaign in the past. When considering what amount should be ideally allocated towards VFR travel in their budget, many maintained 0%. At times this was linked to the accommodation sector because 'we have many accommodation operators as members we need to meet their needs' (Victoria DMO). At other times this was because 'VFRs grow naturally because the region is growing' (Queensland DMO) while for others it was because 'general marketing would capture VFRs anyway' (Victoria DMO) and as such it did not require any funds set aside.

Conversely, another theme that came through in 2009 was that small amounts of around 5%, 5–10%, and 15–20% were reasonable. A small number reported higher figures within the range of 25% and 40%. Some felt that, ideally, it should match the size of the market share. At times this was suggested as a temporary budget allocation, rather than ongoing, referring to the economic crisis. These respondents felt that marketing to VFR travellers had 'more appeal now because of poor economic conditions' (Tasmania DMO). As such, 'due to the present economic climate I could justify around 10%' (Queensland DMO). Another stated that they could justify '25% towards VFR in this economic climate. Last year I would have said 0%. There is a need to be innovative and take the dollars out of international and put those dollars into VFR to trial it' (Western Australia DMO).

Those themes were unchanged four years later. There continued to be a strong theme that no money should be allocated towards targeting VFR travel because 'at this stage there is insufficient data to justify any allocation' (South Australia DMO). In addition, 'the region has a strategic focus of growing overnight stays in commercial accommodation' (New South Wales DMO). However, similar to 2009, some respondents felt that a small amount of around 5%–10% was suitable. There was one respondent who felt it should be proportionate with the visitation level, so for their region should be 44% (New South Wales DMO).

Destination appeal

Respondents were asked what destinations they thought were best suited to attracting VFRs and almost all of them in both 2009 and 2013 stated that they considered particular types of destinations would be more suited to attracting VFR travellers. While different aspects were evident, the key theme was that DMO managers felt that certain destinations had an advantage when it came to attracting VFR travellers. One of the themes that came through for this was that destinations that had 'events' (Northern Territory DMO) were best suited to attracting VFR travellers. Another theme was related to the transit route – that destinations needed to have 'easy access' and 'cheap flights' (New South Wales DMO). Therefore 'those close to a major city' (South Australia DMO) were seen as better suited to attracting VFR travellers.

Others felt that 'destinations that are appealing' (Victoria DMO), that are 'tourism areas' (New South Wales DMO) and offer 'a holiday experience' (New South Wales DMO) were best suited. In this sense, it was linked with those destinations 'that are already popular. This is based on my experience living in a wide range of places. When I live in popular places I get many more VFRs' (Queensland DMO). This seemed to indicate that DMO managers around Australia believed that VFR travellers were influenced by particular types of destinations rather than just the people.

Do VFRs come naturally?

Without exception, all the respondents in both 2009 and 2013 felt that VFR travellers could be influenced to travel to destinations to visit friends/relatives. Some stated this with great conviction: 'can be influenced – absolutely' (South Australia DMO, Queensland DMO), 'can definitely be influenced' (New South Wales DMO), 'no doubt' (Queensland DMO, Western Australia DMO). One respondent stated that VFR travellers 'can be influenced and planning to do this with our new campaign' (Queensland DMO). A strong theme in the responses was that the way to influence VFR travellers was 'through the locals' (New South Wales DMO, South Australia DMO) because 'VFRs are influenced by the host' (South Australia DMO). The key was 'to convince locals that the attractions are good enough' (Western Australia DMO). One respondent stated that VFR travellers 'can be influenced, which is why we target local residents' (New South Wales DMO).

The other theme was to use marketing to influence them. Influencing VFR travellers 'depends on what's on offer. For example an event. A discount voucher book would be very effective' (South Australia DMO). Others felt that marketing techniques could be used to 'influence trips and behaviours' (Queensland DMO) such as 'spend' (Queensland DMO), 'how much they do when they are here' (South Australia DMO) and to 'affect the length of stay and frequency of visit' (Queensland DMO).

Discussion

Many DMO managers were unaware of the proportion of their market that were VFR travellers, and most knew nothing about the characteristics and behaviours of those VFR travellers. Many also assumed that VFR travellers would be aligned with the profiles and characteristics of the leisure market. A key finding that arose from the discussions was that DMOs tend to focus on the leisure and business markets and few focus any marketing efforts towards VFR travel, assuming that they will reach VFR travellers through their generic marketing activities.

This finding that DMO managers felt that they reached VFR travellers through their general marketing was in contrast to the findings by

Morrison, Woods *et al.* (2000). Their research indicated that only 15.8% of DMOs in Australia and New Zealand stated that VFR travellers were included in the general marketing of the region. Furthermore, they found that 71.3% of those DMOs had some specific initiative to attract VFR travellers, although they did find that only 31.4% had used a specific VFR marketing promotion.

In spite of the lower knowledge and attention that Australian DMO managers had of VFR travel, they did assume that local businesses would benefit from those visits. More industrialised forms of tourism such as attractions were frequently nominated, as well as less industrialised forms of tourism such as retailers, restaurants, cafes, pubs and clubs. However, of the most industrialised form of tourism, commercial accommodation, more than half of the DMO managers expected that there would be no benefit from VFR travel. Because of this assumption, many respondents also stated that they would have difficulty in trying to develop a dedicated VFR campaign because their board of directors comprised many accommodation operators.

Alternatively, some thought that because they had many accommodation operators as members, they were obliged to care for the stakeholders' interests. Since many perceived that VFR travellers do not use commercial accommodation, they assumed that VFR travel was unrelated to serving the interests of their members. This aligns with the research undertaken by Morrison, Woods *et al.* (2000) that showed that one of the largest perceived disadvantages of VFR travel by DMOs was 'the lack of use of commercial accommodation facilities' (110). As a result, VFR travel was often not identified in DMO marketing plans. Alternatively, it may have been identified as a major market segment, but resources were not allocated in order to operationalise this aspect of the plan.

A very clear overall theme that came through was that marketing to VFR travellers had often not occurred to DMO managers as a possible campaign to attempt. They knew it existed. They knew it was a large segment. Trying to optimise this segment generally did not occur to the DMOs. Interestingly, the process of answering questions about VFR travel in 2009 and thinking about it for a lengthy period caused many respondents to realise that this may be an opportunity. This metamorphosis of thinking about VFR travel in 2009 did lead to one of the authors of this chapter being contacted by several of the DMO managers after conducting the telephone interviews to gain further information about the 'market'. A number of those DMOs then undertook research and/or campaigns into VFR travel and requested materials to assist them and/or requested research to be conducted within their destination to inform a campaign into VFR. One of those campaigns has been the very successful *Discover Your Own Backyard* VFR marketing campaign, which was introduced in 2011. Destination Melbourne Limited developed an outstanding toolkit that explains to local communities and partners how they can implement the *Discover Your Own Backyard* campaign. Destination Melbourne together with four councils within Melbourne commissioned research (Backer & Lynch, 2011) on the VFR 'market' in Melbourne to ascertain VFRs' economic impacts on the city to help inform the campaign.

The *Discover Your Own Backyard* VFR marketing campaign is an excellent example of a VFR marketing success story. Another outstanding case study is VisitBritain 2012. The *Share Your GREAT Britain* programme enlisted the help of residents of England, Wales and Scotland to invite their relatives and friends to come and visit. Another excellent example is Washington State Tourism's *Share Your Washington* campaign in the US. The *Discover Your Own Backyard* VFR campaign is discussed in detail in Chapter 7, along with six other successful VFR campaigns. While six of those case studies are DMO campaigns, one was launched by a transport company, V/Line, which developed the incredibly successful *Guilt Trip* campaign to guilt VFRs into visiting their friends and relatives more often.

Conclusion

In contrast to the research undertaken by Morrison, Woods *et al.* (2000), all DMO managers who participated in this research in 2009 and 2013 felt that VFR travellers could be influenced rather than just come naturally. However, this may be a result of timing, as more has been learnt about VFR travel over the past 15 years, which may have influenced the vastly different responses. Secondly, as Morrison, Woods *et al.* (2000) stated, the interviews involved one person's opinions to represent the organisation and other people within the same organisation may have different views. Coupled with the high turnover rate within DMOs, attitudes can change rapidly (Morrison, Woods *et al.*, 2000). This point can be highlighted by a comment from one respondent in this research, who outlined that VFR travel had become a major priority for their organisation since he'd started in that position 11 months prior to the interview.

Other factors might also account for the differences between the findings of this research and those of Morrison, Woods *et al.* (2000). This study involved interviewing DMOs at the regional level only and the interview was conducted with the CEO. Conversely the research by Morrison, Woods *et al.* (2000) was sent to 'all the state, provincial, and territorial tourist offices' although it also included a 'random sample of regional tourism organisations' (105). In addition, it was sent to the marketing directors rather than the CEOs and it is not known who actually filled in the survey form. The contrasting findings could also reflect changing economic conditions rather than indicate a trend.

However, this study confirms the broad findings by Morrison, Woods *et al.* (2000), that VFR travel is not well understood by DMOs. Therefore, the potential opportunity in maximising expenditures and experiences by VFR travellers is not fully exploited. In particular, there is still a wide belief that VFR travellers do not stay in commercial accommodation. As a result, few commercial accommodation operators are aware of VFR travel being a potential market segment. It was clear that this had not changed in any way between 2009 and 2013. However, since 2009, a number of major VFR campaigns have been launched, with clear successes. Some of those success stories are discussed in Chapter 7. Perhaps, the circulating of information about those successful VFR campaigns through DMO circles may encourage further interest in VFR travel by industry.

References

Backer, E. (2007) VFR travel – An examination of the expenditures of VFR travellers and their hosts. *Current Issues in Tourism* 10 (4), 366–377.

Backer, E. (2010) Opportunities for commercial accommodation in VFR. *International Journal of Tourism Research* 12 (4), 334–354.

Backer, E. (2012) VFR travel: It *is* underestimated. *Tourism Management* 33 (1), 74–79.

Backer, E. and Lynch, D. (2011) *VFR Travel Research Project: Melbourne*. Ballarat: University of Ballarat.

BBC World News (2009) Family traffic: Fast track program. See http://news.bbc.co.uk/player/nol/newsid_8040000/newsid_8040900/8040921.stm?bw=bb&mp=wm&news=1&nol_storyid=8040921&bbcws=1# (accessed 13 August 2009).

Braunlich, C. and Nadkarni, N. (1995) The importance of the VFR market to the hotel industry. *The Journal of Tourism Studies* 6 (1), 38–47.

Hay, B. (1996) An insight into the European experience: A case study on domestic VFR tourism within the UK. In H. Yaman (ed.) *VFR Tourism: Issues and Implications. Proceedings from the Conference Held at Victoria University of Technology* (pp. 52–66). Melbourne: Victoria University of Technology.

Hu, B. and Morrison, A. (2002) Tripography: Can destination use patterns enhance understanding of the VFR market? *Journal of Vacation Marketing* 8 (3), 201–220.

Jackson, R. (1990) VFR tourism: Is it underestimated? *The Journal of Tourism Studies* 1 (2), 10–17.

Lee, G., Morrison, A.M. and Lehto, X. (2005) VFR: Is it really marginal? A financial consideration of French overseas travellers. *Journal of Vacation Marketing* 11 (4), 340–356.

McKercher, B. (1994) *Report on a Study of Host Involvement in VFR Travel to Albury Wodonga*. Albury-Wodonga, Charles Sturt University.

Minichiello, V., Aroni, R. and Hays, T. (2008) *In-depth Interviewing: Principles, Techniques, Analysis*. Frenchs Forest NSW: Pearson Education.

Morrison, A., Verginis, C. and O'Leary, J. (2000) Reaching the unwanted and unreachable: An analysis of the outbound long haul German and British visiting friends and relatives market. *Journal of Tourism and Hospitality Research* 2 (3), 214–231.

Morrison, A., Woods, B., Pearce, P., Moscardo, G. and Sung, H. (2000) Marketing to the visiting friends and relatives segment: An international analysis. *Journal of Vacation Marketing* 6 (2), 102–118.

Navarro, R. and Turco, D. (2004) Segmentation of the visiting friends and relatives travel market. *Visions in Leisure and Business* 13 (1), 4–16.

Seaton, A. (1994) Are relatives friends? Reassessing the VFR category in segmenting tourism markets. In A. Seaton (ed.) *Tourism: The State of the Art* (pp. 316–321). Chichester: Wiley.

Seaton, A. (1996) Making (even more) sense of the AFR category in tourism analysis. In H. Yaman (ed.) *VFR Tourism: Issues and Implications*. Melbourne: Victoria University of Technology.

Seaton, A. and Palmer, C. (1997) Understanding VFR tourism behaviour: The first five years of the United Kingdom tourism survey. *Tourism Management* 18 (6), 345–355.

3 Are Relatives Friends? Disaggregating VFR Travel 1994–2014

Tony Seaton and Caroline Tie

Introduction

Neglect of the VFR category has been a recurrent charge levied at academics and industry planners by writers who have engaged with this category of tourism over the last three decades (Backer, 2008; Denman, 1988; Jackson, 1990; Seaton, 1994). It has been seen as a Cinderella category, unrecognised or marginalised in planning and research terms, compared to the big, ugly sisters of leisure and business tourism, regarded as tourism's main money spinners.

This chapter examines the charge of neglect in relation to an issue that appeared on VFR agendas in the 1990s. It is whether VFR travel might benefit in research and planning terms by being disaggregated into its two nominal components: those visiting friends and those visiting relatives. The chapter looks at the history and results of disaggregation with particular comparisons between those revealed in the first major study in 1995 and a more wide-ranging, multidisciplinary programme undertaken in 2009, partly under the European Union Interreg 4a directive, the results of which were made available in 2011.

Origins of the VFR Disaggregation Debate

The proposal to split the VFR travel category was first made in a paper presented at an international conference at the University of Strathclyde in 1994 (Seaton, 1994). The rationale for it was an intuitive belief that hosting and paying visits to relatives was a different kind of experience, with different rules of engagement, from doing so to friends, and that the differences might be important ones for tourism planners to take account of in market targeting. A number of specific, hypothesised differences were predicted in the paper, and also some pragmatic consequences the disaggregated results might have for market targeting by tourism organisations.

The opportunity to explore these issues came quickly and unexpectedly when, in response to the paper, the Northern Ireland Tourist Board offered to make available to the university a data set on international visitors to Northern Ireland between 1991 and 1993, derived from an international passenger study in which VFR travellers had been differentiated into three groups: those visiting friends (VFs); those visiting relatives (VRs); and those visiting both (VFVRs). The data, previously unknown to the Strathclyde researchers, were gratefully accepted and became the basis for systematic investigation of some of the hypotheses made in the original paper. The results were published a year later (Seaton & Tagg, 1995) in a journal article paper that identified detailed differences and similarities in behaviour between the three disaggregated groups, across 15 variables of comparison which included socio-demographic features and trip descriptors.

The Northern Ireland Disaggregation

The results of the study are presented in Table 3.1 which comprises the differences and similarities in behaviour of VFs and VRs across 11 of the original 15 variables.[1] VFVRs have been excluded from the table since they comprised only 3.3% of VFR travellers.

The study revealed two general insights into the nature of VFR travel – its composition and the nature of differences in VF and VR behaviours contained within it. Both insights have, to a greater or lesser extent, been supported by what has been revealed about VFs and VRs since.

The law of composition revealed by the analysis may be easily stated – that in any VFR population, VRs will always dominate in numerical terms. The Northern Ireland data showed that 77.3% of VFR travel in Ireland was to relatives, with only 19.5% to friends. VRs were thus almost four times as numerous as VFs, a balance that had never previously been suspected. Though the proportionate balance has varied, every study since has revealed a balance weighted significantly to VRs.

In addition to this key structural feature, the disaggregation revealed a number of striking contrasts within a category that had, until then, been seen as a homogeneous one. The differences were in: previous visits to destination, ethnic connection and type, party size and type, occupation/social status, age, length of stay, timing of trip/season, spending, activities and motivation.

The nexus of variables here associated with each of the two main categories of VFR travellers suggests that the traveller visiting relatives is an older, serial, repeat visitor, going home to parents or siblings, alone or with a companion and/or children, for a longish break, spending less on outside hospitality/entertainment/ sightseeing, but enjoying certain home-based recreations such as fishing and golf.

Table 3.1 Profiles and characteristics of VFs and VRs

	VF	*VR*
Previous visits to destination	Most on first or second trip (47.2%)	Most have made nine visits or more (75.6%)
Ethnic connection	Yes (13.6%)	Yes (77.6%)
Main ethnic connection	Born in N.I. (52.9%) Parents/grandparents born in N.I. (47.1%)	Born in N.I. (84.5%) Parents/grandparents born in N.I. (15.5%)
Party size/composition	Mainly singles (63.5%) and couples (17.1%)	Singles (50.2%), Couples (21.8%), families with children (19.4%)
Occupational status/ Social grading	Mainly social grades ABC1 (62.1%); significant student group (9.8%)	Mainly social grades ABC1 (67.9%). Highest AB total (34.9%)
Age	Young, mainly 16–34 (60.1%)	Older, mainly 35–65+ (58.8%)
Timing/Season	Mostly spring/summer trips (60.7%)	Mostly spring/summer trips (58.7%)
Length of stay	Mainly short breaks (54.9% stayed 1–4 nights)	Mainly long stays (53.8 stayed 9 days or more)
Spending differences	Spend most on drinks/ entertainment, least on shopping; total spending concentrated over shorter stays	Spend most on shopping and on gifts and souvenirs, least on drinks/ entertainment
Main differences in activities engaged in	More sightseeing (Giant's Causeway 56.5%); less sport and festival attendance (golf 5.1%; fishing 3.9%; festival/event 3.5%)	Less sightseeing (Giant's Causeway 38.2%); more sport and festival attendance (golf 14%; fishing 8.4%; festival/event 6.2%)
Motives and satisfactions	People nice/friendly (64.6%); scenery (43.9%); pubs, drink, Guinness (7.8%)	People nice/friendly (52.3%); scenery (35%); pubs, drink, Guinness (4.6%)

The VF, by contrast, appears younger, more likely to be alone or with one companion, more disposed to party and spend out of the house, sightsee and be more impressed by the people and the scenery than the more blasé VR. Of the two categories, the VF traveller acts more like the common idea of a tourist than the VR who, it could be said, may be following an obligatory ritual that is more person-directed and less place-centred.

Not all these contrasts have since been supported in other places, but the two typologies offer behavioural templates that can be considered and compared with VF and VR populations elsewhere.

Both groups tended to be in higher social grades than the general population and travel during the summer or spring. They were also both likely to have an ethnic connection with Northern Ireland but the VR was more likely to be first generation.

If the Northern Ireland study had been continued to the present it would now provide a fascinating longitudinal data set for understanding differences in VF and VR behaviour over time. Due to administrative changes, however, brought about after the 'peace process' collaboration between the North and South of Ireland, responsibility for tourism research changed, and Ireland's visitor surveys ceased to include data on VFR disaggregation.

There was little significant discussion of splitting the category, or available data for comparing with the 1995 study, until Backer's work between 2005 and 2009 (Backer, 2008, 2009). She mounted a survey of VFR travellers staying with hosts at the Sunshine Coast in Australia, which allowed some comparisons between VF and VR behaviour using some of the variables tracked in the 1995 paper. The results supported some, but not all, of the Northern Ireland findings. Among the similarities were her conclusions that:

- Though there were no significant differences in the adult composition of VF and VR parties, VRs travelled with significantly more children.
- VRs visited their hosts significantly more often than VFs.
- Though VF and VR trips were fairly evenly distributed throughout the year, VR travel peaked in December ahead of VF travel, with 20.6% VRs travelling compared with 13.5% VFs. January was the next most popular month with 9.8% VR travellers and 10.1% VF travellers, a finding which indicates the importance of major festivals and holidays (Christmas and New Year here) as the travel occasion for family reunions (Backer, 2007: 164).

The most interesting similarity between Backer's results and those of the 1995 study was on purpose of visit. She found that only 63.4% of VF travellers were staying with hosts for VFR reasons, compared to 80.6% of VRs who gave it as their main reason. VFs were more likely to be staying with friends and relatives for 'leisure-based' tourism experiences of beaches, theme parks, relaxation etc. (Backer, 2007: 165). This mirrors the Northern Ireland data that showed a greater interest in sightseeing, eating and drinking out-of-house by VFs compared with VRs.

The Kent Research Programme

The 1995 disaggregation study had ended by advocating further research and, in particular, 'specially designed VFR research instruments' that would afford greater depth of analysis and include more detailed questions tracking 'motivations and activities' (Seaton, 1995: 16–17). This desideratum was most fully met between 2009 and 2011 in a path-breaking programme of research that may be seen as a model for any tourism organisation with a serious interest in understanding VFR tourism behaviour and marketing. It was the work, not of an academic institution or NTO, but Kent County Council, a regional destination agency in the UK with a particularly high level of VFR visitors, working in partnership with a tourism consultancy and regional administrators in Pas-de-Calais in Northern France.

The purpose of the study was to improve knowledge of the VFR category by:

(1) assessing national and regional VFR patterns in quantitative terms over the previous five years, using available visitor studies with a review of VFR initiatives elsewhere, nationally and regionally;
(2) mounting a multi-methodological programme of research into VFR behaviour that discriminated between VRs, VFs and VFVRs, and which also provided insight into the perspectives of both VFR hosts and VFR guests.

The research programme, the focus of this chapter, comprised three elements:

(1) an online survey of Kent residents who had hosted a visit by friends and/or family in the previous 12 months (VFR hosts), which received 1229 valid responses from a total of 1499 responses received;
(2) an online questionnaire survey of people who had visited Kent to visit friends/family over the same period, based on 672 valid responses from a total of 896 responses received;
(3) focus groups with Kent residents who had hosted, or been guests of, at least one overnight VFR visit in the previous year.

The programme was conducted by a consultancy, the Tourism Company, in conjunction with staff from Visit Kent. Invitations to the public were sent to Kent's database and a link posted to the board's Facebook and Twitter accounts. The survey went 'live' for two weeks in January and February 2009. It tracked: age and gender composition; frequency of VFR trips; expenditure; hosting at home, in commercial accommodation or on neutral ground; attitudes to friends versus family; differences between VF and VR hosting and visiting.

The questionnaire surveys

Just over half of respondents (52%) reported that they had recently hosted an overnight visit from relatives, while only 30% reported an overnight visit by friends. Eighteen percent said that they had hosted a visit by a group made up of both friends and family. These results supported the finding, discussed earlier, that VRs dominate VFs in VFR disaggregation analyses.

This balance had been confirmed in other studies between the Northern Ireland and the Kent Study, internationally and domestically. In 2008, for instance, domestic VFRs in the UK constituted 52% of VR travellers while VFs were 27% (UKTS, 2008). In the same year 77% of VFR trips by overseas tourists to Britain were by VRs. In 2002 ETC's indicated that the balance of VRs to VFs was 64% to 32% with 4% describing themselves as both VFVRs (Kent, 2011: 9).

An additional point of interest about both family/relative hosts and guests was that they mainly comprised immediate, primary members – parents, brothers and sisters – not uncles, aunts and cousins. Of the visits, 74% fell into this category with 20% of visits being from other relations (e.g. aunts and uncles, grandparents). This finding was consistent with the Northern Ireland data on 'ethnic connection' which showed that 84.5% of VRs were first generation natives returning home, rather than those more distantly connected. The generational factor has been found to be a key one in diasporic travel, where both Ali and Tie found that first generation Pakistanis going home to their country of origin, and Chinese-Sarawakian émigrés going 'back' to China on tours, have different motives and experiences from younger, second and third generation travellers (Ali & Holden, 2006; Tie & Seaton, 2013).

VFR profiles

More than two-thirds of visitor respondents to the Kent visitor questionnaires (67%) were female with the remainder (33%) being male. Respondents were more likely to be middle aged. Fifty-two percent of respondents were aged 35–54 years, compared with 35% of the general population. By contrast, 12% of respondents were aged 16–34 years old, compared with 30% of the general population. However, there were fewer in the 65 years and over age bracket (11% compared with 21% amongst the general population).

The social status of VFRs was determined by using Mosaic[2] geo-demographic information based on postcode data from respondents. This revealed that the profile of the VFR sample was higher than that of the general population of Kent County, comprising group categories typically associated with middle and high earners. For example the group

'Middle income families living in moderate suburban semis' made up a fifth of VFR respondents (20%) but only accounts for 13% of the county's population. The group 'couples with young children in comfortable modern housing' accounted for 8% of respondents compared with 6% of the Kent population. Conversely only 2% of respondents were classified as 'elderly people reliant on state support', half the proportion (4%) that exists within the county.

Class differences in home entertaining and hosting staying visits by non-family members have been known to sociologists in the UK for over 50 years since the ethnographic studies by Wilmott and Young (1962) reported that working class people in the East End mainly received family as their guests.

Length of visit

The majority of stays were longer than one night with stays of three nights or longer not uncommon; 71% of overnight visits by friends, and 79% by relatives, lasted more than one night, while 51% of visits by relatives were longer than three nights, compared with 35% for friends.

Frequency/number of VFR visits made in last 12 months

Most VRs were regular visitors. Respondents were asked to indicate how many overnight VFR trips they had taken to see friends or family in the previous 12 months. There were more overnight visits to see relatives than friends. The average number of overnight visits to relatives made during the previous year was 2.9 compared with 2.2 for visits to friends.

Host respondents corroborated the dominance of VR visitors, saying they had received on average 3.5 overnight visits by relatives in the previous 12 months, while the average number of overnight visits by friends was 2.5. Two-thirds of respondents (66%) had hosted two or more visits by relatives with the equivalent figure for visits by friends being 60%.

Motives

The majority of all VFR visits were for the purpose of visiting the host, but the strength of this person-centred motive varied. VF hosts were more likely to say that their visitors came 'Just to visit me/us' than VRs (62% versus 50%), but there was also a recognition that leisure motives featured slightly more for VFs than VRs. Thirteen percent of VFs were said to be combining a visit with the chance to have a day out/holiday/ evening out, a response made by only 9% amongst those with relatives visiting (Table 3.2).

Table 3.2 Motives for visiting friends and relatives (n= 1229)

Main reason for visit	Friends %	Relatives %
Just to visit me/us	62	50
Christmas/New Year	5	20
Family Event	7	12
Combine with day/holiday/evening out	13	9

This seasonal pattern can be compared with the Backer (2009) results in Australia presented earlier. Despite differences in the seasonal conditions in the UK and Australia, VFs were significantly more likely to visit in December in both Kent and Australia. Other findings of the Kent disaggregation were that VFs were slightly more likely to pre-plan than VRs (47% compared with 41%), which is consistent with the greater touristic orientation noted earlier. Financial outlay was higher among hosts that had relatives visiting (£135 versus £116, which is around US$227 versus US$195), but the higher figure may be due to the fact that relatives tend to stay longer than friends, rather than indicating a higher spend per day.

The focus group discussions

Like the quantitative surveys, the groups were divided into two sets of respondents, one made up of people who had, in the previous year, hosted visits from friends, and the second group made of respondents who had been guests. The samples included a broad spread of age (18–65), gender, life stage and social class. The aims were to track how guests and hosts managed and organised visits from friends and relatives, and identify opportunities for influencing the process in ways that would benefit tourism in Kent.

The groups suggested that on average respondents had been guests three times over the past 12 months, involving an average of six to seven people, staying a total of 12 nights. Visits by family/relatives, as opposed to friends, accounted for 60% of the total, once more confirming the invariant dominance of VR over VF travellers.

The 'host' discussion group included comments on timing and occasions. Holidays, especially Christmas and Easter, and school holidays were a popular time for people to get together, but family events such as birthdays, anniversaries or the birth of a baby also acted as a trigger. Some of the comments and occasions mentioned in the verbatims included:

Like it's my Dad's sixtieth birthday in a couple of weeks' time and my Mum's got three different couples staying for one night.

For me visits have purely been based around my daughter and her first eight months.

There was also comment on the stresses of hosting in-laws, some of whom appeared to outstay their welcome:

One or two nights you can live with but a week is a bit much really.

Among the general views of hosts were that: when people visit, the hosts generally feel a responsibility to entertain them and want people to have an enjoyable time. This may involve visiting attractions and places of interest, the coast and countryside, and eating out in pubs and restaurants. Although several respondents suggested that entertaining at home was an important element in the mix. Most seemed to have an itinerary or suggestions in mind and plan something ahead, but weather and time of the year were important determinants of what happened on the day as well as the views of the guests. There was some indication that people played safe in picking trips for guests and chose places that they knew in order to avoid disappointment. One explained that this was why 'we go to National Trust properties.'

There was interesting discussion around the cost to both VF and VR hosts and guests of VFR trips which produced agreement that group reductions and special deals by tourism and hospitality organisations targeted at different types of VFR traveller could be attractive as inducements. Options discussed included: local tourist weeks where residents could get free or reduced entry into participating attractions; vouchers or passports with 2-for-1 offers or admitting a resident free when accompanied by an out of town visitor; clubs for local residents offering special access or offers.

The most interesting group responses were on opinions that involved perceptual differences between hosting friends and relatives. Friends were freely chosen guests, often closer to the age range and interests of the hosts. Families, on the other hand, were an obligatory 'given', involving mixed age groups where there could be a greater clash of interests and tastes among those involved. Some from the guest group saw the presence of children as a liability to hosts and preferred to stay in a hotel rather than impose their kids on their hosts.

My lot are toddlers you know, they've got two kids as well, and they stay at the Hilton Hotel and they say it is much easier to get to, it's near everyone and is just easier that way, rather than putting on you and children.

But it was not just children that might be a problem:

Sometimes there are people staying in your house who are very sensitive and that you like having in your house, and sometimes parents in-law or more distant relatives can cause some difficulties.

Yet hosting relatives might, paradoxically, be less 'high maintenance' than friends, because the host could get away with less effort in not having to take them out and entertain them. Some respondents felt they had to put on a show for friends, to impress them or at least, keep their end up. Keeping up came with hospitality costs, as these comments indicate:

> Friends…you make sure you have a nice bottle of malt in or whatever.
>
> You spend more money when you are entertaining friends. You put in the extras or special treats, more alcohol for friends rather than relatives.
>
> [You are] more likely to take them [friends] out to restaurants than eat at home.
>
> For me, my mum and dad…we don't need to impress them too much and with friends we want to go out and have more of a fun time.

The Two Studies Contrasted

It is impossible to make exact comparisons between the Northern Ireland and Kent studies over the two time periods, due to the difference in: methodologies (quantitative in Northern Ireland; mixed quantitative/ qualitative in Kent); the samples, destinations (regional versus national/ international); and the double perspectives of host/guest in the Kent study, not the other. However, despite these substantive differences, the two studies touched on a sufficient number of common issues in VFR disaggregation to make it worth trying to bring out some of their points of contact and contrast. Table 3.3 attempts a side-by-side résumé of what the two studies convey about VFs and VRs.

The Kent study may be seen as a flag placement in newly discovered VFR territory, constituted by its multi-methodological ingenuity and variety, its procedural sequencing, the substantive issues it sought to monitor, the issues it revealed and the strategic applications it proposed for Kent tourism (not discussed in this chapter).

The research and the ideas generated from it were rated as 'Brilliant' by Ruth Wood, Tourism Officer for Kent:

> It changed our perceptions and those of our tourism industry stakeholders about the VFR category and its opportunities…It threw up things neither we or the industry had really thought about before, not least the group discussions with their disclosures about the normally unexpressed stresses both hosts and guests may feel in hosting relatives and friends, that may lead both to secretly wish that they or their guests took commercial accommodation. This is clearly an opportunity for local accommodation brokers and one which we are looking at

Table 3.3 VF and VR comparisons: Northern Ireland (1995) and Kent, UK (2011)

	VF 1995	VF 2011	VR 1995	VR 2011
Previous visits to destination	Most on first or second trip	Had made fewer trips than VRs	Most had made nine trips or more	Most had made more than three trips per annum
Party size/ composition	Mainly singles and couples	Mainly singles and couples	Singles, couples, families with children	More likely to include children
Occupational status	Mainly social grades ABC1s; significant student group	Mainly upper Mosaic lifestyle groups	Mainly social grades ABC1, especially ABs	Mainly upper Mosaic lifestyle groups
Age	Young, mainly 16–34	Younger than VRs	Older, mainly 35–65+	Middle-aged bias
Timing/season	Mostly spring/ summer trips	More outside Christmas period during year	Higher numbers around Christmas	Higher numbers around Christmas
Length of stay	Mainly short breaks	Shorter stays than VRs	Mainly long stays	Longer stays
Spending differences	Spend most on drinks/ entertainment, least on shopping; total spending concentrated over shorter stays	No precise data but some comment that hosting friends involves more expenditure than relatives	Spend most on shopping and on gifts and souvenirs, least on drinks/ entertainment	No precise data but some comment on expense, particularly for families, and cost sharing by host and guests
Main differences in activities engaged in	Lower levels of sightseeing, but higher levels of golf, fishing, festivals	Less out of house activities	More sightseeing, but lower levels of golf, festivals and events	More likely to enjoy sightseeing and spending on entertainment
Motivations and satisfactions	More likely to rate touristic factors – scenery, pubs, drink and people – highly	Likely to combine VFR motive with holiday/ journey break	Lower rating of touristic factors: scenery, pubs, drink, people	More motivated by specific family events/occasions

highlighting in humorous poster campaigns. (R. Wood, personal communication, 21 July 2014)

The study was also influential in the development of 'write and invite' inducement campaigns, which the study had benchmarked in other places as part of the review. These initiatives support and encourage local people to contact their friends and relatives and invite them to stay. Typically this involves a press campaign to raise awareness of the economic importance of tourism and the provision of postcards which residents can download from a website. Kent has since produced a range of six invitation postcards with customised messages for residents to send to relatives and friends inviting them back, addressed, among others, to grandparents, grandchildren, distant relatives overseas and to young people and their friends.

The research programme and its findings had been disseminated to industry stakeholders in the county and the implications for different tourism organisations discussed. The methodology of interviewing and conducting focused groups with both hosts and guests, and disaggregating the data into VFs and VRs (and also VFVRs, not analysed here), was recognised as innovative and fascinating in its results. When asked if the programme would be repeated, Ruth Wood answered that Visit Kent would 'love to do so' and 'delve deeper' into some of the factors that had been uncovered, but that the issue was always money. The programme had cost £15,000 (US$25,254), which had been half funded through the EU Interreg initiative.

Irrespective of its specific results, the Kent programme offers a useful procedural framework for research-led, strategic VFR planning by destination agencies and industry organisations. Table 3.4 provides a matrix that reduces the programme to two quartile grids, divided laterally and horizontally, the first by VFs and VRs and the second by Hosts and Guests. Research findings can be inserted into two boxes on the left, and then the policy options (to be discussed, agreed or put into effect) arising from them on the right. The matrix simply schematises the methods and procedures of the Kent programme as a prescriptive tool for others to use as a guide in VFR development.

What it leaves out is the pre-research stage of VFR situation analysis, using secondary data and benchmarking surveys derived from international, national and regional sources, that sets the scene and terms for embarking upon primary VFR research and policy initiatives at a specific destination. Space has prevented discussion of this but it was the start point of the Kent programme. Once the situation analysis has disclosed VFR trends in tourist numbers, trips and revenue potential the matrix can be applied.

Once both host and guest behaviour among VF and VR travellers have been researched and understood, the matrix allows the tourism

Table 3.4 VFR disaggregation research and planning matrix

	Visiting friends		Visiting relatives	
	Research	Policy decisions	Research	Policy Decisions
Host	1. Behavioural profiles	1. Strategic prioritisation	1. Behavioural profiles	1. Strategic prioritisation
	2. Trip features	2. Communication	2. Trip features	2. Communication
	3. Expenditures	3. Incentivisation	3. Expenditures	3. Incentivisation
Guest	1. Behavioural profiles	1. Strategic prioritisation	1. Behavioural profiles	1. Strategic prioritisation
	2. Trip features	2. Communication	2. Trip features	2. Communication
	3. Expenditures	3. Incentivisation	3. Expenditures	3. Incentivisation

organisation to develop regional programmes for specific groups for specific times and occasions (e.g. restaurants and bars may be interested most in young VFs, while transport companies may be most interested in deals for frequent VRs).

Disaggregation and VFR Marginalisation

This chapter has presented some of the thinking about VF/VR disaggregation over the past two decades and commended the Kent study as a milestone in exploring the issue. The final question for consideration is how widely it is recognised as operationally worth doing and for what reasons? There are two quite different answers to these key questions.

The first is to admit that, despite the results and applications of the Visit Kent programme, VFR disaggregation is absent from current UK and Ireland research agendas nationally – and so is strategic interest in VFR as a whole. VisitBritain, Britain's NTO, despite an ambitious 'write and invite' campaign called UK-OK in 2002, aimed at attracting diasporic groups to the UK, which ended with a resolve to maintain aspects of the programme's VFR research, has no plans for special VFR research activity in its latest strategic statement (2013). It does, however, gather and disseminate VFR data through its annual visitor studies. At VisitEngland, the agency responsible for UK domestic tourism, Sharon Orrell, Head of Research, though open-minded about the possibilities of VFR tourism research, has been unable to make it a priority due to cutbacks made after the 2008 economic crisis. In Northern Ireland VFR travel was disaggregated in the 1990s when VFR had grown to be 40% of its tourism because of the decline in recreational tourism due to political violence and bombings. Once holiday tourism made a come-back and VFR travel diminished, disaggregation ceased.

The lesson is simple. Interest in VFR, including disaggregation, depends upon destination factors and conditions. Visit Kent was able to make VFR a priority category and devote resources to custom-built research for two reasons: first, the dramatic growth of VFR travel in the UK up to 2009 and its disproportionate volume in Kent, where it constituted 56% of the county's tourism compared to an average elsewhere in the UK of 38%. Second, its geographical position as an east-coast county with gateway sea ports to and from Northern France allowed it to attract EU funding under the Interreg programme with French tourism partners.

Other destination agencies, national and regional, will have a harder case to make for prioritising VFR, because the importance of the category will vary greatly for many reasons – marketing, geographical (including transport access), political, financial and socio-demographic. The relative 'marginalisation' of VFR travel by NTOs is not a function of either ignorance or negligence, but a reflection of the realities of destination management in different places. This was discussed in detail in the previous chapter, whilst successful cases are highlighted in Chapter 7.

The World on the Move: Immigration, Migration and the Diasporic Explosion

There is evidence that realities in many places internationally and domestically are changing. The last two decades have seen unparalleled population movements within Europe, including Britain, which are part of vaster global shifts of immigration and emigration. The volume of VFR travel is strongly related to the history of immigration of the destination (Lehto *et al.*, 2001), and this issue is discussed in the next chapter. Every immigrant and emigrant is potentially a VFR return-traveller or host-receiver of the future. According to Tham (2006), the field of VFR travel has strong links with community settlement, migratory trends and family attachments. Reports show that the growth in the migratory patterns to Australia coincides with the increasing inbound tourism numbers of VFR travellers to Australia (AEI, 1999; BTR, 2003). A similar characteristic was found in research by Langolis *et al.* (1999) – that the inbound tourists from the UK entering Poland had strong personal ties to the country, either in the form of family roots or historical settlement. Therefore, there are strong evidences to argue that the growth of the VFR travel market is strongly correlated to the increase in multinational families dispersed through the effects of migration (Parr *et al.*, 2000).

Typically, there would appear to be a strong connection between (re)enhancing kinship relationships and VFR travel. The principle of using travel and tourism to maintain and enhance the connections amongst friends and relatives at a destination is supported by research. For example, in research with the Commonwealth Eastern Caribbean community of Toronto in Canada, Duval (2004) found that the primary purpose of return visits to the Caribbean was to maintain social and cultural ties. He (2004: 285) argues that: 'the theme of maintaining social and cultural ties centres on and incorporates the visits as a means to sustain ties with family members and friends'. Similar motivations were also found amongst the Vietnamese residents of Australia (Nguyen & King, 1998) and the Afro-Caribbean community of Manchester in England (Stephenson, 2002). Although the visiting of family may be undertaken for the purposes of strengthening ties and reunion, this form of travel may also be motivated by a sense of fulfilling family and societal obligations (Duval, 2004; Stephenson, 2002). A similar social convention and imperative is also observable amongst the first generation Sarawakian-Chinese who were born in China and emigrated to Sarawak – they strongly emphasised the importance of maintaining familial relationships and filial piety in their motivations for tourism participation (Tie & Seaton, 2013). Their journeys to China are not regarded as a casual or hedonistic affair but are motivated by a combination of duty and obligation. Their emphasis on family connections and loyalty towards their place of origin reflects their understanding of tourism as being defined by the visiting of relatives in China, and those living in diasporic communities in other countries.

The student VFR

One aspect of this internationalisation with implications for VFR disaggregation is the burgeoning world of student tourism. A study conducted by Bischoff and Koenig-Lewis (2007) looked at the role of university students in attracting friends and relatives to their place of study and showed that the average frequency of visits was fairly high and their value to the local economy significant. Fifty percent of all VR visits were day trippers, whilst over 90% of VF trips involved an overnight stay, a balance that underlines the utility of disaggregating the category to distinguish differences in behaviour between friends and relatives.

In his study of international students in Australia, Tham's (2006) research found that international students had a strong influence on the VFR market and also on the places visited, because of their familiarity with the surrounding environment. In the UK and Ireland overseas students have been the mainstay of postgraduate numbers in British and Irish universities for more than a decade. In Kent, where there are a number of colleges and universities, Visit Kent has already become aware of the role of students in attracting VFR trips and of the cultural factors that make entertaining friends and relatives different.

In advanced industrial societies children increasingly work and play away from where they originated geographically and friends may become more important than family, a tendency that would affect VF/VR balances which have previously been strongly weighted to relative visiting, rather than visiting friends. There is also a phenomenon which VisitBritain has observed – that of UK expatriates settling in retirement homes in Spain, France, Cyprus and other warm climates but making frequent returns to family and vice versa.

Splitting the category and studying its internal components in depth as discrete entities may cease to be a research luxury and become a managerial requirement for planners attempting to understand and exploit the changing social relations of travel generation.

VFR travel, modern mobilities and the social scientist

The second answer to questions about the value and future of disaggregating VFR travel in tourism management is that managerial factors are not the only, or even, perhaps, the most, important ones for consideration. Irrespective of its existence as a commercial market opportunity, the domain of visiting friends and relatives is a vast and important field of human behaviour, worthy of serious examination for its own sake. It has been a major and frequent subject for novelists, playwrights, filmmakers, poets, artists and composers. How many multimedia stories, images and myths have been created around journeys and visits between relations and friends? However, unlike many other domains of family behaviour (e.g. class, poverty, religion, education, gender), it has attracted little explicit attention from social scientists.

VFR behaviour, as the Kent group discussions hinted, takes place on a playing field underwritten by personal politics, implicit rules of encounter and avoidance, and unspoken tensions, which may be activated when humans temporarily interact away from their own ground, or on it, in the presence of others about whom they may have mixed feelings before, during or after the occasion. The roles of host and guest must be tacitly understood, negotiated and performed harmoniously through a myriad of finely judged decisions in word and deed: what should you *do* with friends when they come? How long should a friend or relative stay? What should a host or guest pay for during a visit and how should it be decided? Is it permissible for a visitor or host to go off and leave a host/guest during a visit? Who talks to whom, what about and for how long? How soon can a visitor go without giving offence? How much freedom of the house does a guest have? How do guests know when the host wants them to go? These micro-political issues in leisure and tourism encounters present relatively unexplored but promising territory for academic researchers – the social psychologist, the sociologist, the human geographer, the anthropologist, as well as the tourism manager and market researcher.

Understanding the social and psychological micro-dynamics of VFR may demand and authorise non-mainstream research methodologies (e.g. unobtrusive observation, critical incident analysis, depth interview, grounded theory) and include disaggregated study of VF and VR populations in both their host and guest roles. The end results may be the theorisation of abstracted issues that have not previously been identified as part of VFR discourse. One may be the relative balance of discretionary choice and constrained obligation in the entertainment of friends and relatives and how they are reflected in the structure and duration of a VFR experience.

Another topic that lies at the heart of VFR hosting concerns the reciprocal expectations behind giving. In the book that made his name as a sociologist/anthropologist, Mauss (1954) famously laid bare the hidden expectations of exchange and reciprocity that underlie gift *giving*, often articulated in the hospitality cliche 'There is no such thing as a free lunch'. The Roman author Seneca had, more than a millennium earlier, written a longer book similar to that of Mauss, analysing what he called 'benefits', which elaborated the responsibilities of gift receiving as much as giving (Seneca, 1620: 1–163). Both works provide a suggestive start point for exploring the concept of exchange in disaggregated VFR travel as an immediate and long-term factor. In modern times, it has been observed that social relations created by new mobilities are in a state of continuing revolution. Thus, understanding the internal character and dynamics of VFR travel, as the Kent model attempted to do, may be as important for academics and policy makers as it is for tourism managers.

Notes

(1) The four excluded are 'country of origin', 'accommodation stayed in', 'method of travel to Ireland' and 'those travelling by sea'. These were thought to be less important/interesting for this chapter, and there were small differences between VFs and VRs in their responses to them.
(2) Mosaic is a lifestyle system of social grading in the UK based on post code addresses that uses a range of data (residential, educational, occupational, socio-demographic) to classify the population into 69 types aggregated into 15 groups.

References

AEI (1999) *Overseas Student Statistics 1998*. Canberra: Department of Employment, Education, Training and Youth Affairs.

Ali, N. and Holden, A. (2006) Post-colonial Pakistani Mobilities: the embodiment of the 'myth of return' in tourism. *Mobilities* 1 (2), 217–242.

Backer, E. (2008) VFR travel: An examination of the expenditures of VFR travellers and their hosts. *Current Issues in Tourism* 10 (4), 366–377.

Backer, E. (2009) VFR travel: An assessment of VFR versus non-VFR travellers. Unpublished PhD thesis, Southern Cross University, Australia.

Bischoff, E. and Koenig-Lewis, N. (2007) VFR tourism: The importance of university students as hosts. *International Journal of Tourism Research 9*, 465–484.

British Tourism Authority (2002) Final Report, 'UK-OK'. London: British Tourist Authority.

BTR (2003) *International Visitor Survey 1999–2002*. Canberra, Australia.

Denman, R. (1988) *A Response to the VFR Market: A Response to the English Tourist Board and Regional Tourist Boards*. London: British Tourist Authority.

Duval, D.T. (2004) Conceptualizing return visits: A transnational perspective. In T.E. Coles and D.J. Timothy (eds) *Tourism, Diasporas and Space* (pp. 50–61). London: Routledge.

Gitelson, R.J. and Kerstetter, D.H. (1994) The influence of friends and relatives in travel decision-making. In J.L. Crotts and W.F. van Raaij (eds) *Economic Psychology of Travel and Tourism* (pp. 59–68). New York: Haworth.

Jackson, R.T. (1990) VFR tourism: Is it underestimated? *The Journal of Tourism Studies* 1 (2), 10–17.

Kent County Council and the Tourism Company (2011) *Visiting Friends and Relatives Study: Final Report.* SusTRIP – 'Sustainable Tourism Research and Intelligence Partnership', European Union, June 2011.

King, B. (1996) VFR – A future agenda. In H.R. Yaman (ed.) *VFR Tourism: Issues and Implications* (pp. 70–84). Melbourne: Victoria University of Technology.

Langolis, S., Theodore, J. and Ineson, E. (1999). Poland: Inbound tourism from the UK. *Tourism Management* 20, 461–469.

Law, R., Cheung, C. and Lo, A. (2004) The relevance of profiling travel activities for improving destination marketing strategies. *International Journal of Contemporary Hospitality Management* 16 (6), 355–362.

Lehto, X.Y., Morrison, A.M. and O'Leary, J.T. (2001) Does the visiting friends and relatives typology make a difference? *Journal of Travel Research* 40 (2), 201–212.

Mason, J. (2004) Managing kinship over long distances: The significance of 'the visit'. *Social Policy and Society* 3 (4), 421–429.

Mauss, Marcel (1954) *The Gift: Forms and Functions of Exchange in Archaic Societies.* London: Cohen and West.

Morrison, A., Woods, B., Pearce, P., Moscardo, G. and Sung, H. (2000) Marketing to the visiting friends and relatives segment: An international analysis. *Journal of Vacation Marketing* 6 (2), 102–118.

Morrison, A.M. and O'Leary, J.T. (1995) The VFR market: Desperately seeking respect. *The Journal of Tourism Studies* 6 (1), 2–5.

Moscardo, G., Pearce, P., Morrison, A.M., Green, D. and O'Leary, J.T. (2000) Developing a typology for understanding visiting friends and relatives markets. *Journal of Travel Research* 38 (3), 251–259.

Nguyen, T.H. and King, B. (1998) Migrant homecomings: Viet kieu attitude towards travelling back to Vietnam. *Pacific Tourism Review* 1, 349–361.

Parr, N., Lucas, D. and Mok, M. (2000) Branch migration and the international dispersal of families. *International Journal of Population Geography* 6, 213–227.

Seaton, A.V. (1994) Are relatives friends? Reassessing the VFR category in segmenting tourism markets. In A.V. Seaton (ed.) *Tourism: The State of the Art* (pp. 316–321). Chichester: John Wiley.

Seaton, A.V. and Tagg, S. (1995) Disaggregating friends and relatives in VFR tourism research: The Northern Ireland evidence 1991–1993. *The Journal of Tourism Studies* 6 (1), 6–18.

Seneca (1620) *The Workes of Lucius Annaeus Seneca Newly Inlarged and Corrected by Thomas Lodge.* London: Willi Stansby.

Stephenson, M. (2002) Travelling to the ancestral homelands: The aspirations and experiences of a UK Caribbean community. *Current Issues in Tourism* 5 (5), 378–425.

Tham, A.M-E. (2006) Travel stimulated by international students in Australia. *International Journal of Tourism Research* 8 (6), 451–468.

Tie, C. and Seaton, A.V. (2013) Diasporic identity, heritage and 'HomeComing': How Sarawakian-Chinese tourists feel on tour in Beijing. *Tourism Analysis* 18, 227–243.

UKTS (2008) The UK Tourist - Statistics 2007. VisitBritain, VisitScotland, Wales Tourist Board. Edinburgh: TNS Travel and Tourism.

Wilmott, P. and Young, M. (1962) *Family and Kinship in East London.* London: Penguin.

4 The VFR and Migration Nexus – The Impacts of Migration on Inbound and Outbound Australian VFR Travel

Brian King and Larry Dwyer

Introduction

There is increasing scholarly recognition that the process and experience of migration stimulates tourism generally and VFR travel in particular. It is evident that such links operate in both directions, with migration influencing VFR travel and vice versa (Williams & Hall, 2002). The interrelationship has prospective implications for policymakers with an interest in understanding migration and tourism. However, there has been minimal evaluation of the proposed link to date and most approaches have adopted a qualitative approach. The present chapter addresses this gap and connects with Chapter 6 which explores the experiences of migrants who are involved in hosting their visiting friends and relatives.

Changing migration and tourism flows have created a dynamic environment for those seeking to understand the interconnections. This chapter explores the relationship and how it has changed over time. There has been an increasing global dispersal of diasporic communities and this has led migrants to travel extensively between their new and old countries. As their income levels and spending capacities have grown, diaspora travel has expanded in both scale and scope. Familial and friendship ties have prompted overseas settlers to stay connected with those who have remained in their country of origin (Basch *et al.*, 1994). Migrants also retain strong emotional and social attachments (Nguyen & King, 2002). Having settled and established themselves in a new country, they proceed to make return visits to previous countries of residence or of origin (Feng & Page, 2000). Tourism may also be stimulated by subsequent visits from friends and relatives (VFR). There is likelihood that permanent migration will be triggered as outbound tourism increases from countries that have been recipients of inward migration (King, 1994; King & Gamage, 1994).

This chapter draws upon Australian trends to explore migration as a determinant of VFR travel flows and vice versa. The authors investigate whether the link between migration and VFR travel is stronger than is the case for overall tourism. In common with other sections of this book which have noted the widespread underestimation of the VFR phenomenon, this has also occurred in Australia as a result of official approaches to classification and data collection. Official Australian government inbound and outbound tourism statistics refer to visiting relatives (VR) and exclude any consideration of visiting friends. The Australian context is of particular interest because the migrant intake of about 200,000 (190,000 places in 2013–2014) is substantial, particularly when considered in the context of a resident population of only 23 million.

The Evolution of Tourism and Migration to Australia

Inward migration has always played a prominent role in nation building. Immigration policies during the post-Federation (1901) years gave preference to British or European immigrants and became known as the White Australia Policy. Through the 1970s and 1980s these were progressively amended to become more welcoming of Asian migrants. During the post-war years, the Australian government showed an increasing interest in cultural pluralism (often termed 'multiculturalism') which recognises and celebrates the contributions to national development by migrants from different origins and cultures. This has helped to reinforce Australia's strengthening relationship with the Asia-Pacific region as a source of both migrants and leisure travellers, including VFRs.

Australia's migrant intake accelerated and diversified after the recession of the early 1990s, with arrivals peaking in the early years after the millennium. Given the importance of tourism to national development (Tourism Research Australia 2010, 2014a, 2014b), it is unsurprising that the migration/VFR nexus is a potentially fruitful area of research. As has been noted by Dwyer *et al.* (1993), the impacts of migration vary in different jurisdictions. While the substantial scale and value of VFR travel in Australia is outlined in other parts of this book, the present chapter explores how tourism and migration have shaped one another over time. More specifically, the authors focus upon the links between migration (flows and stocks) and VFR travel (inbound and outbound) flows. These offer the prospect of providing insights into the responsiveness of tourism flows to migration numbers and a quantitative perspective of VFR travel. Intuitively, the link between migration and VFR travel is more obvious than in the case of linkages between migration and other forms of tourism. In particular, the chapter discusses the influence of migration on VFR and non-VFR travel and on total tourism in the context of the inbound and outbound markets. The final section of the chapter offers suggestions for further research.

Migration and VFR Travel Numbers

Putative links

When settlers depart from a source country to establish themselves overseas, it may stimulate tourism through visits by friends and relatives, by visits from settlers themselves and return visits to their country of origin. Increasing visitation from a particular origin country may in turn stimulate additional permanent migration to the destination. Completing the cycle of influence, the scale of permanent migration may influence visitation to a country for holiday, visiting friends and relatives, business and study purposes. The influences may manifest themselves in various ways.

Higher permanent migration produces a larger pool of friends and relatives in the source country with an incentive to visit. The primary impact is evident where permanent residents communicate with kin, friends and/or associates in the home country and draw their attention to Australia's attractions. Such communications may prompt leisure-focused trips where visitors are accommodated by relatives for part of the time and use dedicated tourist facilities at other times. Friends and relatives who are resident overseas may visit another country to participate in life transition events associated with migrants living in that country, including weddings, funerals and birthdays. The links between tourism and migration and educational travel are also identifiable when graduates remain in their country of study after graduation.

Though ultimately discretionary in nature, such opportunities involve varying levels of social obligation and may prompt prospective tourists to travel to a particular country in preference over alternative destinations. Some visits may be subsidised by relative(s) in that destination. In the absence of such assistance, because of financial constraints, it is likely that international travel would simply not occur. Permanent migrants in a country who visit their country of origin for friends and relatives (VFR) purposes may 'promote' their new home, whether explicitly or implicitly, thereby prompting additional applications for permanent residency, as well as stimulating short-term visits. In the case of refugees who possess fewer resources, the influence on tourism is likely to be longer term. Visitation may also be prompted where contact has been made with relatives or friends resident in a third country.

It has been widely observed that permanent migrants enrich cultural life and enhance a country's appeal as a varied and interesting destination. The establishment of restaurants, shops, events and other related facilities (such as 'Chinatown') exemplify this phenomenon, which also influences domestic travel. Short-term visitation by people from the country of origin strengthens the community in the adopted country and builds sustainability by maintaining the shared language and cultural traditions for international tourists without friends and/or relatives in the host country (Timothy, 2002). Awareness that their compatriots have settled in a particular country may contribute to visitation. Permanent migrants who retain or forge business links with their country of origin may stimulate Australia's trade and associated business travel.

Increased migration into a country may prompt an increase in the domestic accommodation stock that can be accessed by friends and relatives who are visiting from overseas. Given that a substantial proportion of VFRs can travel at less cost because of being accommodated in the homes of friends and relatives, this may have had the effect of boosting the proportion of VFR travellers within the overall category of tourists to Australia. The provision of accommodation on a non-commercial basis acts as a subsidy and price incentive for travel to Australia. The distinction between VFR motives and accommodation is explored in more depth in the following chapter. Though many of the prospective causal links have not been substantiated in the literature, it seems logical that VFR travel between countries will be influenced by previous migration patterns. In the case of Australia, the phenomenon of 'chain migration' creates a pool of residents who can stimulate tourist visits by relatives and friends. Such travel is most likely in cases where kinship bonds have been particularly strong.

Empirical studies

Jackson (1990) discussed the migration-tourism link, noting that the total flow of VFR within Australia as a proportion of the size of country of birth migrant groups 'is significantly and directly related to the proportion of recent migrants'. He argued that VFR is both a cause and an effect of such migration and that changing migration 'will create ongoing changes in the nature of VFR travel' (15). The re-shaping of friendship and kinship networks that result from migration may generate VFR travel flows (Jackson, 1990; Dwyer et al., 1993; King, 1994; Paci, 1994; King & Gamage, 1994; Seaton & Tagg, 1995; Yuan et al., 1995; Feng & Page, 2000). VFR travel flows will depend on both the characteristics of the network and the attractiveness of the place (Boyne et al., 2002; Williams & Hall, 2002).

A recent study of migration-VFR travel links (Dwyer et al., 2014), comparing the census years 1991 with 2006, found that migration was the second placed determinant of VFR arrivals after income in the case of both years. A 10% increase in migration would have produced additional

VFR flows of 4.9% and 6.6% respectively for 1991 and 2006. The study also found that relative price levels between Australia and origin countries assumed greater importance for inbound VFR travel in 2006 over 1991, while the importance of income and transportation costs declined. The reduced importance of income may relate to the fact that VFR travellers in Australia increasingly opt to stay with friends and relatives rather than in commercial accommodation (Backer, 2007, 2010, 2011). The same study also showed that in 1991 migration was the third most important determinant of VFR-related departures, behind income and transport costs. However, by 2006 migration had become the most important determinant, even exceeding income as an influence. In 1991 a 10% increase in migration would have produced an additional 5.5% in VFR outbound flows. By 2006 the comparable figure had increased to 7.1%. The relative price level between Australia and origin countries assumed greater importance for VFR travellers in 2006 over 1991, while income, transportation costs and population declined in importance. While outbound VFR travellers have become more responsive to changes in migration numbers, they have become less sensitive to changes in income, transportation costs and relative prices (Dwyer et al., 2014).

Destination-based attractions have an impact on both tourism generally and on VFR travel in particular (Boyne et al., 2002). The maintenance of family and friendship networks presupposes a degree of mutual travel obligation and may prompt VFR travel in both directions. Such flows are dependent on family relationships, place attachments, leisure attractions of place and location, and the migrant life cycle (Williams & Hall, 2002). According to Crompton (1981), travel offers a means of reinforcing family ties and enhances kinship. Nguyen (1996) indicated that migrant travel reaffirms family ties and protects participants for their social circumstances. Family obligations may provide a rationale for travelling and for choosing destinations. A number of studies (Smith & Toms, 1978; Hollander, 1982; Jackson, 1990; Dwyer et al., 1993) have examined the tourism and migration relationship in the context of migrant impacts on tourism flows. It is evident that members of diasporic communities maintain familial and friendship ties with individuals in the country of origin (Gmelch, 1992; Basch et al., 1994; Nguyen, 1996) as well as strong emotional and social attachments (Philpott, 1968, 1973; Rubenstein, 1979; Nguyen & King, 2002). International labour migration has been responsible for internationalising potential VFR networks, especially among the highly skilled.

Ethnicity has been identified as a powerful driver of return visits from migrants to their friends and relatives in the country of origin (King, 1994). Other recent migrants who share information and observations may also influence VFR-travel decision making. Through the adaption process, migrants refer back to the prevailing conditions in their country of origin alongside the challenges of embracing a new culture. This is influenced by factors such as language ability and the strength of family and kinship ties. The extent of local labour market opportunities may also affect perceptions about adjustments into the host community. A combination of existing and perceived family networks in the new country and links with other recently arrived migrants may build a sense of belonging. From a reading of the migration and acculturation literature one may infer that the strength of family and kinship ties influences the incidence of domestic and international tourism within the host country. Once recently arrived migrants have acquired the necessary resources, international travel becomes a powerful medium for ethnic reunion.

VFR trips by permanent migrants impact on Australia's foreign exchange earnings and terms of trade and contribute to an expansion of imports. Establishing and expanding businesses and jobs produces positive economic impacts, notably in the case of Australian-based travel agencies and tour operators catering to outbound tourists. Dwyer *et al.* (1993) established a clear relationship between migration and tourism flows both inbound and outbound. The authors presented preliminary evidence about the process of maturation, with a tailing off in travel activity once settlers become longer established in Australia. Subsequently, other studies have measured the economic relationship (Dwyer *et al.*, 2014; Forsyth *et al.*, 2012).

Though the relationship between migration and tourism is ongoing, its quantitative significance may have shifted. The present chapter suggests that the migration and tourism phenomena are closely connected, though more recent cohorts from sources such as China and India may have differential impacts from those of earlier migrant cohorts (e.g. from Italy or Greece). The advent of lower real travel costs to and from Australia has influenced tourist movements. More recent migrants (e.g. from Asia and Africa) are increasingly stimulating tourism flows. This prompts the question about whether the migration and tourism relationships of recent arrivals are following a similar pattern to earlier waves of European migrants. In a further exploration of the emerging relationship, Williams and Hall (2002) proposed a model depicting tourism activity as stimulating migration and characterised migration as inducing tourism flows. Such relationships were explored in the context of a geographical extension of friendship, ethnic and kinship networks. While such interdependencies are not new, their scale, intensity and geographical scope have significantly increased over recent decades.

The Influence of Tourism on Migration to Australia

Williams and Hall (2002) noted that increased tourist arrivals into Australia may boost applications for permanent residency. These are more prevalent amongst friends and relatives in the origin country who have visited and been favourably impressed by Australia. The 'family reunion' category of migration to Australia may stimulate both VFR movements and applications to migrate. Australia operates a quota-based migration system, with falling numbers when the quota is tight. 'Transilient' migration is another dimension of the migration-tourist linkage and is prevalent when professionals and managers move internationally for career development (Richmond, 2002). Their period of residence in a particular location may constitute a short- or medium-term pause in their career. 'Skilled' or 'business' migrants are typically posted to a particular country or location, or respond to international advertisements seeking highly skilled personnel. Residence typically extends over a two- or three-year period. Transilient migration exhibits the characteristics of an extended form of tourism, with a substantial average length of stay. The most significant manifestation of this form of migration in Australia is educational travel, with a substantial proportion of international students eventuating as migrants. Such activity may generate visits from friends and relatives who have the means to become tourists and stay in commercial accommodation such as hotels and resorts, rather than in the homes of colleagues or relatives. These visitors are themselves prospective transilient migrants.

Tourist visits may also stimulate the phenomenon of 'retirement migration'. This is exemplified by Americans who have acquired retirement houses in the Bay of Islands, New Zealand and in the case of many British migrants to Australia. Fluctuating living standards in the source country and in the destination may influence when immigration leads to tourism and/or tourism leads to immigration. Migration to Australia from continental Europe diminished greatly once European living standards came closer to par with those prevalent in Australia. In the case of the newly industrialising countries of North East Asia, rapidly rising living standards and middle class affluence extended the numbers who could visit Australia as tourists or take advantage of the skilled migration category for emigration purposes.

The increasing incidence of working and living abroad extends the search for places of retirement and overcomes the traditional obstacle for living abroad: a lack of familiarity. Diasporic movements have shaped the relationship between economically developed migrant-receiving countries and other developed and developing countries. The widespread dispersal of diasporic communities stimulated migrant travel between source and destination countries, prompting a growing demographic phenomenon. Given its global significance, surprisingly little research has examined the characteristics and implications of the travel activities of migrant communities.

'Globalisation' has played a major role in the evolving relationship between tourism and migration. Transient populations who reside in diverse locations may form attachments of varying levels of intensity depending on the intensity of 'sense of place'. Such communities play an important part in shaping place identities through the connections which they form between global and local networks. The tourism and migration literature provides a preliminary conceptualisation of the relationship between the two phenomena. Relevant empirical studies have been conducted by Nguyen and King (2002) and by Boyne *et al.* (2002). The literature has progressively provided a more holistic view of the relationships which connect tourism and diaspora (Nguyen & King, 2002; Coles & Timothy, 2004) and the role of production and consumption (Williams & Hall, 2002). These contributions provide invaluable contextual support for the emerging identification of tourism-migration links. Tourism-migration relationships also illustrate the importance of understanding the impacts on tourism of contemporary global economic and political processes and the circulation of capital and labour (Williams & Hall, 2002). To date, the importance of the VFR component of tourism within such links has been neglected in the literature on globalisation.

Australian inbound and outbound tourism may have varied as a result of decreasing real travel costs, notably the appreciating value of the Australian dollar (though it has fallen from its peak it remains relatively high by historical standards) (Forsyth *et al.*, 2012). Distinctions may also be evident between the experiences and behaviours of migrant groups who have settled during different periods. It is likely that Asians (a larger proportion of the more recent settler groups) are better positioned to stimulate frequent travel activity because of Australia's proximity to their countries of origin. To date there has been little empirical investigation of whether the relationships evident between current migration and tourism resemble those which were applicable to earlier arrivals, notably from Europe.

Diasporas and Tourism

Diasporas have shaped relationships between western nations and many other countries. The wide dispersal of diasporic communities has prompted travel activity by migrants between their new and old countries, creating a phenomenon that continues to expand in both scale and scope. Increasing numbers of migrants are travelling to new destinations and in different ways. For example the growing number of migrants from Ethiopia into Australia has led to travel back patterns that connect Australia and Africa via routes through the Middle East (Filep & Bereded-Samuel, 2012). Assumptions about migrant needs have often been stereotyped and migrant travel motives and destination tastes and preferences are poorly understood. Better information is urgently needed to enhance our understanding of the growth of migration to Australia from emerging sources such as Asia and more recently from Africa.

According to King (1994) migrant travellers display 'a sense of belonging to or identifying with a way of life that has been left behind' (174). This sense of belonging often involves a cultural dimension. Nguyen (1996) explored social and cultural issues underlying migrant travel and observed that travel in certain cultures is prompted by a sense of obligation or compulsion. Migrant identities cross the boundaries between countries which possess very different histories, social values and cultural mythologies and involve interplay between 'home' and 'away'. Migrants' travel motives may include the maintenance of identity and nostalgia, and attachment towards their ancestral home. Travel to the homeland may revive a sense of self and provide a temporary sense of empowerment, belonging and direction. Such visits may help migrants to maintain a balanced life and resolve certain identity-related issues during their adjustment to a new environment. Forming a cultural reconnection with their past may provide protagonists with a buffer from the upheavals associated with migration and assist adaptation to the host country. Migrant travel behaviours may be influenced by personal interests, family ties and obligations and in some cases by spiritual beliefs and religious practices. These may help to explain destination choices, the identity of the decision maker, who travels first and when. Nguyen and King (2002) have proposed that the adapted culture exhibited by migrants is a critical determinant of travel behaviours. Travel to migrant homelands may round out identities and assist environmental adjustment. Migrant travel consumption may be both a consequence and a reflection of adapted culture.

The literature on diaspora tourism has increasingly acknowledged ethnic groups as a growing market segment (Nguyen & King, 2002). Thanopoulos and Walle (1988) and Ostrowski (1991) identified the significance of expatriates and the market for outbound and inbound tourism in destinations. King (1994) has argued that national tourism organisations are neglecting a powerful market segment where the visitor profile is poorly understood. In fact King (1994: 174) indicated that for ethnic reunion travellers such motivation commonly derives from a sense of belonging to or identifying with a way of life that has been left behind. The sense of lost 'roots' is a potent influence for travel and affects successive generations of migrants, not only the first. It is a particularly strong influence in the countries of North America and Australasia whose recent history has been built on migration (King, 1994: 174). The major debate within the tourism literature concerns the classification and measurement of ethnic tourism. The use of VFR as a 'catch-all' category oversimplifies the results and cannot accommodate trip motivations.

Tourism and migration are associated with the creation of place identities and hence connect the local and the global. Held (2004) has noted that the 'explosion of travel migration, fighting, and economic interchange provided an enormous impetus to the transformation of the form and shape of human communities, for the later increasingly became enmeshed in networks and systems of interchange' (2000: 1). A number of empirical studies have tested the relationship between tourism and migration (Boyne *et al.*, 2002). It is most evident in cases where emigration occurs from communities where wider kinship bonds have been intense. Williams and Hall's model (2002) illustrates that tourism leads to migration and that migration in turn leads to tourism activity. Such patterns are a manifestation of friendship and of ethnic and kinship networks. While not a new phenomenon, the scale, intensity and geographical scope of such interdependencies have been accelerating (Dwyer *et al.*, 2014).

Conclusions

A review of the migration and tourism literature has shown that the relationship is belatedly receiving attention from researchers but that the nature of the connections merits further investigation. Migration is a precondition for VFR travel, which is in part an extension of chain migration. VFR travel can flow in both directions along family and kin networks depending on the level of mutual travel obligations. Such travel, therefore, depends on the structure of family and kin relationships and on the prevalence of place attachments. VFR is often not the sole reason for travel but commonly involves a combination of motives that, when pursued at a destination, results in participation in activities that extend beyond VFR. This indicates a need to conduct studies on relationships between migrant travel and its underlying motives. The foregoing discussion has provided some insights to clarify ethnic tourism involving family connections and shared cultural values. Ethnic travellers are defined as those who are explicitly aware of the link between the country visited and their family links. Their primary purpose of travel to an ancestral home is to satisfy a need and demand for ethnic identity. Placing tourism within the framework of temporary and permanent mobility also allows us to see tourism within a wider social context over the life span of individuals as well as to gain a greater appreciation of the constraints that prevent or limit mobility. Coles and Timothy (2004) proposed that the conceptualisation and theory of tourism should consider other mobilities that promote human movement including the creation of extended networks of kinship and community on regional, national and global scales that also promote human movement.

This evaluation has argued that there is a strong quantitative link between migration and VFR travel and also between other forms of tourism and migration. Empirical studies indicate that it is appropriate for tourism stakeholders to consider migration numbers alongside other determinants of Australia's inbound and outbound travel flows such as income, aviation costs and exchange rate changes, which have dominated recent discussions.

By implication, changing migration patterns into Australia will create an ongoing pattern of changes to the various tourism market segments. Observations about such changes should be of interest to tourism and migration-related policy makers, peak industry bodies and stakeholders such as airlines and tour operators.

It has been noted that social networks, cultural traits, ethnic origins and ties are important elements of VFR travel and that their complexity makes it difficult to explain fluctuating trends. The factors affecting VFR travel may provide insights into migrant travel and contribute to forecasting the travel demand of migrants. Accurate forecasting is at the heart of effective tourism planning and decision making, since policy makers, planners and managers must attempt to match supply with future demand. The empirical results can provide important inputs into another neglected area of research, namely determining the economic impacts of migration-induced VFR travel. The estimated elasticities can inform projected changes in VFR travel numbers that may result from future changes in the stock and flows of migrants into Australia. Differences may also be evident between the experiences and behaviours of migrant groups who have settled during different periods.

Overall, this chapter study should enhance understanding of the long-term implications of migration for VFR travel. A comprehensive exploration of the influence of country of origin on migrant travel behaviours should provide a stronger context for understanding the motivations associated with VFR travel and migration. Comparative studies of countries with significant migrant intakes are needed to validate existing studies. In particular, the extent to which the links between migration and VFR travel are equally strong for countries other than Australia remain largely untested. Given that many countries have large migrant intakes, the discussion presented in this chapter has implications for destination managers worldwide.

References

Backer, E. (2007) VFR travel: An examination of the expenditures of VFR travellers and their hosts. *Current Issues in Tourism* 10 (4), 366–377.

Backer, E. (2010) Opportunities for commercial accommodation in VFR. *International Journal of Tourism Research* 12 (4), 334–354.

Backer E. (2011) VFR travel: It *is* underestimated. *Tourism Management* 33 (5), 74–79.

Basch, L., Glick Schiller, N. and Szanton-Blanc, C. (1994) *Nations Unbound: Transnational Projects, Postcolonial Predicaments and the De-territorialised Nation-States*. New York: Gordon and Breach.

Boyne, S. (2001) Hosts, friends and relatives in rural Scotland: VFR tourism market relationships explored. In L. Roberts and D. Hall (eds) *Rural Tourism and Recreation: Principles to Practice*. Wallingford: CABI Publishing.

Boyne, S., Carswell, F. and Hall, D. (2002) Reconceptualising VFR Tourism. In C.M. Hall and A.M. Williams (eds) *Tourism and Migration: New Relationships between Production and Consumption* (pp. 241–256). Dordrecht: Kluwer Academic Publishers.

Coles, T. and Timothy, D.J. (2004) *Tourism, Diasporas and Space*. London: Routledge.

Crompton, J. (1981) Dimensions of the social group role in pleasure vacations. *Annals of Tourism Research* 8 (4), 550–567.

Dwyer, L., Burnley, I., Forsyth, P. and Murphy, P. (1993) *Tourism-Immigration Inter-relationships*. Canberra: Bureau of Tourism Research.

Dwyer, L., Seetaram, N., Forsyth, P. and King, B.E.M. (2014) Is the migration-tourism relationship only about VFR? *Annals of Tourism Research* 46, 130–143.

Feng, K. and Page, S. (2000). An exploratory study of the tourism, migration-immigration nexus: Travel experience of Chinese residents in New Zealand. *Current Issues in Tourism* 3 (3), 246–281.

Filep, S. and Bereded-Samuel, E. (2012) Holidays against depression? An Ethiopian Australian initiative. *Current Issues in Tourism* 15 (3), 281–285.

Forsyth, P., Dwyer, L., Seetaram, N. and King, B.E.M. (2012) Measuring the economic impact of migration-induced tourism. *Tourism Analysis* 17 (5), 559–571.

Gmelch, G. (1992) *Double Passage: The Lives of Caribbean Migrants Abroad and Back Home*. Ann Arbor, MI: University of Michigan Press.

Held D. (ed.) (2004) *A Globalising World? Culture, Economics, Politics* (2nd edn). Routledge: London.

Hollander, G. (1982) *Determinants of Demand for Travel to and from Australia*. Bureau of Industry Economics, Working Paper no. 26. Canberra, Australia.

Jackson, R. (1990) VFR tourism: Is it underestimated? *Journal of Tourism Studies* 1 (2), 10–17. Reprinted in Special Issue *Journal of Tourism Studies* 14 (1), 17–24.

King, B.E.M. (1994) What is ethnic tourism? An Australian perspective. *Tourism Management* 15 (3), 173–6.

King, B.E.M. and Gamage, M.A. (1994) Measuring the value of the ethnic connection: Expatriate travellers from Australia to Sri Lanka. *Journal of Travel Research* 33 (2), 46–50.

Nguyen, T.H. (1996) Ethnic Vietnamese travel from Australia to Vietnam. Unpublished MA thesis, Melbourne, Victoria University.

Nguyen, T.H. and King, B.E.M. (2002) Migrant communities and tourism consumption: The case of the Vietnamese in Australia. In C.M. Hall and A.M. Williams (eds) *Tourism and Migration: New Relationships between Production and Consumption*. Dordrecht: Kluwer Academic Publishers.

Ostrowski, S. (1991) Ethnic tourism: Focus on Poland. *Tourism Management* 12 (2), 125–131.

Paci, E. (1994) The major international VFR markets. *Travel and Tourism Analyst* 6 (August), 36–50.

Philpott, S.B. (1968) Remittance obligation, social networks and choice among Montserratian migrants in Britain. *Man* 3 (3), 465–476.

Philpott, S.B. (1973) West Indian migration: The Montserrat case. *London School of Economics Monographs in Anthropology*, No. 47. London: Athone Press.

Richmond, R.H. (2002) Socio-demographic aspects of globalisation: Canadian perspectives on migrations. *Canadian Studies in Population Special Issue on Migration and Globalisation* 29 (1), 123–149.

Rubenstein, H. (1979) The return ideology in West Indian Migration. *University of Manitoba Paper in Anthropology* 20 (1), 21–38.

Seaton, A.V. and Palmer, C. (1997) Understanding VFR tourism behaviour: The first five years of the United Kingdom Tourism Survey. *Tourism Management* 18 (6), 345–355.

Seaton, A.V. and Tagg, S.J. (1995) Disaggregating friends and relatives in VFR tourism research: The Northern Ireland evidence 1991–1993. *Journal of Tourism Studies* 6 (1), 6–18.

Smith, A.B. and Toms, J.N. (1978) Factors affecting demand for international travel to and from Australia. *Occasional Paper* 11. Australia: Bureau of Transport.

Thanopoulos, J. and Walle, A.H. (1988) Ethnicity and its relevance to marketing: The case of tourism. *Journal of Travel Research* 26 (3), 11–14.

Timothy, D.J. (2002) Tourism and the growth of urban ethnic islands. In C.M. Hall and A.M. Williams (eds) *Tourism and Migration: New Relationships between Production and Consumption*. Dordrecht: Kluwer Academic Publishers.

Tourism Research Australia (2010) *State of the Industry 2010*. Australian Government, Department of Resources, Energy and Tourism, Tourism Research Australia, Canberra.

Tourism Research Australia (2014a) *Tourism's Contribution to the Australian Economy, 1997–98 to 2012–13*. Release: 30 April 2014.

Tourism Research Australia (2014b) *Tourism Update: Updated Results to State of the Industry 2013 – December Quarter 2013*. Release: 9 May 2014.

Williams, A. and Hall, M. (2002) Tourism, migration, circulation and mobility: The contingencies of times and place. In C.M. Hall and A.M. Williams (eds) *Tourism and Migration: New Relationships between Production and Consumption*. Dordrecht: Kluwer Academic Publishers.

Yuan, T.F., Fridgen, J.D., Hsieh, S. and O'Leary, J.T. (1995) Visiting friends and relatives travel market: The Dutch case. *Journal of Tourism Studies* 6 (1), 19–26.

5 VFR Travel: Its True Dimensions

Elisa Backer

Introduction

As outlined in Chapter 1, VFR travel is a form of tourism that is substantial in scale and can be beneficial to industry operators. As the oldest form of travel (Backer, 2011) it is therefore surprising that tourism academic research only commenced in 1990 and that, relative to its size, little research has been done. Seven reasons outlining why VFR travel has been neglected were outlined in 2007 (Backer, 2007) and an eighth was subsequently added (Backer, 2010a). These reasons are presented in Chapter 7 of this book. However, a number of them warrant discussion in this fifth chapter. One of these reasons is 'tourism textbooks'. Despite its size, VFR travel is given, at best, a cursory mention in tourism textbooks and VFR has minimal presence in the relevant texts (Backer, 2009). Present by way of a single column in a table, or by a few paragraphs at best, VFR barely makes it to the index of many tourism textbooks and does not even rate a place in the index of the others. Some improvement in coverage has occurred recently (for example Morrison, 2013; Weaver & Lawton, 2015). However, this still falls short of having a chapter or a book dedicated to such a sizeable field.

Another of the reasons provided to explain why VFR has been neglected relates to discrepancies with the existing data. The size of VFR in terms of purpose of visit is not the same as the size of VFR by accommodation. Compounding this problem is the point that Jackson (1990, 2003) raised with visitors being required to self-classify. By referring to VFR by purpose of visit data, which is generally smaller than the VFR by accommodation data, there is a resulting underestimation of the size of VFR. Furthermore, whichever official dataset is referred to, it only comprises a proportion of VFR travellers and consequentially underestimates the true dimensions of VFR travel. This chapter primarily aims to explain the true dimensions of VFR. It will firstly explain the size, based on an analysis of data in Australia. It will then provide some core characteristics of VFRs relative to non-VFRs, as well as a discussion about the role that is played by hosts.

History of VFR Literature

As introduced in Chapter 1, Jackson (1990) is typically acknowledged as producing the first article dedicated to VFR that was published in a tourism journal. While there were earlier tourism examples where VFR was discussed within the article, VFR was not the focus of the study but part of the analysis. For example, a number of earlier tourism articles used VFR as a form of segmentation in the analysis (i.e. segmented by purpose of visit) (for example Gitelson & Crompton, 1983; Schewe & Calantone, 1978). The sociological aspect associated with VFR dates back even further (for example Havighurst, 1957; Navran, 1967; Rosenblatt *et al.*, 1981; Rosenblatt & Russell, 1975) and VFR has also been analysed in studies that relate to ageing (for example Cowgill & Baulch, 1962). VFR has also been a topic in medical literature, where aspects including definitional constraints (for example Arguin, 2010), health risks (for example Baggett *et al.*, 2009) and health and wellbeing benefits (for example Seeman, 2000) have been considered. These have made VFR a more popular topic than has been the case in the tourism literature.

The volume of VFR travel literature in tourism journals has been relatively scarce given its size, and this was raised earlier through Chapter 1. A content analysis by Griffin (2013), who authors the next chapter in this book, revealed that there were only 39 articles centred on VFR published in tourism journals between 1990 and 2010. However, it is recognised that there have been more articles published in tourism journals since Griffin's work, and that his work did not include book chapters or conference papers. However, these numbers are not great. Of the tourism conferences this author has attended, there has been at most one conference paper dedicated to VFR. Anecdotal evidence from other tourism researchers across the globe suggests that this is the typical experience. Given the size of VFR travel, it is an interesting indicator to have so few conference papers, amongst such a large volume, dedicated to the topic. It serves as an ongoing reminder that VFR travel is indeed still 'desperately seeking respect' (Morrison & O'Leary, 1995: 2).

VFR Travel: It Is Underestimated

In 1990, Richard Jackson's seminal paper (Jackson, 1990) that was reprinted before the journal was discontinued (Jackson, 2003) asked the question 'VFR tourism: is it underestimated?' and, as was revealed in the first chapter, this was answered in 2012 through a response paper, 'VFR travel: it *is* underestimated' (Backer, 2012). In that paper, analysis was undertaken based on primary research and extrapolating it out to a national level to indicate that VFR travel represented 48% of Australia's domestic overnight visitor market. This section will provide an updated analysis of that estimate, based on analysing the raw data from the National Visitors Survey undertaken by Tourism Research Australia (TRA).

Method

An analysis of TRA's National Visitors Survey (NVS) and International Visitors Survey (IVS) was undertaken with data covering the period 2010–2013. For the NVS, TRA conducts interviews with around 120,000 Australian residents aged 15 and over each year. Respondents are interviewed via telephone through a Computer Assisted Telephone Interviewing (CATI) system that involves dialling digits randomly. The survey instrument includes over 70 questions. For the IVS, TRA surveys around 40,000 international visitors aged 15 years and over who are departing the country. The survey is undertaken by Computer Assisted Personal Interviewing (CAPI) in the departure lounges of Australia's eight major airports (Melbourne, Sydney, Brisbane, Perth, Adelaide, Darwin, Gold Coast and Cairns). There are 100 questions in the survey.

The raw data were provided to the author by TRA for the purpose of conducting further research into VFR travel. The data were imported into SPSS and recoded and reformatted according to the VFR Definitional Model. The definitional model provides a conceptual framework for analysing the data based on the definition of VFR being 'A form of travel involving a visit whereby either (or both) the purpose of the trip or the type of accommodation involves visiting friends and/or relatives' (Backer, 2007: 369). This approach allowed the author to aggregate the complete spectrum of VFRs (i.e. travellers who stated a VFR purpose of visit and/or travellers who stayed at the home of friends/relatives). A filter was run on the data to exclude multiple stops and confine the coverage to single stops (to ensure each trip could fit into only one category in the matrix – see Table 5.1). This chapter will focus on an analysis of the 2013 data; however, the data were also analysed across the years 2010–2013 to determine the size of VFR over the four years.

Table 5.1 Size of VFR travel based on domestic overnight visitor data: 2013

	Accommodation: friends & family	Accommodation: commercial
Purpose of visit: VFR	**29.7%**	**7.6%**
	(61.4% VFRs)	(15.8% VFRs)
Purpose of visit: non-VFR	**11%**	**51.7%**
	(22.8% EVFRs)	(non-VFRs)

Results

Results of a range of analyses undertaken are presented in this section. A focus was provided on the domestic 2013 data. It is not possible to merge the data from the NVS and IVS; however, the NVS data were merged to assess whether the 'market' was stable. Information from primary research undertaken in three contrasting regions in Australia is also provided in this chapter.

The size of VFR travel

VFR travel represents a large group of visitors within Australia and accounted for 48.3% of domestic tourism in 2013. The official data for VFR has traditionally been assessed in one of two ways – by purpose of visit *or* type of accommodation. If DMOs rely on either of those statistics to determine the *size* of VFR travel, it will be underestimated. This is because each of those statistics will only assess two of the three types of VFRs (see Table 5.1). There are three different types of VFR travellers. The first type is 'pure' VFRs (PVFRs) who state a VFR purpose of visit and are also staying with friends/relatives. The second type is 'commercial' VFRs (CVFRs) who state a VFR purpose of visit but stay in commercial accommodation. The third type is 'exploitative' VFRs (EVFRs) who stay with friends/relatives but do not report VFR as their main purpose of visit. Those three VFR types can be seen in Table 5.1, which is based on domestic overnight tourism data in 2013 (n=29,987).

As can be determined by referring to the data in Table 5.1, the size of VFR travel in 2013 was 48.3%, with 51.7% being non-VFRs. Of the VFRs, 61.4% of VFRs are PVFRs (which represents 29.7% of all overnight domestic visitors). CVFRs made up 15.8% of all VFRs (or 7.6% of all visitors including non-VFRs); while EVFRs represented 22.8% of all VFRs (11% of the total visitor sample).

VFR travel represents a large proportion of domestic visitors in Australia in every state/territory. The proportion of domestic travellers who were VFR travellers in 2013 was lowest in Northern Territory, comprising 25.6% of all domestic visitors in that year. VFR travel represents a very strong proportion across all other states and territories, particularly Western Australia (49.9%), New South Wales (50%) and South Australia (50.3%). VFR was 48.3% of all overnight visitors in Queensland, 47.9% in the Australian Capital Territory (ACT), 47.2% in Victoria and 42.4% in Tasmania.

The size of VFR travel has remained stable across the four years of 2010–2013, as demonstrated in Table 5.2. The size of VFR based on domestic overnight visitor data (NVS) was 47.9% in 2010, 48.7% in 2011, 48.4% in 2012 and 48.3% in 2013. There was no significant difference between these results, highlighting the stability of VFR travel. The sizes were also considered based on the three VFR types.

Table 5.2 Size of VFR travel based on domestic overnight visitor data: 2010–2013

	PVFR (n)	CVFR (n)	EVFR (n)	All VFR (n)	Non-VFR (n)
2010	28.0% (8,306)	7.2% (2,125)	12.7% (3,752)	47.9% (14,183)	52.1% (15,432)
2011	29.1% (8,684)	7.1% (2,125)	12.5% (3,721)	48.7% (14,530)	51.3% (15,289)
2012	29.4% (6,517)	7.3% (1,621)	11.7% (2,583)	48.4% (10,721)	51.6% (11,424)
2013	29.7% (8,893)	7.6% (2,284)	11.0% (3,302)	48.3% (14,479)	51.7% (15,508)

International VFR travellers

In 2013, 41.3% of international visitors were VFR travellers. In terms of numbers of visitors, the largest source markets were New Zealand, England, Malaysia, Singapore and China. However, the proportion of those markets that were VFRs varied greatly, with strong proportions of visitors from New Zealand and England being VFRs, indicating a potential migration link. The migration-VFR link for Australia was discussed in the previous chapter in this book. International VFR travellers were more likely to be repeat visitors compared to non-VFRs.

Length of stay

The average length of stay for domestic VFR visitors was 3.35 nights, which was the same as for non-VFRs. Of the VFR visitors, PVFRs stayed for 3.5 nights, EVFRs stayed 3.38 nights and CVFRs stayed for 2.70 nights.

International VFRs stayed an average of 27.87 nights, compared with an average stay of 53.71 nights for non-VFRs. Since education purpose of visit is included in international visitor data, these data contribute to the high average international visitor stay.

Generating regions

As presented in Chapter 1, VFRs can come from different generating regions. VFRs were significantly more likely to come from regional areas compared with non-VFRs. Table 1.2 from Chapter 1 similarly highlighted this issue, revealing the differences in the proportion of international visitors across four different local government areas (LGAs). Further, that table depicted the difference between VFRs and non-VFRs in terms of the proportion of international visitors.

International visitors are often statistically more likely to be VFRs than non-VFRs. This was also revealed in a study undertaken at the Sunshine Coast in Australia, which demonstrated that VFRs were significantly more likely to be international visitors than non-VFRs (Backer, 2010b). Domestic VFRs were also found to travel a significantly greater distance compared with non-VFRs (Backer, 2010b).

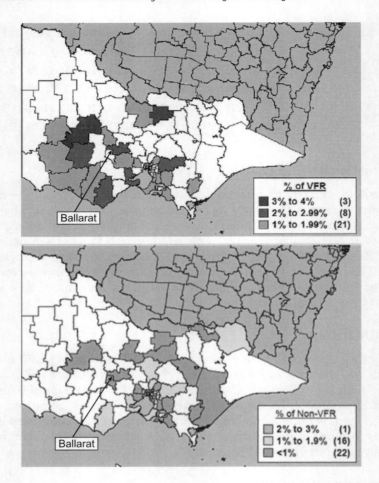

Figure 5.1 Generating region of intrastate visitors to Ballarat based on LGA (VFRs above; non-VFRs below)
Source: Backer and Lynch (2010: 26).

A similar example was outlined in a study in the regional area of Ballarat, about an hour's drive from the Victorian capital city Melbourne in Australia. As depicted in Figure 5.1, the western and southern LGAs were important source markets for instrastate VFRs. In contrast, non-VFRs were more heavily represented by northern and eastern LGAs.

Expenditure

Domestic VFR travellers spent an average of $529 for their trip. This compared to an average of $921 per trip by non-VFR travellers. Of those VFR travellers, the highest expenditure was from those staying in commercial accommodation (CVFRs) who spent on average $825 per trip. These expenditures are what were incurred by the VFR traveller, so do not account for expenditures made by local residents as a result of hosting VFRs.

Trip expenditures for international VFRs were an average of $1,690 compared to $6,677 for non-VFR travellers. Among VFR travellers, those staying with friends/relatives but stating a non-VFR purpose for their trip (EVFRs) had the highest trip spend (of $3,040.45), due to their longer length of stay (45 nights). Those VFRs staying in commercial accommodation (CVFRs) had an average trip spend of $2,878 (and an average stay of 20 nights) while pure VFRs (PVFRs) spent an average of $1,128.37 during their visit in Australia (and stayed an average of 25 nights).

It is worth reflecting on the point made in Chapter 1 regarding how averaged data can shield some of the detail at regional levels. Superficially it would appear that the results from the official national data sets reinforce the thinking that VFRs are of less value to local economies since they spend less money. However, primary research undertaken in a range of contrasting regions has highlighted how the relative difference can vary based on destination. It also revealed that VFRs can outspend non-VFRs in certain categories.

For example, research undertaken by the author in Australia's Sunshine Coast (South-East Queensland) revealed that VFR travellers (n=229) spent a mean of $1,873.89 over the duration of their stay in the destination region, compared with non-VFR travellers (n=509) who spent $2,023.33. The categories of expenditures are outlined in Table 5.3. As outliers skewed the data, the assumption of normality was violated, and data were converted to logarithmic functions. The raw and log means are presented in Table 5.3; the t-tests were performed on the log means. Where the Levene's homogeneity of variances test was significant, an adjusted t-test (equal variances not assumed) was used. Based on these results performed at the 95% confidence level, non-VFR travellers spent more than VFR travellers on groceries, dining out and accommodation, while VFR travellers spent more on entertainment. Overall, non-VFR travellers spent more than VFR travellers.

The same survey instrument was also applied to the North Queensland city of Townsville, where VFRs outspent non-VFRs on dining out, liquor and shopping. However, non-VFRs spent significantly more than VFRs on accommodation and attractions. The average daily expenditure for non-VFRs was $213.78 compared to VFRs' $313.70 but the differences were not significantly different at the 95% confidence level.

At a contrasting destination, Ballarat in regional Victoria, non-VFRs were found to outspend VFRs for accommodation and attractions, and there was no significant difference (at the 95% confidence level) for dining

Table 5.3 Relationship between trip expenditures for VFR and non-VFR travellers at the Sunshine Coast

	VFR mean (Log/SD)	Non-VFR mean (Log/SD)	Levene's F-test	t-value	p
Groceries	$185.99 (1.51/1.02)	$179.54 (1.80/.76)	53.61*	−3.90*	0.000
Leisure shopping	$437.29 (1.72/1.14)	$273.36 (1.61/1.11)	0.037	1.22	0.222
Restaurants/ cafes	$431.85 (2.12/.86)	$395.92 (2.29/.68)	14.99*	−2.62*	0.009
Fuel	$64.08 (1.12/.90)	$60.04 (1.25/.84)	5.04*	−1.80	0.073
Entertainment	$41.23 (.46/.88)	$28.50 (.32 /.76)	16.79*	2.16*	0.031
Activities	$40.61 (.47/.85)	$46.45 (.38/.84)	3.50	1.29	0.198
Liquor	$119.72 (1.35/.98)	$92.88 (1.28/.98)	1.36	0.88	0.378
Attractions	$224.49 (1.10/1.21)	$175.06 (1.15/1.18)	0.64	−0.51	0.612
Accommodation	$269.59 (0.78/1.24)	$715.78 (2.46/.85)	119.79*	−18.63*	0.000
Car hire/taxis	$52.17 (.27/0.78)	$52.85 (.32/.84)	2.56	−0.79	0.428
Total expenditure	$1,873.89 (2.86/.69)	$2,023.33 (3.09/.45)	34.91*	−4.57*	0.000

*Significant at the 95% level

out, leisure shopping, fuel, groceries, liquor, entertainment and car hire/ taxis. The total daily expenditures for non-VFRs were $318.42, which was significantly more than VFRs' $191.77 (at the 95% confidence level).

These few examples highlight that it is important to understand VFR at a regional level in order to provide adequate information to inform marketing campaigns, as the average data may not be appropriate at each regional level. In addition, analysing the expenditure of VFRs without consideration of the hosts' expenditure can also omit part of the detail.

The role of the host

The next chapter in this book pays attention to the role of hosts in regards to the immigration-VFR relationship. However, the role of hosts is important to understand in a very broad way. It is not possible to assess the role of hosts with the NVS data, as the surveys gather visitor data only. However, in the primary research undertaken by the author at a number of contrasting destinations, hosts were also surveyed to ensure a complete assessment of VFR travel could be obtained.

As McKercher (1995) stated, 'no system exists in Australia to examine hosts' involvement in VFR travel or their contribution in total VFR spending' (247). Whilst there have been a number of studies that examined the role of VFR hosts (for example Beioley, 1997; Litster, 2007; McKercher, 1994, 1995) those studies had not combined VFR expenditures with hosts' expenditures to gain a complete understanding of the total expenditure. In order to gain this level of understanding, the expenditures incurred by local residents (n=625) in hosting VFR travellers were aggregated with the VFR expenditures (n=229) that were identified in Table 5.3. These were then compared with non-VFR travellers (n=509).

Expenditures across different categories can be borne by VFR travellers and/or their hosts. They may take turns in paying for restaurant bills. Even if dining at the local residents' homes, VFR travellers may purchase the groceries and even cook the meal. Expenditures and hosting can vary enormously between each different travel party. Aspects such as life cycle stage, age, income and health may influence these relationships.

To be more accurate with these calculations, a series of steps occurred to merge the different data sets (VFR and hosts). These were performed in Excel prior to inserting the formula into SPSS to generate the results. Firstly, the residents' average expenditures for hosting travel party trips were divided by length of stay (from the residents' survey) to establish the mean daily expenditures on each category. Then each expenditure category for the VFR (from the visitors' survey) was calculated based on adding the daily expenditure to the multiplication of the residents' daily expenditure and length of stay. Thus, the formula adopted for each separate expenditure category was: expenditure (category) VFR and host = daily VFR expenditure (category) + (nights staying * residents' daily expenditure).

A t-test of the log data for all pairwise comparisons within each row concluded that the expenditures for VFR travellers with their hosts is greater than non-VFR expenditures for groceries, leisure shopping, fuel, entertainment, activities, liquor and attractions. Non-VFR travellers had a significantly higher expenditure on accommodation. There was no significant difference at the 95% level for restaurants/cafes, or car hire/taxi. With the higher non-VFR expenditure on accommodation offsetting the higher VFR expenditure on many categories, there was no significant difference between the total expenditures for the two groups at the 95% confidence level. Thus, both groups expended similar total expenditures, but the extent of the benefit is experienced differently across the industries. The results of this can be located in Table 5.4.

The same process was followed for data from Townsville and Ballarat. In Ballarat, the combined hosts' plus VFR expenditures were not significantly different, whilst in Townsville, the VFR expenditure was significantly higher than non-VFR expenditures once the outlay by local residents was included. Such findings reinforce the importance of understanding VFR at each local level.

Table 5.4 Trip expenditures for VFR travellers combined with hosts relative to non-VFR travellers

	VFR mean (Log/SD)	Non-VFR mean (Log/SD)	Levene's F-test	t-value	p
Groceries	$295.99 (2.10/.55)	$179.54 (1.80/.76)	7.814*	5.999*	0.000
Leisure shopping	$489.77 (2.12/.72)	$273.36 (1.61/1.11)	84.630*	7.411*	0.000
Restaurants/ cafes	$519.91 (2.37/.56)	$395.92 (2.29/.68)	0.204	1.585	0.113
Fuel	$97.90 (1.68/.48)	$60.04 (1.25/.84)	121.423*	8.882*	0.000
Entertainment	$55.53 (1.17/.63)	$28.50 (.32 /.76)	0.770	14.745*	0.000
Activities	$54.75 (1.19/.60)	$46.45 (.38/.84)	14.305*	14.877*	0.000
Liquor	$163.60 (1.85/.55)	$92.88 (1.28/.98)	198.941*	10.018*	0.000
Attractions	$260.06 (1.77/.75)	$175.06 (1.15/1.18)	331.820*	8.554*	0.000
Accommodation	$269.59 (0.78/1.24)	$715.78 (2.46/.85)	119.791*	−18.627*	0.000
Car hire/taxis	$52.17 (.27/0.78)	$52.85 (.32/.84)	2.564	−0.794	0.428
Total expenditure	$2,262.37 (3.02/.54)	$2,023.33 (3.09/.45)	14.690*	−1.662	0.097

*Significant at the 95% level

Discussion

Assessing the profiles and characteristics regarding VFR travellers relative to non-VFRs helps to explain VFR travel. Despite the growth in research into VFR travel over the past two decades, relative to its size, the field remains misunderstood and neglected by tourism practitioners and academe. To date, scholars have failed to discuss this area of tourism in any serious way. With so few VFR articles in tourism journals and, until this book, scarcely a mention about VFR travel in tourism books, it is axiomatic that VFR has been unable to earn a place in higher education tourism teachings. Lack of education about VFR is likely to contribute to the problem of tourism organisations largely overlooking the VFR travel phenomena, since discussions on the potential of it to industry is unlikely to occur in the course of the studies for future tourism marketers and managers.

The conceptualisation of VFR travel by integrating the two traditional forms of assessments of VFR, trip purpose and accommodation, through the VFR Definitional Model has ensured more understanding of the size and nature of VFR trips. In Australia, the size of VFR travel has been consistently underestimated for a range of reasons, but one of these reasons is through having no ability to determine its size. The inability to know the true dimensions and the size of VFR is a contributing force resulting in its ongoing failure to be taken more seriously.

It is hardly surprising that minimal marketing specifically towards VFR travellers has been undertaken, given its perceived secondary status in tourism. As little is known about VFR travel, not much effort seems to be placed on dedicating resources towards research in this area, as was revealed in Chapter 2. As a result, operators have been traditionally disinclined to undertake dedicated VFR travel campaigns, and few organisations have developed marketing activities that are focused on VFR travel. Some of those few are discussed in Chapter 7 in this book. King (1996) believes it is just as well that so little marketing has been done in the area of VFR travel given the 'absence of adequate research', which may cause campaigns to 'miss their mark' (85).

Within this discussion concerning marketing, it is useful to highlight that much of the literature discussing VFR travel often refers to it being a 'market', as identified in Chapter 1. However, in cases where VFR travellers are staying with friends or relatives, there are no property rights being exchanged, and therefore VFR travel in those cases is not really a market. Visitors staying with friends and relatives do not tend to pay their host for their lodging and, as such, there has been no property exchange. The whole concept of a market involves exchange between buyers and sellers, who are connected by four flows. These flows are communication, products/services, money and information (Kotler *et al.*, 2013). Without the host acting as a seller and receiving money in exchange for goods (the accommodation), VFR travel cannot be considered as a market.

Certainly VFR travellers enter into market transactions – for instance, as they enter a theme park the seller is receiving something in return for the transaction. Those VFR travellers staying in commercial accommodation are also entering into market transactions. However, as an entirety VFR travel cannot be categorised as a market. The assertion that VFR travel is a worthwhile market segment cannot really be given and, in the broad manner in which it is used, authors are only really borrowing the term. For, indeed, VFR travel is only a market segment for some organisations and operators. While VFR travellers may spend money and become involved in activities that involve market transactions, their accommodation, if staying with friends or relatives, is a form of non-marketised tourism. As such, the trip itself may involve both non-marketised and marketised activities.

This chapter has explored some critical characteristics of VFR travellers relative to non-VFR travellers in Australia. It has included a discussion on the expenditures by hosts. This enabled an examination of VFR travel through combining the residents' expenditures with those of the VFR travellers and then comparing those total expenditures to non-VFR travellers. Since some of the expenditures for VFR trips are assumed by the VFR host, 'by factoring in hosts' expenses, a more complete estimate of the economic impact of VFR travel would emerge' (McKercher, 1996: 703). Despite being raised by McKercher (1996) almost two decades ago as an important aspect of understanding VFR travel, the role of the host has received negligible attention. By factoring in those expenditures born by hosts as a direct result of having friends/relatives visit, a more complete understanding of VFR travel can be revealed. This can be particularly important for operators of restaurants, cafes and theme parks, where the combination of the VFR travel party and the hosts results in a large group and therefore can be a lucrative segment. As revealed in this chapter, across many categories, VFR travel was not, in terms of expenditure, any less important than non-VFR travel. In fact, across most of the categories, expenditure for VFR travel was higher than for non-VFR travel.

Conclusion

Visiting friends and relatives (VFR) travel has been highlighted through previous research as being historically ignored and underestimated. Despite the size of VFR, and the prior research into VFR, namely since Jackson's (1990) seminal article, VFR remains largely ignored by tourism marketing practitioners and is 'one of the most neglected areas of study' (Page & Connell, 2009: 94). While VFR travel is one of the largest and most significant forms of travel, and is recognised as being a sizable form of travel worldwide, 'VFR travel remains well-known but not known well' (Backer, 2009: 2).

The future challenge for VFR travel is to be understood well enough to be given greater respect by academics and industry practitioners. This chapter has provided details showing a range of VFR characteristics in Australia as well as each of the three VFR types. The key aspect that this chapter provides for an international readership is that official data that only show the proportion of VFRs that state a VFR purpose of visit and/ or stay with friends/relatives are not revealing the size of VFR travel. Just because someone has come to a region for VFR purposes does not mean that they will stay in their host's home. VFR travellers also stay in commercial accommodation (Backer, 2010a) and as such can provide a useful segment for commercial accommodation operators to target. As revealed in this chapter, VFRs staying in commercial accommodation make up 15.8% of all VFRs in Australia, and in some regions this proportion has been found to be even higher (e.g. Ballarat, Sunshine Coast and Townsville). This chapter has also revealed the impact that hosts' expenditures can provide. The role of the host is very important as a source of information, for the VFR will rely heavily on the knowledge provided by the host on what to do in the region. It is therefore critical for local residents to have a good level of awareness about their region in order to provide reliable information to VFRs. The term VFR is readily recognisable by tourism students, academics and practitioners. However, while those people will know what VFR stands for, they are unlikely to know much about the behaviours of VFR travellers. It is hoped that this chapter contributes towards existing knowledge so that VFR travel will be more than just well-known, but also known well.

References

Arguin, P. (2010) A definition that includes first and second generation immigrants returning to their countries of origin to visit friends and relatives still makes sense to me. *Journal of Travel Medicine* 17 (3), 147–149.

Backer, E. (2007) VFR travel – An examination of the expenditures of VFR travellers and their hosts. *Current Issues in Tourism* 10 (4), 366–377.

Backer, E. (2009) The VFR trilogy. In J. Carlsen, M. Hughes, K. Holmes and R. Jones (eds) *See Change: Proceedings of the CAUTHE Conference, 10–13 Feb, 2009*. Fremantle, WA, Australia: Curtin University, WA, Australia.

Backer, E. (2010a) Opportunities for commercial accommodation in VFR. *International Journal of Tourism Research* 12 (4), 334–354.

Backer, E. (2010b) *VFR Travel: An Assessment of VFR Versus Non-VFR Travellers*. USA: VDM Verlag Dr. Müller.

Backer, E. (2011) VFR travellers of the future. In I. Yeoman, C. Hsu, K. Smith and S. Watson (eds) *Tourism and Demography* (pp. 74–84). Oxford: Goodfellow Publishers.

Backer, E. (2012) VFR travel: It *is* underestimated. *Tourism Management* 33 (1), 74–79.

Backer, E. and Lynch, D. (2010) *VFR Travel Research Project: City of Ballarat*. University of Ballarat: Ballarat.

Baggett, H., Graham, S., Kozarsky, P., Gallagher, N., Blumensaadt, S., Bateman, J., Reed, C. (2009) Pretravel health preparation among US residents traveling to India to VFRs: Importance of ethnicity in defining VFRs. *Journal of Travel Medicine* 16 (2), 112–118.

Beioley, S. (1997) Insights. *Four Weddings, a Funeral and a Holiday – The Visiting Friends and Relatives Market* 8 (7), B1–B15.

Cowgill, D. and Baulch, N. (1962) The use of leisure time by older people. *The Gerontologist* 2 (1), 47–50.

Gitelson, R. and Crompton, J. (1983) The planning horizons and sources of information used by pleasure vacationers. *Journal of Travel Research* 2 (3), 2–7.

Griffin, T. (2013) Research note: A content analysis of articles on visiting friends and relatives tourism, 1990–2010. *Journal of Hospitality Marketing & Management* (June 2013), 1–22.

Havighurst, R. (1957) The leisure activities of the middle-aged. *American Journal of Sociology* 63 (2), 152–162.

Jackson, R. (1990) VFR tourism: Is it underestimated? *The Journal of Tourism Studies* 1 (2), 10–17.

Jackson, R. (2003) VFR Tourism: Is it underestimated? *The Journal of Tourism Studies* 14 (1), 17–24.

King, B. (1996) VFR – A future research agenda. In H. Yaman (ed.) *VFR Tourism: Issues and Implications Proceedings from the Conference held at Victoria University of Technology*, 85–89. Melbourne: Victoria University of Technology.

Kotler, P., Bowen, J. and Makens, J. (2013). *Marketing for Hospitality and Tourism* (6th edn). Upper Saddle River: Pearson Higher Ed. USA.

Litster, J. (2007) *2006 Survey of Central Queensland Residents Who Host Visiting Friends and Relatives: Methodology.* Rockhampton: University of Central Queensland.

McKercher, B. (1994) *Report on a Study of Host Involvement in VFR Travel to Albury Wodonga.* Albury-Wodonga: Charles Sturt University.

McKercher, B. (1995) An examination of host involvement in VFR travel. In R. Shaw (ed.) *Proceedings from the National Tourism and Hospitality Conference, 14–17 February 1995. Council for Australian University Tourism and Hospitality Education* (pp. 246–255). Canberra, ACT: Bureau of Tourism Research.

Morrison, A.M. (2013) *Marketing and Managing Tourism Destinations.* London: Routledge.

Morrison, A. and O'Leary, J. (1995) The VFR market: Desperately seeking respect. *The Journal of Tourism Studies* 6 (1), 1–5.

Navran, L. (1967) Communication and adjustment in marriage. *Family Process* 6 (2), 173–184.

Page, S. and Connell, J. (2009) *Tourism: A Modern Synthesis.* China: South-Western Cengage Learning.

Rosenblatt, P.C., Johnson, P.A., Anderson, R.M., Anderson, M. and Rosen, P.C. (1981) When out-of-town relatives visit. *Family Relations* 30 (3), 403–409.

Rosenblatt, P.C. and Russell, M.G. (1975) The social psychology of potential problems in family vacation travel. *The Family Coordinator* 24 (2), 209–215.

Schewe, C. and Calantone, R. (1978) Psychographic segmentation of tourists. *Journal of Travel Research* 16 (3), 14–20.

Seeman, T. (2000) Health promoting effects of friends and family on health impacts in older adults. *American Journal of Health Promotion* 14, 362–370.

Weaver, D. and Lawton, L. (2015) *Tourism Management* (5th edn). Milton: Wiley.

6 The Experience and Implications of Immigrant Hosts

Tom Griffin

Introduction

Personal relationships are a major influence in global travel, with more than one-quarter of all international trips motivated by the desire to visit friends and relatives (UNWTO, 2011). Although interest in VFR has been rising in recent years (Griffin, 2013b) the study of visiting friends and relatives (VFR) travel as a whole has received comparatively little attention from both academics and practitioners, largely driven by the (mis)perceptions of limited value (Backer, 2007, 2011; Lee et al., 2005; Morrison & O'Leary, 1995; Poel et al., 2006; Seaton & Palmer, 1997; Seaton & Tagg, 1995). Much of the research that has been conducted has been visitor-centric, often positioning the focus of inquiry on marketing and business interests. The host experience has received little attention, despite its centrality to the encounter, significant contribution to touristic activity in the hosts' communities and comparatively easy identification as a study subject (Young et al., 2007). Several studies have considered the social impact of tourism on residents as recipients of tourism development (e.g. Andereck et al., 2005; Andereck & Vogt, 2000; Gursoy et al., 2010; Nunkoo & Ramkissoon, 2011a, 2011b), but VFR requires residents' inclusion as consumers and producers of tourism development and experiences, not just as passive recipients (Griffin, 2014; Shani & Uriely, 2012). The experiences and implications of immigrants hosting visiting friends and relatives are therefore worthy of consideration; and are explored further in this chapter.

VFR Travel and Immigration

VFR travel and immigration are two phenomena with inextricable links, as newcomers to a community invariably have networks that extend the boundaries of their new home region (Asiedu, 2008; Brown, 2010; Feng & Page, 2000; Uriely, 2010; Williams & Hall, 2000). Not only do immigrants use their vacation time and funds to visit their home community, but they become attractions, triggering visits that otherwise would not have occurred (Williams & Hall, 2000); the symbiosis between immigration and VFR is substantial.

The reasons for immigration are manifold (Boyne *et al.*, 2002) and VFR will affect different migrant groups in various ways. Ex-patriate retirees in gated communities (Williams *et al.*, 2000), international university students (Bischoff & Koenig-Lewis, 2007; Michael *et al.*, 2004) and new residents (Shani & Uriely, 2012; Young *et al.*, 2007) will experience hosting in different ways depending on the temporary or permanent nature of their stay, the social and physical environment of their community, their life stage and many other factors. It must also be acknowledged that many immigrants are unlikely to host VFRs at all for economic or social reasons. As immigration continues to rise (UN-DESA & OECD, 2013), advances in communication technology enable distant relationships to be maintained with greater ease than ever before. The opportunity to maintain connections with those who are geographically distant is vastly different for contemporary migrants. Whereas a common consequence of migration in years past would be an expectation that families would be forever separated, technological enhancements in communication and transport mean that for many migrants (but of course not all) connections are more easily maintained and nurtured in today's world (Burrell & Anderson, 2008; Sturgess & Phillips, 2009; Vertovec, 2001). Rather than replacing the need for face-to-face interaction, new technology in communications can actually provide ongoing stimulus for maintaining relationships and can give impetus for additional touristic travel to occur.

The 'Hosting' Literature

VFR hosts create touristic demand in their communities, direct and filter visitor experiences and participate in additional non-routine activities themselves. Studies that have covered hosting are often concerned with the hosts' propensity and frequency to host, their spending and participation in activities and influence over guest behaviours (Backer, 2007, 2008, 2010; Bischoff & Koenig-Lewis, 2007; Gitelson & Kerstetter, 1994; McDonald & Murphy, 2008; Michael *et al.*, 2004; Tham, 2006; Shanka & Taylor, 2003; Williams *et al.*, 2000; Young *et al.*, 2007). This is indicative of the marketing and economic development focus of much VFR travel research (Shani & Uriely, 2012) that positions hosts as vehicles to increase tourism revenues. However, hosting should also be viewed from the perspective of the individual host, considering the implications regarding attachment to their visitors, as well as to their community. This is particularly pertinent for immigrants who may not be very familiar with their new communities and may have limited regular access to established personal networks.

Leisure and Integration

The experience of immigration and issues of integration have been studied extensively (e.g. Berry, 2001; Cheong *et al.*, 2007; Pedraza-Bailey, 1990; Portes, 1997; Rudmin, 2003), and some researchers have considered the links between leisure participation and the social cohesion of immigrant groups (Stodolska, 1998, 2000; Stodolska & Yi, 2003; Tirone & Shaw, 1997). The transnational realities of immigrants create a great number of influences and pressures on their identity, often stirring internal tensions (Vertovec, 2001). Additionally, interaction with the new community and its culture can cause immigrants to experience:

> a clash, a culture shock, [as they] are thrown out of their closed every day life-world…[This] cannot be underestimated in its far-reaching consequences. A person's life-world is a person's guarantee of survival in a particularly structured environment…[and w]hen this guarantee is taken away, the world may become a chaotic and threatening jungle. (Mainil & Platenkamp, 2010: 64)

Interpreting, engaging and adapting to new cultures can be a tumultuous experience. An individual is forced to query the meaning, morals and logic of the new environment, which in turn can lead to a critical reflection and questioning of one's own culture, cultivating feelings of identity loss and existential crises (Mainil & Platenkamp, 2010). Positive interaction with the host community is important to help establish cultural bridges and improved integration.

Various authors have considered the role of leisure in forming, maintaining and evolving identity and integration among immigrants. Broadly speaking, the literature supports the notion that participation in leisure activities has potentially positive effects on the development of social capital and integration among immigrants (e.g. Doherty & Taylor, 2007; Stodolska, 1998). Of course, leisure is manifested in different cultures in various ways, with diverse interpretations of concepts such as recreation, play and freedom. This means that immigrants may initially find it awkward to translate the host culture's expression of leisure (Chick, 1998; Stodolska & Livengood, 2006; Tirone & Pedlar, 2000). For example, Tirone and Shaw (1997) conducted a study with immigrant women in Nova Scotia, Canada, and noted that:

> Research on the leisure of women from diverse cultures cannot be based on the assumption that leisure meanings are the same as the North American conceptualization…Moreover, since leisure cannot be understood in isolation from the rest of social life, the application of…leisure related concepts to all aspects of life may be a useful way

to explore the potential relevance of leisure in the lives of immigrant women. (226)

Stack and Iwasaki (2009) interviewed 11 Afghani refugees in Winnipeg, Manitoba, Canada, and found several key themes. Prior to immigration, participants' social networks consisted mainly of family members and were the major source of their leisure experiences. Because of immigration these networks were no longer available on a routine basis, and the opportunities to participate in leisure, and gain the associated benefits, were lost. The difficulty of overcoming the ruptured family ties and their unfamiliarity with the local culture were barriers to interaction with other community members. Leisure settings provided participants with structured opportunities to learn and improve skills such as English, increased awareness of the local culture and helped establish a forum where they could also share their own culture, leading to the development of personal connections with other immigrants and residents.

Leisure experiences that acknowledge immigrants' cultural expectations can be extremely beneficial in developing human and cultural capital. In a study conducted on newcomer participation in park activities in Alberta, it was found that active engagement with newcomers through a targeted orientation programme by the park authorities led to very positive results and outcomes (Lange *et al.*, 2011). Newcomers that participated in the programme improved their English language abilities and gained higher levels of literacy around environmental knowledge and issues. In addition, the connections that newcomers established with the physical environment, previously inaccessible due to physical and psychological barriers, proved important not only in improving their sense of comfort in Canada and attachment with their new home, but also for remembering and reflecting on their own homeland and the landscapes that influenced their upbringing and identities. Leisure, therefore, can be seen to intertwine several elements of immigrants' lives and is reflected in their culture and lived experiences, as well as being a vehicle for interaction and integration with the world around them.

In summary, leisure that bridges prior cultural expectations with new surroundings has the power to forge attachments and understandings between immigrants and their unfamiliar surroundings.

Interaction in VFR for Host, Guest and Place

When attention turns to the experiences that VFR facilitates for immigrant hosts, there are several aspects that become connected when building on the previous discussion of leisure in general. The ways in which many people consume tourism experiences have become more complex in a world of increasing immigration and interconnectedness (Havitz, 2007;

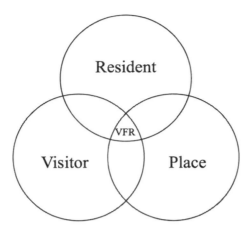

Figure 6.1 The interactional elements of VFR

Larsen *et al.*, 2007). Larsen (2008) criticises much tourism research for producing 'fixed dualisms between the life of tourism and everyday life: extraordinary and ordinary, pleasure and boredom, liminality and rules, exotic others and significant others' (21). A refreshing idea is introduced: a large proportion of tourism activity is actually not an escape but an opportunity to carry out social obligations within a value system that is embedded within the actors' everyday routines. In a world of increasing immigration, tourism plays a more complex role than just satisfying motives of escapism and fun, but allows participants to combine leisure experiences while fulfilling social duties (Larsen *et al.*, 2007).

The experience of spending time with loved ones and old friends can have ramifications for host and guest during the trip in terms of shared experiences, but also on the personal relationships with each other post-trip, as well as with the place itself (as destination for the visitor and home for the host). The VFR experience is unique in that it requires resident, visitor and place to interact together unlike any other tourism-related experience (Figure 6.1). The interactions facilitated by the VFR encounter therefore have implications that are distinct from other forms of tourism for the resident, visitor and place.

Co-presence with visiting friends and family

Hosting enables rich and meaningful interactions for immigrants with visiting friends and family that are less likely to occur with new acquaintances. A hosting experience allows newcomers to use long-term relationships and the cultural references they contain as a basis for interpretation of their new surroundings and culture; it is a type of conversation that is simply not possible to have with new neighbours and colleagues, and can enrich and embellish the meanings created in the shared moments, providing an additional layer of meaning construction and satisfaction (Hallman & Benbow, 2007).

Co-presence, or simply being with someone, 'affords access to the eyes...[which] enables the establishment of intimacy and trust' (Urry, 2002: 259). Co-present interactions are part of a fluid ongoing rapport that is '"thick" with information...deliver[ing] far more context than any other form of human exchange' (Boden & Molotch, 1994: 259). Being in the presence of people with whom we are comfortable and whom we trust allows self-reflection through interpreting their reactions to our own actions; co-presence with these people teaches us a lot about ourselves. VFR travel facilitates a different form of co-presence with friends and family than what occurs when the parties live in close proximity. Distance and separation from those with whom we are close, those with whom we have shared formative experiences in the construction of identities, means that the time spent together becomes a more intense and acute experience than if it were to happen more regularly. The limited frequency and availability of co-presence for distant parties therefore means that VFR encounters are often driven by leisure (Havitz, 2007; Mason, 2004). As discussed previously, this has implications for integration and well-being.

The simple conversations that occur during hosting, which are often built on years of shared context, can have foundational effects and can transform the construction of meaning with routine places. As has been suggested by Shotter (1993):

> although our surroundings may stay materially the same at any one moment in time, how we make sense of them, what we select for attention or to act upon, how we connect those various events [together], dispersed in time and space...and attribute significance to them, very much depends upon our use of language. (2)

Sharing experiences with people we are close to and with whom we share a cultural language adds significance to the experience; attending a festival or shopping in a market for the first time with a visiting friend or relative helps construct additional meaning and attachment with that place for the immigrant host. Interaction with place is important, as physical environments provide backdrops and context to personal interaction, as festivals or locations become part of personal culture (Crouch, 2000). A visit of a friend or relative might inspire the immigrant host to link or compare this new place with previous shared experiences or inspire the host and guest to reminisce about other events that would otherwise be forgotten. All of this reduces the substitutability of the new place in the formation of individual and communal identities, giving some prominence to these new places (Milligan, 2003). A trip to a park will differ for a lone newcomer than a trip to that same place with a close friend from the home culture, as 'co-presence with people is imbued with *co-presence with and in a place*' (Mason, 2004: 427 [original emphasis]).

The change of role from newcomer and outsider for the immigrant host in their everyday lives to expert and guide in their hosting role can also help to shift meaning attachment. For example, Shani and Uriely (2012) found domestic migrant hosts in Israel were inspired to seek new places to visit and as a result became more attached to and familiar with their new region, finding enjoyment as both tourist and guide and appreciating the opportunity of 'being with close significant others' (431).

This improved and strengthened attachment that bridges the old and new can enhance the feeling of home within foreign spatial boundaries; memories can be established in and linked to physical locations, souvenirs can be bought at museum gift shops or in new neighbourhoods and photos taken at local tourist attractions with visiting guests can be displayed, all acting as physical cues to bridge the past and new and helping to build a new home.

Social capital

The concept of *social capital* is useful for identifying, describing and potentially measuring the benefits of hosting for immigrants and their communities. Where economic capital is found in bank accounts, and human capital refers to skillsets, social capital is found in our personal networks (Portes, 2000). Bourdieu (1986) defines social capital as 'the aggregate of the actual or potential resources which are linked to possession of a durable network of more or less institutionalized relationships of mutual acquaintance and recognition' (248). Visiting in itself becomes part of the expectations of what friends and family should do. Mason (2004) found that the VFR encounters of UK residents of Pakistani origin were rich in kinship significance and important in nurturing relationships;

> Although visiting (and being visited by) local and UK-based kin was both a routine and significant part of life, visits to kin in Pakistan needed to be more carefully engineered to ensure that the act of visiting took place. Visiting in this sense was a fundamental act of kinship in itself, and one that is tied up with cultural and religious understandings of social interaction and obligation and the ritual etiquette involved in being a guest of one's kin (p. 424).

In addition, Mason (2004) found that VFR trips acted as a focal point and stimulation for nourishing the relationship between host and guest between visits: 'Evoking as well as experiencing visits, past and future, helped to sustain family narratives of kinship networks...[T]he life of the visit, in both experiential and symbolic terms, extended well beyond the temporal confines of the event itself' (423). The effort of travel demonstrates commitment, imbues self-worth and corroborates the value of the relationship for those involved.

Immigration can significantly disrupt an individual's networks from which they would routinely draw from for financial help, advice, general social contact and well-being. The hosting experience can refresh personal relationships that are traditional sources of social capital for the immigrant. Whether it is in the form of personal loans from parents, or emotional support, or help with home improvements, or advice on business and finance, the hosting experience provides that interaction that enables those exchanges to be maintained and nurtured. Social capital can be traded during the trip and can provide the foundations for subsequent exchanges. In seeing their friend or family member's new home, visitors gain perspective about how their help is used; actually visiting and establishing their own personal connection with the place where their friend or family now lives may help contextualise requests – for example, for a loan to fix the roof or a car to get them to work. Further, help such as childcare so often provided by grandparents and family at home can only be received after travel has occurred. Hosting provides immigrants with valuable opportunities to maintain and draw upon social capital that could otherwise be faded and out of reach.

Implications for the community

There are several implications about immigrants and hosting for the broader community. VFR experiences are distinct from those of other types of visitors because of the interaction between them, the host and place. This can affect how they consume the community as a destination and their perceptions of it. Their experiences are filtered through a resident, adding a perception of authenticity to their vacation that other visitors are not afforded. This can help a community communicate itself to visitors more genuinely and ultimately aids the generation of valued word-of-mouth forms of marketing that carry additional weight because of their perceived authenticity (Hall, 2007; Yu *et al.*, 2012).

As previously discussed, VFR increases not only visitation to a destination but also the number of resident hosts who participate in touristic activity within their home communities. The increased number and variety of individuals who participate in the construction of place meaning can enrich the overall cultural development and image of a destination. As Gieryn (2000) has noted: 'Places are doubly constructed: most are built or in some way physically carved out...[but t]hey are also interpreted, narrated, perceived, felt, understood, and imagined' (465). The cultivation of culture within a community, with input from multiple stakeholders who have connections across the globe, can enhance the appeal of a destination manifested in festivals and events that offer a community the opportunity to present themselves and define who they are (Derrett, 2003; Dwyer *et al.*, 2010; Ziakas & Costa, 2010). The impact is cyclical, as described by Derrett (2003):

> [Resident hosts] share their special space and favourite places with visiting friends and relatives [which] assists in healing, awareness raising, and...understanding issues of [local] sustainability...[T]he values, interests, and aspirations of individuals are influenced by their biophysical environment (space and place)→ which leads to a sense of community→ that influences how the community celebrates→ that affects the community's well-being→ that in turn informs the environment in which individuals and groups define their values and beliefs. (52)

In facilitating a wider variety of people to engage and co-construct the cultural meaning of a place, VFR and hosting can actually make a community a more interesting, representative and dynamic place to live and visit. This potential for increased awareness amongst residents of their own environment is consistent with aspects of sustainability that consider the fostering of cultural input from various sections of a community as vital for socio-cultural adaptation, and the innovation and integration of new ideas making the community a more vibrant and appealing destination (Mundt, 2011). Ultimately, the successful integration of immigrants is vital for communities to prosper (Frideres, 2008; Penninx, 2005), and hosting can help bridge those connections.

Hosting immigrants also has economic implications for communities. Immigrant residents who attend attractions or festivals for the first time because of hosting may return after their guests have left, opening up a new and potentially regular consumer base for local businesses. A further important impact relates to how the hosting of friends and relatives encourages immigrant residents to stay and spend in their own community when they might themselves otherwise take vacations in their home countries. VFR visitors are also more likely to patronise a greater diversity of businesses because of the higher propensity to stay in and visit non-touristic areas of a destination (Scheyvens, 2007). Many VFR travellers will spend more time in residential and peripheral areas of a community outside of the core tourist zones. Compared with other visitor groups, it is likely that the economic impact of VFR traveller spending could affect a more diverse number of businesses with potentially lower economic leakages (Asiedu, 2005; Caffyn, 2012; Sandbrook, 2010; Scheyvens, 2007). VFR is also less prone to the fragility of much tourism demand and has shown resilience in times of uncertainty. The personal relationships that immigrants have around the world will often trump obstacles such as airfare increases or even health scares that might otherwise discourage international trips (Griffin, 2013a; Scheyvens, 2007).

Conclusion

The experience of hosting for immigrants has a variety of implications. At an individual level, immigrants can experience familiar interactions with guests, re-connecting with their historical sense of place, and are also motivated to participate in activities leading to new connections with their new surroundings. This, in turn, can help shape a sense of community identity, enhancing a cosmopolitanism that augments destination appeal. The relative lack of attention by academics to this broad field of study is surprising. It is a potentially fruitful source of questions around identity formation, integration and possible critical approaches to the way in which destinations market themselves, while disregarding the substance and value attached to the touristic activities of their immigrant residents. For destination marketing practitioners there are various opportunities to engage immigrant residents as ambassadors, promoting an authentic representation of the community to otherwise unengaged markets around the globe. For integration services too, there is the potential to consider the role that hosting can play in an immigrant's settlement experience and to offer support, encouragement and advice about how to benefit most from the experience. It is most likely that as migration continues to accelerate, and technology permits relationships to be sustained at a distance, the demand for VFR travel and its significance for our communities will also continue to rise. Failure to better appreciate the phenomenon will at best result in missed opportunities for destinations. It may also lead to a lack of understanding about what is arguably the greatest force in world travel today and in the future: our personal relationships with those in distant lands.

References

Andereck, K.L., Valentine, K.M., Knopf, R.C. and Vogt, C.A. (2005) Residents' perceptions of community tourism impacts. *Annals of Tourism Research* 32 (4), 1056–1076.

Andereck, K.L. and Vogt, C.A. (2000) The relationship between residents' attitudes toward tourism and tourism development options. *Journal of Travel Research* 39 (1), 27–36.

Asiedu, A. (2005) Some benefits of migrants' return visits to Ghana. *Population, Space and Place* 11 (1), 1–11.

Asiedu, A.B. (2008) Participants' characteristics and economic benefits of visiting friends and relatives (VFR) tourism – an international survey of the literature with implications for Ghana. *International Journal of Tourism Research* 10 (6), 609–621.

Backer, E. (2007) VFR travel: An examination of the expenditures of VFR travellers and their hosts. *Current Issues in Tourism* 10 (4), 366–377.

Backer, E. (2008) VFR Travellers – Visiting the destination or visiting the hosts? *Asian Journal of Tourism and Hospitality Research* 2 (1), 60–70.

Backer, E. (2011) VFR travel: It *is* underestimated. *Tourism Management* 33 (1), 74–79.

Backer, E. (2010) Opportunities for commercial accommodation in VFR travel. *International Journal of Tourism Research* 12 (4), 334–354.

Berry, J.W. (2001) A psychology of immigration. *Journal of Social Issues* 57 (3), 615–631.

Bischoff, E.E. and Koenig-Lewis, N. (2007) VFR tourism: The importance of university students as hosts. *International Journal of Tourism Research* 9 (6), 465–484.

Boden, D. and Molotch, H. (1994) The compulsion of proximity. In R. Friedland and D. Boden (eds) *NowHere: Space, Time and Modernity* (pp. 257–286). Berkeley, CA: University of California.

Bourdieu, P. (1986) The forms of capital. In J.G. Richardson (ed.) *Handbook of Theory and Research for the Sociology of Education* (pp. 241–258). New York, NY: Greenwood Press.

Boyne, S., Carswell, F. and Hall, D. (2002) Reconceptualising VFR tourism: Friends, relatives and migration in a domestic context. In C.M. Hall and A.M. Williams (eds) *Tourism and Migration: New Relationships between Production and Consumption* (pp. 241–56). Dordrecht: Kluwer.

Brown, K.G. (2010) Come on home: Visiting friends and relatives – The Cape Breton experience. *Event Management* 14 (4), 309–318.

Burrell, J. and Anderson, K. (2008) 'I have great desires to look beyond my world': Trajectories of information and communication technology use among Ghanaians living abroad. *New Media & Society* 10 (2), 203–224.

Caffyn, A. (2012) Advocating and implementing slow tourism. In T.V. Singh (ed.) *Critical Debates in Tourism* (pp. 373–379). Bristol: Channel View Publications.

Cheong, P.H., Edwards, R., Goulbourne, H. and Solomos, J. (2007) Immigration, social cohesion and social capital: A critical review. *Critical Social Policy* 27 (1), 24–49.

Chick, G. (1998) Leisure and culture: Issues for an anthropology of leisure. *Leisure Sciences* 20 (2), 111–133.

Crouch, D. (2000) Places around us: Embodied lay geographies in leisure and tourism. *Leisure Studies* 19 (2), 63–76.

Derrett, R. (2003) Making sense of how festivals demonstrate a community's sense of place. *Event Management* 8 (1), 49–58.

Doherty, A. and Taylor, T. (2007) Sport and physical recreation in the settlement of immigrant youth. *Leisure/loisir* 31 (1), 27–55.

Dwyer, L., Forsyth, P., King, B. and Seetaram, N. (2010) *Migration-Related Determinants of Australian Inbound and Outbound Tourism Flows*. Gold Coast, Queensland: STCRC.

Feng, K. and Page, S.J. (2000) An exploratory study of the tourism, migration-immigration nexus: Travel experiences of Chinese residents in New Zealand. *Current Issues in Tourism* 3 (3), 246–281.

Frideres, J. (2008) Creating an inclusive society: Promoting social integration in Canada. In J. Frideres, M. Burstein and J. Biles (eds) *Immigration and Integration in Canada in the Twenty-First Century* (pp. 77–101). Kingston, Ontario: Queen's University.

Gieryn, T.F. (2000) A space for place in sociology. *Annual Review of Sociology* 26, 463–496.

Gitelson, R. and Kerstetter, D. (1994) The influence of friends and relatives in travel decision-making. *Journal of Travel & Tourism Marketing* 3 (3), 59–68.

Griffin, T. (2013a) Visiting friends and relatives tourism and implications for community capital. *Journal of Policy Research Tourism, Leisure and Events* 5 (3), 233–251.

Griffin, T. (2013b) A content analysis of articles on visiting friends and relatives tourism, 1990–2010. *Journal of Hospitality Marketing and Management* 22 (7), 781–802.

Griffin, T. (2014) A paradigmatic discussion for the study of immigrant hosts. *Current Issues in Tourism*, 17 (6), 487–498.

Gursoy, D., Chi, C.G. and Dyer, P. (2010) Locals' attitudes toward mass and alternative tourism: The case of Sunshine Coast, Australia. *Journal of Travel Research* 49 (3), 381–394.

Hall, C.M. (2007) Response to Yeoman *et al.*: The fakery of 'the authentic tourist'. *Tourism Management* 28 (4), 1139–1140.

Hallman, B.C. and Benbow, S.M.P. (2007) Family leisure, family photography and zoos: Exploring the emotional geographies of families. *Social & Cultural Geography* 8 (6), 871–888.

Havitz, M.E. (2007) A host, a guest, and our lifetime relationship: Another hour with grandma Havitz. *Leisure Sciences* 29 (2), 131–141.

Lange, E., Vogels, P. and Jamal, Z. (2011) *Learning a Language, Learning the Land: Newcomers, Parks, and Language Learning Research and Evaluation Report*. To Edmonton Community Adult Learning Association; Alberta Tourism, Parks and Recreation; Edmonton Mennonite Centre for Newcomers; City of Edmonton, Natural Areas Conservation; and Mountain Equipment Co-op.

Larsen, J. (2008) De-exoticizing leisure travel. *Leisure Studies* 27 (1), 21–34.

Larsen, J., Urry, J. and Axhausen, K.W. (2007) Networks and tourism: Mobile social life. *Annals of Tourism Research* 34 (1), 244–262.

Lee, G., Morrison, A.A., Lehto, X.Y., Webb, J. and Reid, J. (2005) VFR: Is it really marginal? A financial consideration of French overseas travellers. *Journal of Vacation Marketing* 11 (4), 340–356.

Mainil, T. and Platenkamp, V. (2010) Narrative analysis as a tool for contextual tourism research: An exploration. *Tourism Culture & Communication* 10 (1), 59–75.

Mason, J. (2004) Managing kinship over long distances: The significance of 'The visit'. *Social Policy and Society* 3 (4), 421–429.

McDonald, S.M. and Murphy, P. (2008) Utilizing and adapting leisure constraints models to enhance 'short-break' vacations: Case study of Melbourne, Australia. *Journal of Vacation Marketing* 14 (4), 317–330.

Michael, I., Armstrong, A. and King, B. (2004) The travel behaviour of international students: The relationship between studying abroad and their choice of tourist destinations. *Journal of Vacation Marketing* 10 (1), 57–66.

Milligan, M. (2003) The individual and city life: A commentary on Richard Florida's 'Cities and the Creative Class'. *City & Community* 2 (1), 21–26.

Morrison, A.M. and O'Leary, J.T. (1995) The VFR market: Desperately seeking respect. *Journal of Tourism Studies* 6 (1), 2–5.

Mundt, J.W. (2011) *Sustainable Tourism: Reconsidering a Concept of Vague Policies*. Berlin: Erich Schmidt Verlag, KG.

Nunkoo, R. and Ramkissoon, H. (2011a) Developing a community support model for tourism. *Annals of Tourism Research* 38 (3), 964–988.

Nunkoo, R. and Ramkissoon, H. (2011b) Residents' satisfaction with community attributes and support for tourism. *Journal of Hospitality & Tourism Research* 35 (2), 171–190.

Pedraza-Bailey, S. (1990) Immigration research: A conceptual map. *Social Science History* 14 (1), 43–67.

Penninx, R. (2005) Integration of migrants: Economic, social, cultural and political dimensions. In M. Macura, A.L. Macdonald and W. Haug (eds) *The New Demographic Regime: Population Challenges and Policy Responses* (pp. 137–152). Geneva: United Nations.

Poel, P., Masurel, E. and Nijkamp, P. (2006) The importance of friends and relations in tourist behaviour: A case study of heterogeneity in Surinam. In M. Giaoutzi and

P. Nijkamp (eds) *Tourism and Regional Development: New Pathways* (pp. 219–238). Burlington, VT: Ashgate Publishing.

Portes, A. (1997) Immigration theory for a new century: Some problems and opportunities. *International Migration Review* 31 (4), 799–825.

Portes, A. (2000) Social capital: Its origins and applications in modern sociology. In E.L. Lesser (ed.) *Knowledge and Social Capital* (pp. 43–67). Boston, MA: Butterworth-Heinemann.

Rudmin, F.W. (2003) Critical history of the acculturation psychology of assimilation, separation, integration, and marginalization. *Review of General Psychology* 7 (1), 3–37.

Sandbrook, C.G. (2010) Putting leakage in its place: The significance of retained tourism revenue in the local context in rural Uganda. *Journal of International Development* 22 (1), 124–136.

Scheyvens, R. (2007) Poor cousins no more valuing the development potential of domestic and diaspora tourism. *Progress in Development Studies* 7 (4), 307–325.

Seaton, A.V. and Palmer, C. (1997) Understanding VFR tourism behaviour: The first five years of the United Kingdom tourism survey. *Tourism Management* 18 (6), 345–355.

Seaton, A.V. and Tagg, S. (1995) Disaggregating friends and relatives in VFR tourism research: The Northern Ireland evidence 1991–1993. *Journal of Tourism Studies* 6 (1), 6–18.

Shani, A. and Uriely, N. (2012) VFR tourism: The host experience. *Annals of Tourism Research* 39 (1), 421–440.

Shanka, T. and Taylor, R. (2003) International student graduation ceremonies: An opportunity for local tourism services providers. *Asia Pacific Journal of Tourism Research* 8 (2), 13–22.

Shotter, J. (1993) *Conversational Realities: Studies in Social Constructionism*. London: Sage Publications Limited.

Stack, J.A.C. and Iwasaki, Y. (2009) The role of leisure pursuits in adaptation processes among Afghan refugees who have immigrated to Winnipeg, Canada. *Leisure Studies* 28 (3), 239–259.

Stodolska, M. (1998) Assimilation and leisure constraints: Dynamics of constraints on leisure in immigrant populations. *Journal of Leisure Research* 30 (4), 551.

Stodolska, M. (2000) Changes in leisure participation patterns after immigration. *Leisure Sciences* 22 (1), 39–63.

Stodolska, M. and Livengood, J.S. (2006) The influence of religion on the leisure behavior of immigrant Muslims in the United States. *Journal of Leisure Research* 38 (3), 293–320.

Stodolska, M. and Yi, J. (2003) Impacts of immigration on ethnic identity and leisure behavior of adolescent immigrants from Korea, Mexico and Poland. *Journal of Leisure Research* 35 (1), 49–79.

Sturgess, P. and Phillips, C. (2009) Google, email and Facebook: Internet literacy to improve the health and well-being of newly arrived refugees and migrants. A Pilot Study. *MSJA*, 9.

Tham, A.M-E. (2006) Travel stimulated by international students in Australia. *International Journal of Tourism Research* 8 (6), 451–468.

Tirone, S. and Pedlar, A. (2000) Understanding the leisure experiences of a minority ethnic group: South Asian teens and young adults in Canada. *Loisir et société* 23 (1), 145–169.

Tirone, S.C. and Shaw, S.M. (1997) At the center of their lives: Indo Canadian women, their families and leisure. *Journal of Leisure Research* 29 (2), 225–244.

UN-DESA and OECD (2013, Oct. 3–4). *World Migration in Figures.* See www.un.org/esa/population/migration/documents/World_Migration_Figures_UNDESA_OECD.pdf (accessed 1 April 2014).

UNWTO (2011) *UNWTO Tourism Highlights.* Madrid: UNWTO.

Uriely, N. (2010) 'Home' and 'away' in VFR tourism. *Annals of Tourism Research* 37 (3), 854–857.

Urry, J. (2002) Mobility and proximity. *Sociology* 36 (2), 255–274.

Vertovec, S. (2001) Transnationalism and identity. *Journal of Ethnic and Migration Studies* 27 (4), 573–582.

Williams, A.M. and Hall, C.M. (2000) Tourism and migration: New relationships between production and consumption. *Tourism Geographies* 2 (1), 5–27.

Williams, A.M., King, R., Warnes, A. and Patterson, G. (2000) Tourism and international retirement migration: New forms of an old relationship in southern Europe. *Tourism Geographies* 2 (1), 28–49.

Young, C.A., Corsun, D.L. and Baloglu, S. (2007) A taxonomy of hosts visiting friends and relatives. *Annals of Tourism Research* 34 (2), 497–516.

Yu, X., Kim, N., Chen, C.C. and Schwartz, Z. (2012) Are you a tourist? Tourism definition from the tourist perspective. *Tourism Analysis* 17 (4), 445–457.

Ziakas, V. and Costa, C.A. (2010) 'Between theatre and sport' in a rural event: Evolving unity and community development from the inside-out. *Journal of Sport & Tourism* 15 (1), 7–26.

7 Implementing VFR Travel Strategies

Elisa Backer and Brian Hay

Introduction

Visiting friends and relatives (VFR) travel has been highlighted through previous research and through a number of the preceding chapters as being historically ignored and underestimated by both researchers and tourism marketing practitioners. As noted in Chapter 5, scholarly interest into VFR really only commenced in 1990, and for the next two decades only 39 tourism journal articles dedicated to VFR were published (Griffin, 2013). Due to definitional issues, the scale of VFR travel both in terms of the number of trips and their value remains unclear. The value of the segment is consistently raised in the literature (Backer, 2007, 2010a, 2011, 2012; Braunlich & Nadkarni, 1995; Hay, 1996, 2008; Jackson, 1990, 2003; King, 1996; McKercher, 1994, 1995; Morrison *et al.*, 1995; Seaton, 1994; Seaton & Palmer, 1997; Seaton & Tagg, 1995; Yaman, 1996). Given the size and potential impact of the VFR market, it is surprising that the quantity of VFR research is so limited.

However, a new wave of academic research which seeks to better understand the full economic, social and political impact of VFR travel may be encouraging an awakening in industry circles, resulting in the development of more specific and targeted VFR campaigns. This chapter outlines seven case studies – from Australia, Scotland, Ireland and Wales – and discusses the rationale for such campaigns. The conclusions outline the common themes and issues from the case studies, and in particular highlight the need for the campaigns to provide clearer evidence of the economic, social as well as political benefits from VFR travel.

Background

One factor contributing to the underestimation of VFR travel may be that secondary data are commonly used as the source, and such secondary data do not provide a robust measurement for VFR travel (Backer, 2012). Almost half (45.5%) of the VFR articles published in tourism journals between 1990 and 2010 used secondary data (Griffin, 2013). However, secondary data only indicate how many travellers stated VFR as a purpose of visit *or* how many travellers stayed with friends and relatives. The official data do not attempt to measure VFR by aggregating the three types ('pure' VFRs – who stay with friends/relatives and state VFR as the purpose of visit; 'commercial' VFRs – who state VFR as the purpose of visit but stay in commercial accommodation; and 'exploiting' VFRs – who stay with friends/relatives but state a non-VFR purpose of visit). Therefore, by using accommodation data (which aggregates pure VFRs and exploiting VFRs) or purpose of visit data (which aggregates pure VFRs and commercial VFRs), one of these three groups of VFRs is always left out; so the size of VFR travel is underestimated.

In Australia, the size of VFR has been estimated to be 48% of the nation's domestic overnight travel market when the three VFR types are aggregated (Backer, 2012). Given the size of the 'market', it is therefore somewhat surprising that providers and suppliers of tourism services in both the public and private sectors have not made stronger efforts over the years to capitalise on the potential opportunity through developing campaigns to maximise its yield. Eight reasons have been outlined to explain why VFR continues to be ignored (Backer, 2010a).

(1) Lack of a definition.
(2) Discrepancy with existing data.
(3) Difficulties with measurement.
(4) Lack of lobbying.
(5) Perceived minor economic impact.
(6) Lack of discussion in tourism textbooks.
(7) Perceived to be difficult to influence.
(8) VFR is not 'sexy'.

However, more recently, awareness has been growing to demonstrate that VFRs are not only large by size but also spend money broadly throughout local economies, and they do in fact utilise commercial accommodation (Backer, 2010a; Braunlich & Nadkarni, 1995). The research to date has reported on VFR profiles and characteristics and considered the hosting of VFRs. However, there remains a gap in the extant literature that investigates the industry voice – the development and evaluation, or lack thereof, of VFR campaigns.

Research undertaken in Australia in 2009 indicated that there was a general lack of understanding of VFR travel by destination marketing organisations (DMOs) (Backer, 2010b), and that there was little consideration throughout the nation of setting aside any marketing funds to try to capitalise further on the VFR market. However, VFR may be starting to gain additional recognition in both academic and industry spaces. A content analysis of VFR articles revealed that VFR is 'receiving an increasing amount of attention, from a growing variety of scholars applying more varied approaches' (Griffin, 2012: 781). In addition, recently a number of VFR marketing campaigns have begun to develop, driven perhaps by the economic conditions since the global financial crisis (GFC), causing traditional markets to decline and so forcing the sector to look towards alternatives. In order to explore that trend, seven case studies of VFR marketing campaigns were examined in detail to understand VFR travel from the practitioner's perspective.

Discussion of Case Studies

In recent years there have been a number of very significant VFR campaigns both in Australia and in other destinations, such as: 'Your Favourite Spot' in Brisbane, 'I Love Frankston' in Victoria and 'London for Londoners'. In the most recent case discussed in this chapter, Tourism Australia and British Airways teamed up to develop a VFR campaign aimed at encouraging the British to visit their friends and relatives who have moved to Australia. This chapter provides an overview of seven VFR campaigns which were featured during the period from 2000 to 2014. Four of the cases are from Australia, including three within the state of Victoria. The Australian cases are varied in their size and structure and provide examples which are instructive for industry and researchers. Since intimate knowledge was obtained about three of the Australian cases due to one of the authors working closely with the organisations, it was felt that the detail of the cases would provide rich and valuable information that could be transferable to regions throughout the world and therefore provided a valuable addition to this book. The case studies will be discussed in chronological order.

Case study 1, Wales: Homecoming – Hiraeth 2000 – It's time to come home (2000)

In an effort to capture the emotional global appeal surrounding the 2000 millennium celebrations, a number of destinations took the opportunity to raise their profile, including Australia, New Zealand and Israel (Morgan & Pritchard, 2001). One of the largest marketing programmes linking tourism and the millennium was in the UK, where it is estimated that a grouping of national agencies spent some £30bn (around US$50bn) on associated capital projects (Brown, 2001). Using the emotional appeal of the millennium, a number of destinations across the world sought to appeal to their diaspora market to come home for the event. Wales was no exception and a campaign was launched in 1998 by the Wales Tourist Board (WTB, the national DMO for Wales). The campaign was closely associated with the establishment of the new (in 1999) Welsh Assembly, which had delegated powers from the UK parliament for a number of functions, including tourism. The campaign used the dual language (English/Welsh) tag line 'Homecoming 2000 – Hiraeth 2000 – it's time to come home', which targeted local, national and international tourists with an existing affinity to Wales.

The campaign was supported by £6.2m (around US$10.45m) from the UK Millennium Festival Fund, at a time when the WTB's total overseas marketing budget was £1.5m (around US$2.5m). The campaign aimed to maximise visitation to Wales in 2000. It focused less on marketing to an overseas country as a whole, but rather on regions in some key overseas countries with strong links to the Welsh diaspora (USA, Canada, Australia, New Zealand and South Africa) along with additional segments from Asia and Europe (Wales Tourist Board, 1998). Within these countries, two segments were seen as offering the greatest potential (descendants with Welsh lineage who had never been to Wales and people who had relocated away from Wales for career or business reasons but who did make visits back home). Groups with connections to Wales were also targeted as secondary market segments, such as those who had studied in Wales, sport touring groups and those with an interest in Welsh culture.

As outlined by the Wales Tourist Board (WTB, 1998) the campaign aimed to:

(1) create a focus for additional tourism promotion for the millennium year;
(2) create a marketing initiative to motivate defined target segments, coupling their emotional bond with Wales to the millennium;
(3) stimulate a commitment at regional and community level to building a critical mass of events and products under the homecoming theme.

The campaign was formally launched in late 1998, with four key elements, namely: a dedicated website; harnessing of Welsh residents' VFR connections; exploitation of links to Welsh expatriate communities across the world; and public relations led events.

The marketing campaign consisted of a number of elements. First, the WTB invited people to send a personalised message and a 'moving reminder' by filling in a reply slip and providing the WTB with contact details of the person they wished to return to Wales, and no matter where they lived in the world, they all received an information pack, video and brochure about Wales. Second was the development of the homecoming website, which by the end of the year-long campaign had received almost one million hits. This was at a time when web-based marketing was still relatively new. The third element was connecting with the myriad of Welsh Societies across the world and updating the WTB society's database. Each registered society was sent marketing materials about the event so that they could develop a relationship with the local expatriate community; and through such societies, they also developed an 'Ambassadors for Wales' programme.

There is always a difficulty in evaluating most marketing campaigns, especially those aiming to develop long-term changes in perception. Output measures from the campaign included 70,000 requests for information including the WTB video, and in a survey of 11,000 of these respondents, over 90% recalled the strap line 'Wales 2000 – it's time to come home', 44% had actually visited Wales in 2000, 54% said the WTB material had influenced their decision, with 42% saying they would visit Wales in 2002 (Morgan *et al.*, 2003). The WTB calculated a return on investment of 77:1, with £22m (around US$37m) generated from a WTB budget of just over £275,000 (around US$463,550) (Wales Tourist Board, 2001). In addition, some 1 million visits were recorded to the Homecoming website, and around £1m (around US$1.69m) in press coverage was generated.

Despite the initial success of the campaign, its long-term impact was undermined by two external events – namely the outbreak of foot and mouth disease in Wales in Spring 2001, which deterred UK visitors, and the terrorist attacks on New York in September 2001, which deterred USA visitors, a key market for the campaign (Morgan *et al.*, 2003). Although the WTB is looking at the possibility of repeating the event, to date no firm plans have been developed.

Case study 2, Scotland: Homecoming Scotland (2009)

Whether you are Scottish or simply love Scotland, you are invited to come home – home to the land of your ancestors so you can experience a living culture. (Ministry for Enterprise, Energy and Tourism, Scottish Government, 2007)

In 1999 the Scottish parliament was established and took direct responsibility for a number of functions, including economic development and tourism. In 2007 Scotland elected the Scottish National Party (SNP) whose stated aim is the political independence of Scotland, and as the largest political party, they formed the new Scottish government. However, lacking an overall majority, they had to rely on other parties to achieve their plans, and this encouraged a degree of cross party cooperation. One of their early announcements was support for Homecoming Scotland (HS), an idea first formed under the previous Labour administration. However, there was always an underlying perception that the SNP would use HS for their own political ends, moving Scotland towards independence, so this marketing initiative was caught up in the national political debate and subject to intensive political scrutiny. An example of this is when a HS promotional poster sought to portray Scotland using a group of stereotypical white, kilted Scots. This poster was quickly redrawn, as it was devoid of any of Scotland's ethnic minorities.

Like most marketing events, HS was developed from a previous campaign, in this case the experience of the 1999 Orkney Homecoming (Basu, 2004), which focused on Canadians who had a family connection to Orkney. HS was funded through various governments grants totalling some £8.5m (around US$14m) (Morrison & Hay, 2011) and is a classic example of the centrality of public-private partnership and the catalytic role government agencies can play in channelling investment and marketing to develop a nationally focused theme.

Although HS was a Scottish government initiative, its day-to-day management was devolved to VisitScotland (the national DMO), which acted as the agency to deliver the programme. It consisted of a programme of around 400 events, which ran from January to November 2009, and focused on five themes: Burns (Scotland's National Poet), Golf, Whisky, Great Minds and Innovations and Scottish Clans and Ancestry. Central to HS was the levering of incoming tourist demand through links with the Scottish diaspora community, estimated at between 28m and 40m worldwide (Eirich & McLaren, 2008). As well marketing to the Scottish overseas diaspora community in Canada, USA, Australia, New Zealand and Europe, the campaign was also aimed at the domestic diaspora market, Scots living in other parts of the UK. It is worth noting that the campaign had no presence in South Africa or in the Caribbean, both with strong historic ties to Scotland.

As well as a series of national and international marketing campaigns, HS also provided support to many locally managed events, which were also branded as HS events. They were part funded by grants of between £5,000 and £50,000 (around US$8,428–US$84,284), either to provide support to existing planned events or to encourage new events designed to attract visitors of Scottish birth, descent or affinity to Scotland.

The HS campaign was criticised for focusing too much on the traditional images of Scotland – of tartan and idealised images of rural Scotland. The messages in the marketing material played heavily on emotional connections through the use of words such as: *reconnect, homeland, native shores, come home, kindle pride*. These intangible emotions, when combined with more tangible anchors such as specific major events, like the national Gathering of the Scottish Clans, appealed to the overseas markets – but questions were asked as to why Scotland always looked backward to its past and was not portrayed as a more outward looking and modern country.

There were a number of difficulties out of the control of the campaign, such as delays in completing the national Robert Burns museum, one of the five key themes of HS, and the liquidation of the company managing the Gathering of the Clans, a key event in the HS calendar. Also many organisations and companies used the Homecoming brand for their own marketing purposes, as it was made freely available to all who wanted to exploit it. Thus HS lost some control of the brand, which was used sometimes to market products that had little to do with the event. There were also a series of unforeseen international events that may have affected the HS programme. These included the released Libyan bomber being greeted in Tripoli by the Scottish flag, the closure of a major whisky plant, Harris Tweed Company's decision to drop Scotland as a brand selling point and the almost complete collapse of the Royal Bank of Scotland, which had become an international symbol of the new dynamic economy of Scotland.

In terms of its success, VisitScotland (2010) estimates include £28m (around US$47m) of public relations activity, 15% increase in trips from Europe, 200,000 new names added to VisitScotland database, 87% awareness of the event in Scotland, 86 international tourism businesses developing HS themed products and 25 million visits to the HS websites. The short-term tactical measurement focus of 'success' tends to highlight economic measures, such as increases in visits, but it could be argued that the real benefits are intangible and long term, such as changes in visitors' and residents' perceptions, but they are much more difficult to measure. HS was repeated in 2014 and it was again caught up in a national political debate about the future governance of Scotland, as it was seen as part of the SNP's wider marketing programme to persuade the people of Scotland to vote in the 2014 referendum on whether Scotland remains part of the UK or becomes an independent country.

Case study 3, Mildura, Australia: Be a tourist in your own town (2009–2013)

In 2013, this marketing campaign entered its fifth year and has become so well established that it is now a core element in Mildura's Tourism Week. Mildura is a regional city in Victoria, Australia, about 475 kilometres (295 miles) northwest of Melbourne. What is interesting about this campaign is that the target market is not the visiting tourists, but their hosts – the residents who live and work in Mildura. The campaign was started in response to a number of external factors, some of which the town had no control over. This included being a long distance from major population centres and also, in particular, the effects of ten years of drought followed by two years of floods. There was a perception that, during the drought years, residents were talking down the town, effectively dissuading friends and relatives from visiting and therefore not taking advantage of both the economic and social benefits that tourism could bring to the town. As a result of the floods, the Murray River (Mildura's primary tourism asset) was transformed and revitalised, along with its associated creeks, tributaries, billabongs, flora and fauna. This new rejuvenated environment provided locals with an authentic reason to invite friends and relatives to 'come and see the Murray like you've never seen it before' (Mildura Tourism, 2011: 3).

The campaign was initiated, led, managed and funded by Mildura Tourism with around A$40,000 (around US$37,580) from their resources, along with matching funds of more than A$40,000 from local media and commercial sponsors. The campaign initially made use of the traditional marketing outlets, including local television and radio, along with a 16-page full-colour free A4 brochure, which featured all the town's most popular tourism products, as well as location maps. This particular product proved to be popular not only with tourism operators, but also with local residents who kept it and used it as a reference for themselves.

Before the marketing element of the campaign commenced, it was recognised that the residents of the town had a limited knowledge about local tourism products. Therefore, the campaign first focused on persuading local tourism operators such as attractions, shops and restaurants that they had opportunities to grow their businesses by better educating the local community. The marketing concept was designed to encourage local residents to use their local tourism facilities, which was operationalised through what was titled as 'mates rates specials'. At the heart of the campaign was a belief that the most effective marketing tool was 'word of mouth', and there could be nothing stronger than your friends and relatives asking you to visit. The town residents, after they became much more aware of the local attractions, acted as knowledgeable tourism marketing ambassadors by not only encouraging the original visit, but also in encouraging their visitors to make return trips.

As the campaign developed over a number of years, while still focusing on the VFR market, it also encouraged tourism operators to consider developing their existing products, especially new tourism products that could inspire repeat visitation. The campaign also encouraged locals to make more use of local tourism facilities by taking short breaks within the region.

In order to assess the effectiveness of their marketing campaign, rather than undertaking a traditional tourism survey to gather data, Mildura Tourism gathered data and information from local residents' access to daily information distributed through their website and Facebook. In accessing these services, local residents were able to take part in daily prize competitions, and this provided information on subjects such as: preferred travel months (December–February and March–May), origins of VFR (mainly Melbourne and Regional Victoria) and their travel experiences (river, wineries and restaurants).

In terms of measurable results, data suggest that the campaign had the support of the local community. In 2009, the first full year,

30 operators took part in the campaign, with around 100 events attended by approximately 3,300 residents. In 2012, this had grown to 84 operators with around 400 events attended by more than 6,000 local residents (R. Trowbridge, personal communication, 23 August 2013). Although such data is always useful, perhaps the most important change was in the attitude of local residents, as, anecdotally, the campaign resulted in much higher civic pride in the community (R. Trowbridge, personal communication, 23 August 2013). In addition, there was also extra expenditure associated with VFR travel, such as spending by the hosts on food and drink. There was also a notable increase in the tourism businesses working together for mutual benefits, as they recognised the education role played by Mildura Tourism in developing a co-operative approach to tourism marketing (R. Trowbridge, personal communication, 23 August 2013).

In 2013, the fifth year for the VFR campaign, the total value of the six-week promotional campaign was A$103,094 (around US$96,860); with A$55,363 (around US$52,016) from local business partners supporting the campaign and A$47,731 (US$44,845) from Mildura Tourism (Mildura Tourism, 2013). According to Mildura Tourism (2013) the campaign has assisted in building strong relationships with the campaign suppliers and that 'after each year every sponsor and campaign partner has indicated their willingness to support the next year's campaign...which has already commenced for 2014' (Mildura Tourism, 2013b: 2).

Case study 4, Melbourne, Australia: Discover your own Backyard (2011–2012)

Destination Melbourne Limited (the local DMO) launched the campaign in September 2011 in partnership with 11 local councils in the Melbourne metropolitan area, with an overall aim to increase the yield from VFR trips and encourage dispersal of VFR travel across the whole of the Melbourne metropolitan area. The rationale for the campaign was:

(1) VFR travel was a key market for Melbourne, with some 2.7 million people visiting their friends and relatives, with VFR listed as the main reason to visit the city by domestic overnight visitors.
(2) Residents are the gatekeepers and the greatest source of influence over the behaviour of VFR travellers, and the hosts' local knowledge can influence the VFR experience much more than any destination marketing campaign, provided they are effective in disseminating this knowledge to their friends and family.
(3) Local government is the best organisation to educate residents on becoming better hosts, as they have a deep understanding of the local community's strengths and are skilled in communicating to their local residents and businesses.

The overall marketing campaign budget was $A250,000 (around US$234,885) in 2011/12.

Given the need for Destination Melbourne to work with residents, the objectives of the marketing campaign were to:

(1) Educate residents about the tourism products in their area.
(2) Make the residents aware of the power of VFR travel and for residents to act as ambassadors for the area to their visiting friends and relatives.
(3) Create a sense of community pride in the local area.

These aims were operationalised into a campaign that focused on promotional advertising in local newspapers and the placement of a number of editorial pieces, featuring stories from local residents along with press releases. There was also a competition for local residents that encouraged them to collect stories about their favourite places in the area, some of which featured in the local press, along with information about events and editorial promotions. These activities were supported by posters, flyers and emails, and the campaign also made use of social media by placing information, videos and material on social media sites such as Facebook, YouTube, Metacafe, Flickr, DailyMotion and Twitter.

As with the other case studies, it is difficult to isolate solely the impact of the VFR campaign from the impact of other marketing campaigns. However, up to March 2012 VFR travel trips increased by 4% (to 2.4 million) and VFR nights increased by 8.6% to 7.2 million compared to the previous year. By contrast, the more traditional holiday/leisure tourism trips only increased by 1.9%, and their nights actually decreased by 3%. However, perhaps the biggest change was in the mindset of local residents about the importance of tourism to the Melbourne area, but this is difficult to measure and quantify.

In terms of impact, qualitative feedback from councils and operators provides some indication. For example, the tourism officer from Wyndham City Council stated that

> The Discover Your Own Backyard campaign has been a real eye-opener for us, highlighting the value of the visiting friends and relatives market. This market makes up a significant proportion of visitors to the Wyndham region and DML has provided us with a framework to capitalise on this opportunity. (N. Tehan, personal communication, 15 August 2013)

Benefits were also detected at the individual operator level. For example, according to the Director of the Goona Warra Vineyard:

> We must extend our thanks for the very timely program which is dedicated to support small businesses such as ours. We are already seeing

an increasing number of visitors to our cellar door, all stating they had no idea what treasures lay on their doorstep. We could never achieve such far reaching and well-coordinated publicity on our own as a single small operator. (E. Barnier, personal communication, 15 August 2013)

In conclusion, the campaign made much use of connecting with local residents to help them understand the importance of tourism to the Melbourne economy. Destination Melbourne also recognised that for the campaign to succeed it needed buy-in from locals and that nothing works better in tourism marketing than word-of-mouth advertising, in this case 'selling' the destination to the residents.

Case study 5, Victoria, Australia: The V/Line train guilt trip campaign (2012–13)

Growing the visiting family and friends segment is a key focus for V/Line. This market provides a huge boost to regional economies and is an important part of the Victorian State Government's regional strategy. As every country person knows, it's not always easy to get their friends and family in city to come and visit (the country). A well-laid Guilt Trip is a great way of getting your family and friends to visit more often. (V/Line, 2012)

This idea first developed from information about the size of the VFR market in the Melbourne metropolitan area, where around 0.74m of the 2.1m annual VFR trips were undertaken by metropolitan residents in Victoria, Australia (V/Line, 2011). Similar data on the importance of the market was highlighted in research conducted by Tourism Victoria (Tourism Victoria, 2010), which suggested that some 33% of the domestic overnight trips were for VFR purposes. The basic justification for the campaign was to make better use of the spare capacity in the off-peak V/line trains. It was felt by V/Line's ex-General Manager that 'with a little promotion, [V/Line] could not only increase this market but also tap into the emotional engagement these travellers have' (P. Matthews, personal communication, 10 August 2013).

The campaign was unusual in two aspects. First, it focused on two-way Melbourne trips, both inbound and outbound – that is, trips to country stations as well as trips to urban Melbourne stations. Second, it centred around the concept of 'guilt trips'. The marketing concept behind the idea of the 'guilt trip' is to make people feel guilty about not visiting their friends/relatives. The idea was first developed in a V/Line internal brainstorming meeting, which highlighted the tactics used by parents of V/Line staff members to encourage them to visit. The obvious difficulty in such a campaign is that it could focus too much on the negative feelings generated by guilt, and so could fail to reach the core market. To overcome this concern, the campaign used humour by developing marketing material based around birthday cards that a mother would send to her children.

The campaign was built around two bursts of advertising with the first burst in May 2012 when the Victorian Minister for Transport launched the campaign through a series of press, radio, outdoor and online marketing campaigns (see Figure 7.1). The campaign made extensive use of a custom-made unique web-based microsite, in which the users could send guilt-based birthday cards to their friends/relatives. People could even buy a guilt trip for someone else and the ticket would be posted out to them in a guilt trip wallet. The second phase centred on a fictional mother (Louise) who was described as a 'guilt trip master' and ran in October and November 2012, and again made use of online videos, online adverts and traditional press adverts. The 'instructional videos with Louise guiding viewers on the art of giving a good guilt trip…were created in a small country town using locals as talent. This gave the ads an authentic country feel and added another dimension to the campaign' (P. Matthews, personal communication, 10 August 2013).

According to ex-General Manager Marketing and Stakeholder Relations, V/Line, Paul Matthews:

> The thing I like about the guilt trip campaign is the conversation it has created. Radio hosts have encouraged talk back with callers, people have laughed at the humorous and often sarcastic radio advertisements and more importantly, people have travelled taking guilt trips on the train…When V/Line discovered the size of the VFR market, we knew that with some clever marketing, we could not only fill spare seats in the off peak, but play to a sentiment that is always hiding somewhere in people's mind. The long overdue visit to a loved one or old friend. The guilt trip did this perfectly. (P. Matthews, personal communication, 10 August 2013)

Figure 7.1 Posters from V/Line's guilt trip campaign
Source: V/Line (2012).

As with the previous case studies, the impact of the campaign is difficult to measure, except through secondary surrogate measures. V/Line's guilt trip campaign was developed to have a two-year cycle, 2012–13. Evidence of success based on its first year of running includes a 20% increase in enquires about VFR travel to the V/Line call centre, an overall 12% increase in online sales over the campaign period and VFR travellers also increased as a proportion of those travelling from 32% to 35% (V/Line, 2013). There were over 80,000 views on YouTube for its online films (V/Line, 2013). In addition

> The ads rates high in terms of brand difference and talkability. Respondents resonated with the humour conveyed in the ads, helping drive cut-through and recall. Usage intent scored higher than average, in particular for respondents with family and/or friends in regional Victoria. (V/Line, 2013: 1–2)

The success of the campaign could also be measured by the number of marketing awards it won; these included, for example, CSS awards for the best microsite, the Siren Award for the radio adverts, Mumbrella Encore 2012 Award for the fourth favourite radio advert of the year and an IMPACT award from the *Australian Creative* magazine, where it was listed as one of the twelve best marketing campaigns for 2012 (V/Line, 2013).

This marketing campaign had three interesting aspects. First, the campaign had an underlying but barely acknowledged social role, that of re-connecting parents who lived in the country to their children who lived in the town. Normally VFR trips, because of population density, tend to be associated with trips to cities, not to country areas. Reconnecting urban populations to their country roots was thought to do much to enhance the quality of family life for both city and country residents. Second, the campaign had strong political support, with the Victorian Minister for Transport launching the marketing campaign. Third, the campaign stressed very much through the minister's launching speech that it was seen as a means to boost local economies. That is, it was seen as much as an economic activity as a tourism activity.

In conclusion, the campaign was sold on economic grounds, justified on social grounds and supported on political grounds. This locked-in 'triple helix' strength was the key to the success of this campaign.

Case study 6, Ireland: The Gathering Ireland (2013)

The Gathering Ireland (GI) campaign was initiated and financially supported by the Irish government and has been described as the 'largest ever tourism initiative in Ireland' (Tourism Ireland, 2013). It was managed by both Bord Failte (the Irish national DMO) and Tourism Ireland (cross-border Ireland DMO). This makes it unusual, as it is world's only multinational VFR travel campaign. It was developed against a background of a declining overseas tourism market and a serious financial crisis in Ireland, which led to Irish government seeking help from a number of international institutions. Although GI was based broadly on Homecoming Scotland, it was also a repeat of a similar event in held 1953, An TÓstal. With a global Irish diaspora population in excess of 70m (40m in USA), the GI was designed to motivate that diaspora market, as well as those with an affinity for Ireland who also enjoyed Irish culture, heritage, arts and sports. It focused mainly on the USA, but also on the Canadian, UK, Australian and New Zealand diaspora markets. The programme also was designed to provide a base for the people of Ireland and local communities to organise events which enabled them to connect with their relatives through a series of family, local/county and national 'gatherings'.

The aims of the GI were to:

(1) Mobilise citizens, communities and businesses to work collectively and to connect with diaspora groups around the world.
(2) Attract 325,000 additional overseas visitors, generating €168m.
(3) Promote pride in Ireland and raise the profile and standing of the country.
(4) Create a platform for on-going and lasting engagement with the Irish diaspora.

Funding for GI was provided through some €13m direct government aid, and the project was managed through Bord Failte. The strategic goal from the start was to move the campaign from being perceived solely as a national government-run initiative to one that actively engaged with local people and their communities. At the core of the campaign was the concept of the 'gathering', whether a family reunion, village/town reunion or special interest group reunion such as a college class reunion. These local 'gatherings' were supplemented by a series of 26 sponsored and funded national 'gatherings' or events. This approach led to the development of a collaborative management model between the project team at the national DMO and each of the 34 local authorities, who appointed a gathering coordinator to develop links with local tourism community interest groups. It was designed to be 'a project of the people, by the people, for the people', and in order to archive this aim, a series of local town hall information meetings across Ireland was undertaken by the national DMO, and this helped in the formulation of almost 5000 local and family 'gatherings' registered on the GI website.

In conjunction with these campaigns, GI also undertook a domestic communications programme some six months in advance of the main events with the aim of increasing awareness and understanding of the GI, in tandem with the community engagement programme, the main element of which was a six part TV broadcast on RTÉ, the main public TV channel, titled *The Gathering – Homeward Bound*; this was supplemented by 'invite them home' radio broadcasting as well as the development of a strong digital and social media campaign.

According to Ireland (2013), an evaluation of 2013 GI suggested that about 250–275,000 of overseas visitors to Ireland travelled specifically because of the Gathering and that:

(1) The growth in visitor numbers, directly attributable to the Gathering, is estimated to be worth approximately €170 million in revenue.
(2) The Gathering Ireland succeeded in its broad based aim of engaging the people of Ireland to invite ancestral relatives and friends to attend some 5000 local Gatherings across the country.
(3) In addition to the economic value, The Gathering also delivered a social dividend, with a very positive impact on communities.
(4) The Gathering was delivered within its approved budget of €13m government funds.

The major strength of the GI was very much the number of small-scale locally developed events, as the Irish people embraced the concept of bringing family members back home to Ireland. Also of interest was the expansion of the theme to affinity groups (such as sporting clubs), focusing very much on the friends elements of VFR travel. In terms of the future of GI, it is clear there are two options, either to repeat the event in a number of years or to focus on developing the events spurred by GI by making them more sustainable. Although both actions are possible, in a small country with limited tourism marketing budgets, difficult choices need to be made.

Case study 7, Australia: Visit Soon (2014)

The Tourism Australia campaign called 'Visit Soon' was released in April 2014, with the tagline 'Australia has everything...except you'. In a statement to support the rationale underpinning the campaign, Tourism Australia's regional general manager for the UK, Denise von Wald, stated that 'Visiting Friends and Relatives (VFR) represents a large and valuable market' (Edensor, 2014). It was felt that the recovering economic conditions in the UK provided the 'ideal time to be launching such a campaign' (Tourism Australia, 2014). In terms of rationale, it was noted that:

Australia has consistently been the most popular destination country for British emigrants over the past 20 years. With an estimated 40,000 Brits immigrating to Australia every year, and so many 'Poms' now calling Australia home, the Visiting Friends and Family market is huge and one we are very keen to tap into. We know from research that a personal invitation and, with it, the promise of an emotional reunion and prospect of a more 'local' holiday experience, is a critical trigger when it comes to getting relatives and friends living overseas to lock in a visit Down Under (Tourism Australia, 2014)

The link between VFR and the UK was considered strong since VFR 'is Australia's largest visiting segment out of UK, representing 43% of all visitors aged 15 years and above, and contributing 30% (A$90m) (around US$84m) of total UK visitor spending' (Tourism Australia, 2014). In order to grow the market, the campaign was developed to try to tap into the emotional 'pulling power' and made use of social media through video share and invitation messages. In just one day after posting a question on Facebook about who they were missing in Australia, Tourism Australia had received 16,000 likes and close to 2000 comments. Along with joint marketing promotions, British Airways and QANTAS as well as a number of UK tour operators are offering special promotional fares and packages to attract VFR travellers to Australia. Although it is too early to present the results from this campaign, the increase in competition on the UK–Australia air routes from the new Middle-East based airlines presents a direct threat to the legacy airlines that fly this route (BA and QANTAS). So it is perhaps not surprising that they are looking to expand their traditional markets by marketing to the family and friends of recent immigrants to Australia.

Discussion

These seven case studies illustrate the wide range of objectives to be delivered by the various VFR marketing campaigns. However, there was a high degree of commonality in all marketing campaigns, such as: recognition of the key role that residents can play in the success of campaigns, the need to market the tourism product not only in the origin area but also in the destination area, the need to encourage local businesses to see their product as part of the local tourism infrastructure and finally to encourage tourism businesses and the local tourism organisations to work together for the greater need of the local community. In terms of marketing media, it was also clear that both traditional media as well as social media can play a role in helping local residents understand both the products and importance of VFR travel to their area and that the key to success in marketing VFR travel lies in the local people being used to welcome their friends and relatives. As the case studies illustrate, local residents first need to be 'sold' as to the benefits of VFR travel, as they are in both literal and psychological terms the gatekeepers to the product.

As well as these very practical issues, the case studies also highlight the need for the campaigns to provide evidence of not only economic benefits but also community benefits, such as social cohesion by bringing family and friends closer together and the ability to generate a degree of local civic pride in the wider community. What was also clear from the case studies was the need to illustrate that the VFR campaign had support from three different perspectives – namely economic, social and political. Economic in the sense of hard and measurable cash benefits to the area, social by bringing people together so as help in communal and family cohesion and political in terms of gaining the backing of key local power brokers. This triple lock of economic, social and political benefits would appear to be the key to a successful VFR campaign.

The political element carries a high degree of risk, and it only requires a change in the make-up of the stakeholders for even the most successful campaign to crumble. It is argued that one of the contributing reasons why VFR travel has been neglected is because it lacks a lobbying group to champion it (Backer, 2007; Hay, 1996, 2008). In fact, it has been argued that there is actually lobbying against VFR (King, 1996). DMOs can be particularly vulnerable because their strategic direction is often governed by a board of directors. The background, skills and strength of the board members can drive the direction of the organisation; not always for the better. Earlier campaigns such as 'tourism is everyone's business' are not necessarily helpful. The rationale behind this slogan is that every business serves tourists either directly or indirectly and as such everyone is in the business of tourism (Backer & Barry, 2013). The flipside of the statement is that it can be interpreted as meaning that anyone whose business deals with tourists, however intangibly, knows something about tourism. They assume that they have the necessary skills to sit on a DMO board, but the skill sets of some DMO board members are often not suitable and it is disappointing that individuals with no background or training in tourism end up on DMO boards. This can be for political reasons, that they are considered to be well-connected or powerful.

Conclusion

As was argued earlier, the key to drawing these lessons from case studies is not only investigating the commonality of the issues, but also developing an understanding of the reasons for the actions and outcomes of such actions. Sharing information by writing up and publishing reports on VFR campaigns, along with a discussion on the practical lessons learnt and generalising from the case studies, should help other destinations develop their VFR products. In terms of further research, the social benefits of VFR travel have been highlighted. However their output measures need further refinement to provide assurance that developing VFR travel campaigns is beneficial. The impact of the role played by local politics and politicians is poorly understood, as are the motivations for local residents to act as ambassadors for VFR travel. There is a need to explore the impact and workings of VFR travel outside the limited geographical areas in this chapter, so as to investigate the commonality of issues within other destinations. Finally, it is important to note that the term VFR was first developed as a quantification for describing a market segment that was defined by what it was *not* – namely holiday, leisure, business, government or pilgrim trip (United Nations Statistical Commission, 1994). As has been shown by the case studies, it has become much more than a statistical measure and is a key developing market for local communities.

References

Backer, E. (2007) VFR Travel – An examination of the expenditures of VFR travellers and their hosts. *Current Issues in Tourism* 10 (4), 366–377.

Backer, E. (2010a) Opportunities for commercial accommodation in VFR. *International Journal of Tourism Research* 12 (4), 334–354.

Backer, E. (2010b) *VFR Travel: An Assessment of VFR Versus Non-VFR Travellers.* USA: VDM Verlag Dr. Müller.

Backer, E. (2011) VFR travelers: How long are they staying? *Tourism Review International*, 14 (2), 61–70.

Backer, E. (2012) VFR Travel: It *is* underestimated. *Tourism Management* 33 (1), 74–79.

Backer, E. and Barry, B. (2013) Empirical testing of the theory of partial industrialisation in tourism. *Journal of Hospitality and Tourism Management* 20, 43–52.

Basu, P. (2004) My own island. *Journal of Material Culture* 9 (1), 27–42.

Braunlich, C. and Nadkarni, N. (1995) The importance of the VFR market to the hotel industry. *The Journal of Tourism Studies* 6 (1), 38–47.

Brown, G. (2001) Revisiting the millennium: The marketing of Sunrise 2000. *Journal of Vacation Marketing* 7 (3), 247–258.

Edensor, H. (2014) Tourism Australia and BA team up for emotional new campaign. *Travel Weekly.*

Eirich, F. and McLaren, J. (2008) Engaging the Scottish diaspora – Internal document. Edinburgh: Scottish Government's Europe, External Affairs and Culture Analytic Unit.

Griffin, T. (2013) Research note: A content analysis of articles on visiting friends and relatives tourism, 1990–2010. *Journal of Hospitality Marketing & Management* (June 2013), 1–22.

Hay, B. (1996) An insight into the European experience: A case study on domestic VFR tourism within the UK. In H. Yaman (ed.) *VFR Tourism: Issues and Implications. Proceedings from the Conference held at Victoria University of Technology* (pp. 52–66). Melbourne: Victoria University of Technology.

Hay, B. (2008) An exploration of the differences in the volume and value of visiting friends and visiting relatives tourism in the UK. In S. Richardson, L. Fredline, A. Patiar and M. Ternel (eds) *CAUTHE 2008 Where the Bloody Hell Are We? Proceedings of the CAUTHE Conference held in Gold Coast, Australia, 11–14 February 2008* (pp. 488–497). Gold Coast: Griffith University.

Jackson, R. (1990) VFR tourism: Is it underestimated? *The Journal of Tourism Studies* 1 (2), 10–17.

Jackson, R. (2003) VFR tourism: Is it underestimated? *The Journal of Tourism Studies* 14 (1), 17–24.

King, B. (1996) VFR – A future research agenda. In H. Yaman (ed.) *VFR Tourism: Issues and Implications. Proceedings from the Conference held at Victoria University Conference, Victoria, Australia.* (pp. 85–89). Melbourne: Victoria University of Technology.

McKercher, B. (1994) *Report on a Study of Host Involvement in VFR Travel to Albury Wodonga.* Albury-Wodonga.

McKercher, B. (1995) An examination of host involvement in VFR travel. In R. Shaw (ed.) *Proceedings from the National Tourism and Hospitality Conference, 14–17 February 1995. Council for Australian University Tourism and Hospitality Education* (pp. 246–255). Canberra, ACT: Bureau of Tourism Research.

Mildura Tourism (2011) *Annual Report 2010–2011.* Mildura.

Mildura Tourism (2013) *Evaluation Results from Mildura Tourism's 2013 'Be a tourist in your own town campaign'.* Mildura.

Morgan, N. and Pritchard, A. (2001) Contextualising destination branding. In N. Morgan, A. Pritchard and R. Pride (eds) *Destination Branding: Creating the Unique Destination Proposition* (pp. 11–41). Oxford: Butterworth-Heinemann.

Morgan, N., Pritchard, A. and Pride, R. (2003) Marketing to the Welsh diaspora: The appeal to Hiraeth and Homecoming. *Journal of Vacation Marketing* 9, 69–80.

Morrison, A. and Hay, B. (2011) A Review of the constraints, limitations and success of Homecoming Scotland 2009. *Fraser of Allander Economic Commentary* 34 (1), 44–54.

Morrison, A., Hsieh, S. and O'Leary, J. (1995) Segmenting the visiting friends and relatives market by holiday activity participation. *The Journal of Tourism Studies* 6 (1), 48–63.

Seaton, A. (1994) Are relatives friends? Reassessing the VFR category in segmenting tourism markets. In A. Seaton (ed.) *Tourism: The State of the Art* (pp. 316–321). Chichester: Wiley.

Seaton, A. and Palmer, C. (1997) Understanding VFR tourism behaviour: The first five years of the United Kingdom tourism survey. *Tourism Management* 18 (6), 345–355.

Seaton, A.V. and Tagg, S. (1995) Disaggregating friends and relatives in VFR tourism research: The Northern Ireland evidence 1991–1993. *The Journal of Tourism Studies* 6 (1), 6–18.

Tourism Australia (2014) Tourism Australia in new campaign with BA to target UK VFR market. See http://www.tourism.australia.com/news/media-releases/Media-releases-10573.aspx (accessed 24 April 2014).

Tourism Ireland (2013) The Gathering Ireland 2013. See http://www.thegatheringireland.com/ (accessed 24 April 2014).

Tourism Victoria (2010) *Regional Victoria Market Profile Year Ending December 2010.* Melbourne, Australia.

United Nations Statistical Commission (1994) *Recommendations on Tourism Statistics.* New York: UN Press.

V/Line (2011) *Origin-Destination Survey.* Melbourne, Australia.

V/Line (2012) Campaign brief. See http://www.campaignbrief.com/2012/05/regional-train-operator-vline.html (accessed 6 May 2014).

V/Line (2013) *V/Line's Guilt Trip Campaign.* Melbourne, Australia.

VisitScotland (2010) *HS09 Evaluation.* Edinburgh: VisitScotland.

Wales Tourist Board (1998) *Homecoming 2000 – Hiraeth 2000: Draft Programme and Delivery Plan.* Cardiff: Wales Tourist Board.

Wales Tourist Board (2001) *Homecoming/Hiraeth 2000 Campaign. Return on Investment Analysis.* Cardiff: Wales Tourist Board.

Yaman, H. (1996) VFR tourism: Issues and implications. In *VFR Tourism: Issues and Implications, Proceedings from the Conference held at Victoria University of Technology.* Melbourne: Victoria University of Technology.

Part 2

VFR Travel Profiles – Perspectives on Developed and Emerging Countries

8 Visiting Friends and Relatives (VFR) Travel: The Case of Iran

Zahed Ghaderi

Introduction

Visiting friends and relatives (VFR) is an important but overlooked and underestimated travel segment in Iran. Despite the big size of VFR travel, it was assumed that its value was small to decision-makers and tourism marketing practitioners compared to other forms of tourism (Backer, 2007; Seaton & Palmer, 1997). Although there are no official data indicating the exact size of this tourism segment, a recent study showed that 11% of domestic tourists in Iran travelled for the purpose of visiting friends and relatives (Ghaderi, 2011) and this market provided a huge boost to the country's tourism industry. Nevertheless, no study has attempted to explore this market segment, its characteristics, expenditure patterns and size in the country's travel and tourism industry. Not surprisingly, no specific report on VFR travel could even be found in the database of Iran's cultural heritage, handicrafts and tourism organisation to uncover this travel market.

An analysis of the marketing programme of national, provincial and local tourism authorities, and those of private sector operators, revealed that not much attention has been paid to this significant market in Iran. Therefore, further investigation of this large market and its characteristics is imperative. Moreover, this chapter highlights the necessity of a new wave of research to encourage both academics and practitioners to give further recognition of VFR's value in the contemporary travel and tourism industry. It attempts to understand the VFR travel market in Iran; to provide in-depth information about this growing travel market segment; and to identify and analyse major domestic and international VFR market segments. In addition, this chapter also tries to fill the gap in the country's travel and tourism profile and to provide the grounds for future research into this segment. The results of two empirical surveys on domestic tourism and Iran's household travel are used to identify the demographic, socioeconomic profile and travel characteristics of VFR travellers in Iran.

Background

Formally acknowledged as a large form of tourism worldwide, the VFR travel market is likely to be the oldest kind of travel, and travelling for visiting friends and relatives has always been socially important (Backer, 2011, 2012). Various definitions have been suggested for VFR travel and Backer's (2007) definition is the most appropriate one: 'VFR travel is a form of travel involving a visit whereby either (or both) the purpose of the trip or the type of accommodation involves visiting friends and/or relatives' (369). While Backer's (2007) definition of VFR travel covers both criteria of purpose of visit and accommodation use, previous researchers suggested only one criterion – either accommodation use, which is deemed to stay in the homes of friends and relatives (see, for example, King, 1994; Kotler et al., 2006), or purpose of the visit (King, 1994; Kotler et al., 2006; Yuan et al., 1995). Nevertheless, as Backer (2012) and Jackson (1990) point out, not all VFR travellers who stay with their friends and relatives state a VFR travel purpose, and not all tourists who travel for VFR purposes stay with their friends and relatives. King (1996) in his research suggests that VFR travel can be seen from four perspectives: as a motivation for travel, as a trip purpose, as a vocation activity and as a form of accommodation use. Therefore, presenting a generally accepted definition of VFR travel remains challenging among both academics and practitioners. With regard to the size and significance of VFR travel, several authors argue that this market segment is not well researched compared to other kinds of tourism market (see, for example, Asiedu, 2008; Backer, 2007, 2008, 2012a; Bischoff & Koenig-Lewis, 2007; Lee et al., 2005).

A stream of academic research was initiated in the mid-nineties and after this period this market segment received some attention from tourism marketing organisations (Backer, 2007; Lehto et al., 2001; Shani & Uriely, 2012). This growth was due to the recognition that VFR travel was the primary source of tourism in some destinations, and that it might be economically more significant than formerly thought (Backer, 2007; Lee et al., 2005; Seaton & Palmer, 1997). However, different reasons were also raised for historical marginalisation of VFR travel among academics and practitioners, as were outlined in Chapter 7. First, it was assumed that its importance and value was small to tourism practitioners compared to other forms of tourism, likely due to this perception that VFR travel has limited economic impacts on host communities (Asiedu, 2008; Backer, 2007, 2012a; Lee et al., 2005); second, as it happened for reasons outside the control of tourism marketing efforts, it was assumed it could not be stimulated by tourism planners; and third, although it could be stimulated, no particular activity was assumed essential to do so since it would be influenced by the same marketing efforts as those promoting mainstream recreational tourism. A fourth reason has also been suggested which is more political: VFR travel has had no lobbying group championing it by tourism stakeholders compared to other types of tourism activities (Backer, 2007; Hay, 1996; Lehto *et al.*, 2001). A further four reasons were mentioned in Chapter 7.

Initial attempts were undertaken by publishing works either as journal articles or dedicated conferences (Lee *et al.*, 2005). These case studies attempted to outline or segment VFR travellers and take a marketing perspective in their recommendations. Since then, tourism scholars and practitioners have undertaken ad hoc research on this topic and presented their studies either as journal articles or book chapters (see, for example, Asiedu, 2008; Backer, 2007, 2010, 2011, 2012a; Boyne, 2011; Boyne *et al.*, 2002; Hay, 2008; Hu & Morrison, 2002; Jackson, 2003; Lee *et al.*, 2005; Lehto *et al.*, 2001; Morrison *et al.*, 2000; Moscardo *et al.*, 2000; Pearce & Moscardo, 2006; Pennington-Gray, 2003; Shani & Uriely, 2012; Uriely, 2010; Young *et al.*, 2007). These initial efforts have shed some light on the notion of VFR travel and provided the basis for future research in different corners of the world.

These studies, however, were mainly conducted in the developed nations and concentrated on the characteristics of VFR travellers in these countries, but developing countries, especially Middle-Eastern countries, were largely overlooked despite their significant market share of VFR travel. This inattention from both academics and tourism marketing agencies led to a shortage of work in the area of VFR travel. Not surprisingly, both Iranian tourism scholars and practitioners overlooked this important market and, to the best of the author's knowledge, no study spoke about VFR travel in Iran, its characteristics and its market significance. Hence, this research attempts to fill this gap within the context of tourism in Iran.

Method

As mentioned before, there is no specific empirical study focusing on VFR travel in Iran, which outlines the characteristics of the VFR travel market. Hence, research to identify some facts about VFR travel is imperative. The method used for this study was based on the result of an empirical study conducted by the author on domestic tourists in different destinations in Iran (Tehran, Esfahan, Shiraz, Mashhad, Gilan, Mazandaran, Tabriz and Hamadan). Participants were domestic tourists who travelled individually or by organised tours in the aforementioned gateways. In this survey, nearly 1000 questionnaires were distributed to domestic tourists on different dates during April to September 2009 and almost 900 questionnaires were completed and returned for analysis and interpretation. The questionnaire included information on the social status of the travellers, their motives to travel, their destinations, length of stays and the distribution of their spending on different items such as accommodation, transportation and entertainment. Those questionnaires related to VFR travel were selected for further analysis and interpretation. 'VFR main purpose of visit' and 'home of friends and relatives as accommodation' were two criteria to differentiate VFR travellers from other domestic tourists.

In addition, data from a survey on Iranian households conducted by the Statistical Center of Iran (SCI) during summer 2012 (from June until September) was applied, which presented the volume and size of VFR travellers. The SCI has undertaken various surveys on the households' travels indicating their purpose of visits, expenditure patterns, accommodations used, destinations visited and the numbers of domestic trips they have had.

Results

VFR travel profile of Iran

VFR travel is the most unknown travel segment in Iran and it has been overlooked by both academics and practitioners alike. There is no specific study describing the market significance and characteristics of VFR travel in Iran and thus its economic contribution to the country's tourism industry is not fully appreciated. The only reliable information that exists is the results of an empirical survey conducted by SCI in 2012 during the summer, which shows that of 42,555,081 overnight domestic trips, approximately 23,773,399 (56%) were conducted for the purpose of visiting friends and relatives (Statistical Center of Iran, 2012). Similarly, out of 28,316,056 same-day trips, around 7,950,961 trips were undertaken for the purpose of VFR (see Table 8.1).

As Table 8.1 shows, during the summer season approximately 71 million domestic trips took place, of which 44.7% were conducted for the

Table 8.1 Results of national survey of domestic travellers during summer 2012

Main purpose of trip	Same-day trip	Overnight trip	Total
Leisure	7,726,345	8,708,673	16,435,018
VFR	7,950,961	23,773,399	31,724,351
Pilgrimage	3,209,454	6,195,633	9,405,087
Health	4,743,947	2,474,515	7,218,462
Shopping	3,495,379	246,929	3,742,308
Education	44,339	91,544	135,883
Business	324,685	643,569	968,255
Other purposes	820,946	420,826	1,241,772
Total	**28,316,056**	**42,555,081**	**70,871,136**

Source: Statistics Center of Iran (2012)

Table 8.2 Types of accommodations used by domestic travellers during summer 2012

Type of accommodation used	Share %
Public accommodations	5%
Government accommodations	5%
Friends/relatives homes	67%
Rental villas and apartments	11%
Private villas and apartments	6%
Private camps	5%
Other accommodations	2%
Total	100%

Source: Statistical Center of Iran (2012)

purpose of VFR. This share is significantly important in the country's travel and tourism market, which has been neglected in planning and marketing programmes over years. However, no detailed information is provided about the characteristics of VFR travellers in the survey and what kind of accommodation they used during their stay. Nevertheless, the same survey shows that almost 67% of all domestic travellers during the summer used houses of friends and relatives as accommodation whether their main purpose of visit was VFR or other purposes (see Table 8.2) (Statistical Center of Iran, 2012).

As outlined in Table 8.2, friends' and relatives' houses were the main type of accommodation used by domestic travellers, followed by rental villas and apartments with 11% and private villas and apartments with 6%. Other accommodations such as public accommodations, government accommodations and private camps accounted for 5% for each category. The high percentage of travellers using friends and relatives houses reflects the effects of the severe economic crisis on the country's travel and tourism industry, which started in 2011, because of which many tourism businesses, including accommodation sectors, experienced difficult situations (Ghaderi, 2012). To mitigate the financial burden of trips during the economic crisis, travellers stayed with their friends and relatives, as using commercial accommodation was not affordable.

In order to explore more facts about VFR travel in Iran, the results of an empirical study conducted by the author were employed to discover unknown aspects of the VFR travel market. An empirical study of 900 domestic tourists in different tourist destinations in Iran showed that 11% of domestic tourists in 2009 travelled for the purpose of VFR (Ghaderi, 2011) and 9% used the houses of friends and relatives as their accommodation. The study also revealed that VFR travellers were male dominated (56%), while females accounted for 44%. The majority of VFR respondents were between 30 and 55 years old and young singles or couples with children. Almost 90% of VFR respondents stayed with their friends and relatives, and only 10% used commercial accommodation. They stayed an average of three days at their friends' and relatives' houses. The average income level of respondents was approximately IRR9,000,000 (Almost equal to US$950),[1] and they roughly spent IRR3,000,000 to 5,000,000 (Almost equal to US$350-550) per trip. According to this survey, VFR travellers planned their trip on their own instead of using package tours or travel agents or tour operators. The majority of these travellers claimed that they obtained the required information from their friends and relatives, through word-of-mouth, and few used other sources such as internet and printed advertising materials.

In terms of educational background, almost 85% of VFR travellers had university qualifications, while 10% obtained high school diploma and 5% secondary and primary school certificate. Asking occupational activity of respondents, the majority of these visitors (80%) worked for government organisations and private companies, while 20% were self-employed and had a business in the market. In addition to visiting friends and relatives purposes, the majority of VFR travellers stated that they have engaged in out-of-house activities and had visited other natural or cultural tourist attractions located in or around their friends' and relatives' destinations.

The findings also reveal that almost two-thirds of VFR travellers (almost 65%) were repeat visitors and had visited their friends and relatives at least two times while 35% of VFR travellers made only one trip. Enquiring about the mode of travel, transportation to tourist destinations, public transportation (bus and train) was the main mode of travel used by VFR travellers followed by private vehicles. Travellers' tendency to use public transportation can be due to the significant rise in fuel prices in recent years in Iran where the price of fuel has been increased several times (Ghaderi, 2011, 2013).

Discussion of Findings

Although there is a lack of information about the VFR travel segment in Iran, the results of two empirical surveys revealed some facts regarding this important travel market. According to data from the Center for Statistics, almost half of all domestic trips were conducted for the purpose of VFR during the summer survey. This is a significant share of the country's tourism market and highlights the need for considerable attention by tourism stakeholders. Despite the significance of VFR travel, it has been neglected by practitioners, which might be due to the fact that the majority of VFR travellers stayed in the homes of their friends and relatives rather than commercial accommodation.

Nevertheless, evidence shows that VFR spending, although often lower overall than other forms of tourism activities, is significant in certain sectors of expenditure such as on travel, transportation, services and retail (Backer, 2007; Lee *et al.*, 2005; Seaton & Palmer, 1997; Shany & Uriely, 2012). In addition, there are hidden patterns of expenditures in VFR travel that may help to compensate for the lower overall expenditures recorded by tourists; and buying gifts for friends and relatives may even surpass accommodation expenses. This result is in line with Lee *et al.'s* (2005) findings that VFR travellers spent much more than the other tourists across all expenditure categories, especially on shopping, meals and other expenses. Therefore, the common perception that VFR travel is unprofitable is unfounded.

The research undertaken for this chapter revealed that a considerably high proportion of all domestic trips (44%) were made for the purpose of VFR and 67% of respondents stayed in the homes of friends and relatives. Those trips were typically conducted in the peak seasons (during summer and school holidays), which conflicts with both Backer (2012b) and Seaton and Palmer's (1997) research, which suggested that VFR was 'a basis for achieving a more balanced tourism development, [as it was] less dependent on high season' (354).

Domestic VFR travel in Iran is mainly undertaken in peak seasons (school holidays), when a large volume of people from metropolitan areas travel to see their friends and relatives and also stay with them. This volume does not include long-haul or short-haul international VFR travellers (either those Iranians that reside outside the country or non-Iranians who travel to see their friends and relatives in Iran), which have not been considered in the government statistics. Further, this volume does not represent all the VFR travel market in Iran; and this result is consistent with Backer (2012a) that the formal data are only a portion of the total number of VFR travellers, which was discussed in Chapter 5.

Another significant VFR market is Iranians that stay abroad and return to the country to visit their friends and relatives. Although there is no transparent and clear information about the numbers of these people, it has been estimated that the total number is between 5–6 million, who mainly stay in the USA, the UK, the United Arab Emirates, Canada, Germany, France and Sweden (Ebtekar News, 2012). Many of these people visit their friends and relatives at least once per year and make trips to other parts of the country to visit other tourist destinations. This is a huge potential market that tourism marketing agents could encourage to diversify their trip for longer stays. For example, when Iranian immigrants return to the country for visiting their friends and relatives, they will want to visit other cultural and historical attractions in the country. Hence, tour operators can offer various itineraries to attract this group of tourists (ITTO, 2001). Unlike domestic VFR travellers that seem to have low levels of income

(Ghaderi, 2011), this group of VFR travellers usually have high income levels with strong power of purchase. When they come to Iran, they find it very affordable compared to their country of residence (ITTO, 2001).

Furthermore, the result of this study challenges the current belief that VFR travellers spend less money than other types of tourists (Asiedu, 2008; Denman, 1998; Langlois *et al.*, 1999; Lee *et al.*, 2005). On the contrary, it shows that they have spent considerable amounts of money per trip to buy travel necessities such as gifts, food and beverages, and paid travel transportation. These expenses, unlike the suggestion of previous studies (Backer, 2007; Bresler, 2011; Lee *et al.*, 2005; Meis *et al.*, 1995; Seaton & Tagg, 1995), bring considerable economic benefits to communities and other travel stakeholders. Moreover, the result of previous studies reveals that hosts (friends and relatives) spend as much on hosting and entertaining VFR travellers, which contributes to the enhancement of the local economy as well (Asiedu, 2008; Backer, 2007; Lee *et al.*, 2005; Meis *et al.*, 1995). In addition, VFR travellers have disseminated free word-of-mouth advertisement and promotion that could attract other visitors to tourist destinations. This result confirms the findings of Meis *et al.* (1995), Morrison and O'Leary (1995), Backer (2010, 2007) and Young *et al.* (2007) that VFR travellers have spread free word-of-mouth as informal marketing communication in attracting visitors to destinations. Furthermore, VFR travel tends to be less vulnerable to economic downturns compared to other forms of tourism, as was demonstrated in the country's recent economic crisis (Ghaderi, 2012). While other forms of tourism, including leisure and business travel, showed a dramatic decline, VFR travel experienced positive growth and the number has been increasing over the past years (SCI, 2012). This statement is also supported by Daniels and Loveless (2013) and Backer (2012): VFR travel is more resilient to crisis situations than other kinds of tourism activities. In addition, Asiedu (2008) discussed that even during periods of socio-political crises, when western nations issue travel advisory to their citizens to avoid unnecessary travel to such potentially dangerous countries, Ghanaians domiciling outside the country were likely to visit to satisfy pressing family obligations.

The result of this study also illustrated that the majority (almost 90%) of VFR travellers stayed with their friends and relatives and only 10% used commercial accommodation due to the high cost of hotels and sociocultural norms of Iranian community. This result confirms the finding of Pearce and Moscardo (2006) that in developing countries sociocultural norms effectively require VFR travellers to stay with family and friends when visiting even though the main purpose of visit is not VFR. Beside the economic significance, VFR travel has contributed to the solidity and strength of social foundations of Iranian communities. This type of tourism has caused VFR travellers to visit the land of their parents and strengthen the family ties (ITTO, 2001). For instance, travelling to the ancestral homeland to visit relatives has led to the formation of a strong cultural communication and empathy and a sense of unity among hosts and guests, which, from tourism points of view, led to repeat visitation (Boyne, 2001; Hänsel & Metzner, 2011). It is important to note that VFR travel has a significant relationship with repeat visitation and this positive association and its economic value is also emphasised in a number of studies (see, for example, Backer, 2010; Bischoff & Koenig-Lewis, 2007; Gitelson & Crompton, 1984; Meis *et al.*, 1995; Paci, 1994; Tiefenbacher *et al.*, 2000).

Conclusion

This chapter has highlighted the importance and significance of the VFR travel market in Iran, despite the current tendencies to marginalise and underestimate its market share by tourism marketing agencies. It also has illustrated a number of features of domestic VFR travel in Iran, which modifies and extends knowledge. Changes in family structures and demography, and an increasing tendency for parts of extended families to live in disparate locations, which may cross national borders and cover large distances, together with the ease of access to international travel networks, suggest that VFR travel is very likely to be a growth area in contemporary travel and tourism (Carr, 2011). The analysis of VFR travel in Iran provides valuable insight into its structure and identifying features. However, there are major areas of further work. For instance, empirical research on different categories of VFR travellers, their motivations and activities is needed. Further research is also recommended in determining the differences in the profiles and structures of international VFR travel and those of domestic travel. In addition, the economic contribution of VFR travel to the advancement of local economy and the expenditure pattern of VFR travellers in Iran is unclear and research in this area is suggested.

This chapter has practical implications for tourism marketing agencies and policy makers not only in Iran, but also more broadly. First, it highlights the value of VFR travel to authorities and tourism marketing agencies and the importance of paying more attention to this kind of tourism and bringing it in the frontline of marketing programmes of tourism organisations. Second, previous research has often focused on its economic benefits with inadequate research to consider the cultural input that VFR travel could bring. That benefit could contribute to the sustainability of the tourism product in Iran and thus further enhance economic development. Third, the result of this study assists tourism marketing organisations to consider interests and specific needs of VFR travellers in tour programmes and promotional activities. As this chapter and some previous studies revealed (for example Poel *et al.*, 2004), the average length of stay of VFR travellers is twice as long as the average length of stay of leisure tourists, hence tour operators and travel facilitators should try to offer a variety of tour packages in order to be able to satisfy the needs of VFR travellers while visiting their friends and relatives. The results of past VFR studies also indicate that this kind of tourism does not need significant investment (Hänsel & Metzner, 2011; Jackson, 1990). Therefore, even smaller towns without primary and major tourist attractions or scenic beauties can benefit from VFR travel.

Note

(1) It is important to note that this survey was conducted before the economic crisis in Iran started in 2011 which the rate of Iranian Rial (IRR) was US$1 equal to IRR9500. The current rate is three times higher than the rate mentioned in 2009.

References

Asiedu, A.B. (2008) Participants' characteristics and economic benefits of visiting friends and relatives (VFR) tourism – an international survey of the literature with implications for Ghana. *International Journal of Tourism Research* 10 (6), 609–621.

Backer, E. (2007) VFR travel: An examination of the expenditures of VFR travellers and their hosts. *Current Issues in Tourism* 10 (4), 366–377.

Backer, E. (2010) Opportunities for commercial accommodation in VFR travel. *International Journal of Tourism Research* 12 (4), 334–354.

Backer, E. (2011) VFR travellers of the future. In I. Yeoman, K. Hsu, C. Smith and S. Watson (eds) *Tourism and Demography* (pp. 73–86). Oxford: Goodfellow Publishers.

Backer, E. (2012a) VFR travel: It *is* underestimated. *Tourism Management* 33 (1), 74–79.

Backer, E. (2012b) VFR travel: Why marketing to Aunt Betty matters. In H. Schänzel, I. Yeoman and E. Backer (eds) *Family Tourism: Multidisciplinary Perspectives* (pp. 81–92). Bristol: Channel View Publications.

Bischoff, E.E. and Koenig - Lewis, N. (2007) VFR tourism: The importance of university students as hosts. *International Journal of Tourism Research* 9 (6), 465–484.

Boyne, S. (2001) Hosts, friends and relatives in rural Scotland: VFR tourism market relationships explored. In L. Roberts and D. Hall (eds) *Rural Tourism and Recreation: Principles to Practice* (pp. 41–43). Wallingford: CABI Publishing.

Boyne, S., Carswell, F. and Hall, D. (2002) Reconceptualising VFR tourism. In C.M. Hall and A.M. Williams (eds) *Tourism and Migration: New Relationships between Production and Consumption* (pp. 241–256). Netherlands: Kluwer.

Bresler, N. (2011) Decision factors for domestic package tours – Case study of a region in South Africa. *Turizam, International Scientific Journal* 15 (2), 53–64.

Carr, N. (2011) *Children's and Families' Holiday Experience*. London: Routledge.

Daniels, M. and Loveless, C. (2013) *Wedding Planning and Management: Consultancy for Diverse Clients*. New York: Routledge.

Denman, R. (1988) A response to the VFR market: A report to the English Tourist Board and Regional Tourist Boards. London: British Tourist Authority.

Ebtekar News (2012) Iranians stay abroad. See http://www.ebtekarnews.com/Ebtekar/News.aspx?NID=104168 (accessed 2 March 2014).

Ghaderi, Z. (2011) Domestic tourism in Iran. *Anatolia* 22 (2), 278–281.

Ghaderi, Z. (2012) The effects of economic crisis on tourism businesses in Iran. Unpublished research work. Sustainable Tourism Research Cluster.

Ghaderi, Z. (2013) Domestic tourism in Iran. In World Tourism Organization (ed.) *Domestic Tourism in Asia and the Pacific* (pp. 187–212). Madrid: UNWTO.

Gitelson, R.J. and Crompton, J.L. (1984) Insights into the repeat vacation phenomenon. *Annals of Tourism Research* 11 (2), 199–217.

Hänsel, M. and Metzner, T. (2011) Visiting friends & relatives (VFR). In A. Papathanassis (ed.) *The Long Tail of Tourism: Holiday Niches and Their Impact on Mainstream Tourism* (pp. 35–44). Germany: Springer.

Hay, B. (1996) An insight into the European experience: A case study on domestic VFR tourism within the UK. In H. Yaman (ed.) *VFR Tourism: Issues and Implications* (pp. 52–66). Melbourne: Victoria University.

Hay, B. (2008) An exploration of the differences in the volume and value of visiting friends and visiting relatives tourism in the UK. *CAUTHE 2008 Where the Bloody Hell Are We? Proceedings of the CAUTHE Conference Held in Gold Coast, Australia, 11–14 February 2008* (pp. 1–10). Gold Coast: Griffith University.

Hu, B. and Morrison, A.M. (2002) Tripography: Can destination use patterns enhance understanding of the VFR market? *Journal of Vacation Marketing* 8 (3), 201–220.

Iran Touring and Tourism Organization (ITTO) (2001) Iran's Tourism Development and Management Master Plan. Unpublished Report. Tehran, Iran.

Jackson, R.T. (1990) VFR tourism: Is it underestimated? *Journal of Tourism Studies* 1 (2), 10–17.

King, B. (1994) What is ethnic tourism? An Australian perspective. *Tourism Management* 15 (3), 173–176.

King, B. (1996) VFR – A future research agenda. In H. Yaman (ed.) *VFR Tourism: Issues and Implications* (pp. 85–89). Melbourne: Victoria University.

Kotler, P., Bowen, J.T. and Makens, J.C. (2006) *Marketing for Hospitality and Tourism*. New Jersey: Pearson Education.

Langlois, S., Theodore, J. and Ineson, E. (1999) Poland: In-bound tourism from the UK. *Tourism Management* 20 (4), 461–469.

Lee, G., Morrison, A.M., Lehto, X.Y., Webb, J. and Reid, J. (2005) VFR: Is it really marginal? A financial consideration of French overseas travellers. *Journal of Vacation Marketing* 11 (4), 340–356.

Lehto, X.Y., Morrison, A.M. and O'Leary, J.T. (2001) Does the visiting friends and relatives' typology make a difference? A study of the international VFR market to the United States. *Journal of Travel Research* 40 (2), 201–212.

Meis, S., Joyal, S. and Trites, A. (1995) The US repeat and VFR visitor to Canada: Come again, eh! *Journal of Tourism Studies* 6 (1), 27–37.

Morrison, A.M. and O'Leary, J.T. (1995) The VFR market: Desperately seeking respect. *Journal of Tourism Studies* 6, 2–5.

Morrison, A., Woods, B., Pearce, P., Moscardo, G. and Sung, H.H. (2000) Marketing to the visiting friends and relatives segment: An international analysis. *Journal of Vacation Marketing* 6 (2), 102–118.

Moscardo, G., Pearce, P., Morrison, A., Green, D. and O'Leary, J.T. (2000) Developing a typology for understanding visiting friends and relatives markets. *Journal of Travel Research* 38 (3), 251–259.

Paci, E. (1994) The major international VFR markets. *Travel & Tourism Analyst* 6, 36–50.

Pearce, P.L. and Moscardo, G. (2006) Domestic and visiting friends and relatives tourism. In D. Buhalis and C. Costa (eds) *Tourism Business Frontiers: Consumers, Products and Industry* (pp. 48–55). Great Britain: Elsevier.

Pennington-Gray, L. (2003) Understanding the domestic VFR drive market in Florida. *Journal of Vacation Marketing* 9 (4), 354–367.

Poel, P.E.F., Masurel, E. and Nijkamp, P. (2004) The importance of friends and relations in tourist behaviour: A case study of heterogeneity in Surinam. In M. Giaoutzi and

P. Nijkamp (eds) *Tourism and Regional Development: New Pathway* (pp. 219–238). USA: Ashgate Publishing.

Seaton, A. and Palmer, C. (1997) Understanding VFR tourism behaviour: The first five years of the United Kingdom tourism survey. *Tourism Management* 18 (6), 345–355.

Seaton, A. and Tagg, S. (1995) Disaggregating friends and relatives in VFR tourism research: The Northern Ireland evidence 1991–1993. *Journal of Tourism Studies* 6 (1), 6–18.

Shani, A. and Uriely, N. (2012) VFR tourism: The host experience. *Annals of Tourism Research* 39 (1), 421–440.

Statistical Center of Iran (SCI) (2012) National tourism survey results. Tehran: Statistical Center of Iran.

Tiefenbacher, J.P., Day, F.A. and Walton, J.A. (2000) Attributes of repeat visitors to small tourist-oriented communities. *The Social Science Journal* 37 (2), 299–308.

Uriely, N. (2010) 'Home' and 'away' in VFR tourism. *Annals of Tourism Research* 37 (3), 854–857.

Young, C.A., Corsun, D.L. and Baloglu, S. (2007) A taxonomy of hosts visiting friends and relatives. *Annals of Tourism Research* 34 (2), 497–516.

Yuan, T., Fridgen, J., Hsieh, S. and O'Leary, J. (1995) Visiting friends and relatives travel market: The Dutch case. *Journal of Tourism Studies* 6 (1), 19–26.

9 Travel in the United States: An Examination of VFR Travel

Joseph T. O'Leary, Gyehee Lee, Jung Eun Kim and Nandini Nadkarni

Introduction

Visiting friends and relatives (VFR) as a trip purpose and as an activity occurs everywhere in the world. It is a global phenomenon in tourism for a variety of social and eco-political reasons (Lee *et al.*, 2005). Generally in the tourism literature, VFR is treated as a primary trip purpose while some researchers view it as a special kind of destination activity. Some others consider VFR as possessing dual functions, as the motivator (purpose to take a trip) and as a salient activity (Asiedu, 2008). Regardless of the typology, Uriely (2010) argues that VFR travellers experience 'home' and 'away from home' opportunities. They rely upon their hosts' access to non-touristic places in the visited destination and enhance their destination familiarity through participating in the everyday life of local residents, enjoying home traditions, food, language and local norms through their hosts.

Background

The VFR sector has garnered sporadic attention from tourism researchers in the past. Arguments about why VFR travel may not have received more consideration range from it not being perceived to be as valuable as other forms of tourism to that it cannot be stimulated or controlled through marketing activities in the same way as efforts tied to other mainstream tourism efforts (Lee *et al.*, 2005).

VFR value and structure may be even more of an issue now. Tourism demand in the United States grew at a rate of 3.7% per year until entering the economic recession in December 2007. At the same time, GDP grew 2.7% a year. The recession caused the GDP of the United States to fall by nearly 4% and real travel demand to fall 6% over six quarters (Advertising Age, 2009). Using data from the US Travel and Tourism Satellite Account system, Ritchie *et al.* (2009: 5) concluded that '[T]ourism in the United States has been and is being, affected by the current economic crisis, and it appears likely that it will be further affected in the near future'. Specifically the study pointed out that travel demand during the current recession decreased at twice the rate of the GDP decline. The economic downturn has affected not only the frequency of travel but also the purpose of travel and travel behaviours.

Various data sources suggest that VFR is often one of the most important reasons for travel to a destination and one of the leading trip purposes. It also would seem that, with recent economic challenges (e.g. the financial crisis in 2008) taking place globally, the patterns and importance of VFR travel may have also shifted. VFR travel may play a new role as visitors take advantage of opportunities that are perceived to be more cost effective.

With particular reference to the United States this chapter will discuss some of the relevant VFR literature, identify and describe a national profile, characteristics and behaviours of VFR travellers and compare that with their business and general leisure travel counterparts. In addition, considering the economic changes that occurred around 2008, it will further examine differences before and after the recession crisis using survey data from 2006 and 2011. The empirical analysis will be based on a large national data set collected annually from over 60,000 travelling households providing the unique ability to identify trends and forecast US travel behaviour. It does not appear that analysis of this type has been reported in other places.

Literature Review

VFR typology

Generally, VFR travellers have been examined using either motivation or activity. Although most researchers treat VFR based on motivation, Morrison *et al.* (1995) viewed VFR as one of the activities travellers report doing in the destination of their visit rather than as a prime travel motivation. Defining and determining the parameters of VFR as a tourism phenomenon helped marketers and researchers in VFR travel understand better the complexity of the VFR phenomenon (Pearce & Moscardo, 2005). Suggesting that VFR travellers cannot be understood as a single market with homogeneous characteristics, Moscardo *et al.* (2000) classified VFR in the context of five defining factors, including sector, scope, effort, accommodation used and focus of the visit with either friends or relatives. They made a binary classification of VFR for each parameter and then classified the phenomenon into two types: type A for VFR as a main motivation, and type B for VFR as part of activities/motivations. A few studies (e.g. Backer, 2009; Hu & Morrison, 2002; Lockyer & Ryan, 2007; Pearce, 2012; Uriely, 2010) adopted this approach to segment the VFR market. For instance, Lehto *et al.* (2001) concluded that such parameters are useful in that they categorise VFR travellers into five sub-segments. They found significant differences among those VFR groups in terms of their behavioural characteristics and patterns and thus concluded that the parameters used by Moscardo *et al.* (2000) make more practical sense to DMOs (Lehto *et al.*, 2001).

Using United Kingdom travel data, Seaton and Palmer (1997) argued that VFR travellers can be categorised into two types, namely motivational VFR (whose main trip purpose is to visit friends and relatives) and accommodation VFR (stay with their hosts, friends and relatives for accommodation). They suggest that even though the motivational VFR group is differentiated from the accommodation VFR, there are more trip characteristics shared than with other trip purposes (e.g. leisure, business and other tourists). Thus, categorising VFR only based on trip purpose fails to accurately measure the size of the VFR market (Seaton & Palmer, 1997). As discussed, these two typologies suggest that the use of commercial accommodation is a key parameter in defining VFR travellers. This is due to the significance of the accommodation expenditure towards the overall economic contribution to the host destination (Lee *et al.*, 2005; Seaton & Palmer, 1997; Lehto *et al.*, 2001). Regardless of VFR travellers' accommodation use patterns, VFR remains a very significant segment (McKercher, 1996). Using a large national survey collected by the US Dept. of Commerce, Lee *et al.* (2005) differentiated North American bound VFR French travellers (main purpose) in terms of their economic value and divided them based on total expenditure per capita. They found high spending VFR showed a sharp contrast to their low spending counterpart. Interestingly, high spending VFR travellers tended to spend more than general leisure travellers on accommodation, meals and shopping (Lee *et al.*, 2005). They reinforced the heterogeneity of VFR travellers that has been identified in the literature and that their economic contribution is not marginal (Lee *et al.*, 2005).

Economic contribution of VFR

While VFR travel is one of the oldest and largest forms of travel (Backer, 2011), the economic contributions of VFR travel have often been underappreciated (Backer, 2012; Laskai, 2013; Seaton & Palmer, 1997; Seaton & Tagg, 1995). Various sources suggest that VFR is often one of the most important reasons for travel to a destination and one of the leading trip purposes (Asiedu, 2008; Lehto *et al.*, 2001; McKercher, 1996; Morrison *et al.*, 1995). It also has a significant impact on national and regional economies because of the scale and distribution of involvement impacting various travel characteristics (e.g. spending, activity choices, hotel use and food).

McKercher (1996) reported that VFR travel accounts for about 32% of all domestic person-trips in Australia and for up to 50% of domestic visitor-nights in New South Wales and Victoria. One study revealed that of the 18.7 million foreign visitors to the US in 1993, 30% of them came for the purpose of VFR, exceeding the number of business trip arrivals (Braunlich & Nadkarni, 1995). This trend did not seem to change over time in the USA.

The Survey of International Air Travellers conducted in 2001 showed about 23% of all inbound travellers reported they came to the USA mainly for VFR purposes and another 35% for one of their trip purposes (International Trade Administration, 2002). Similarly, Morrison *et al.* (1995) reported that more than 60% of the destination marketing organisations in the USA and Canada indicated that VFR travellers in their area accounted for between 30% and 50% of total domestic travellers. Although more recent statistics are difficult to obtain, it seems reasonable to assert that this trend has been maintained or increased.

Comparing the economic multiplier effect of VFR with general leisure/ business tourism in Sri Lanka, King and Gamage (1994) showed that VFR generated higher tourism income multipliers and more direct and induced incomes than non-VFRs. Navarro and Turco (1994) found in their studies that VFR travellers, when compared to traditional assumptions, contributed positively to the local economy by significantly using commercial accommodation, restaurants, special events and attractions. Morrison *et al.* (1995) supported the high impact of the VFR travellers by showing that the majority of VFR travellers in Queensland not only used commercial accommodation facilities but also had high expenditures at restaurants, night clubs and casinos. They argued that VFR travellers, even if having a primary purpose of visiting friends and relatives, do not automatically stay at their friends and relatives' home. In a study examining the international VFR market to the United States, Lehto *et al.* (2001) found that almost half of international VFR travellers used commercial accommodation. Lehto *et al.* (2001) also reported that international VFR travellers showed significant spending on restaurants, shopping and transportation.

Studies supporting the assumption that VFR travellers use less commercial accommodation facilities argue that the VFR market should be appreciated for its direct economic contribution to the local community. Seaton and Palmer (1997) showed that VFRs spend less than the other types of traveller because they invest less on accommodation and travel packages. However, domestic VFR travellers in the United Kingdom spent more on eating, drinking, shopping, services and entertainment than other tourists. Hay (1996) also found that VFR travellers had higher expenditures on various types of shopping. According to Lee *et al.* (2005), the majority (62%) of VFR travellers spent less than the other types of visitors but a significant proportion (38%) of the group spent significantly higher amounts than other types of leisure and business travellers. The high-expenditure group used commercial accommodations and spent more on eating, shopping and activities than other tourists. Lee *et al.* (2005) and Jackson (1990) concluded that the VFR market can be a segment of international travel that brings significant economic contributions to host communities.

Considering the volume of VFR travel and the extended length of stay, which is usually longer than for business and even for some leisure travel, the economic importance of this market is far from being marginal. McKercher (1996) demonstrated that the incremental expenses assumed by the hosts, in addition to the direct spending from VFR, are largely left unaccounted in the total economic benefits generated from VFR activities. He argued that such host-burdened expenditures account for up to an additional 25% in the forms of host expenditure for food and others to entertain their guest VFRs of the total economic benefits contributed to the host communities (McKercher, 1996). Despite these facts, the prevalent underestimation of the value of this market is often attributed to questions about VFR travellers using commercial accommodation hence devaluing their actual importance (Lee *et al.*, 2005).

Investigation of the recent changes and trends in US VFR Travel

There are only a handful of research examples examining the US VFR phenomenon (Braunlich & Nadkarni, 1995; Hu & Morrison, 2002; Pennington-Gray, 2003). Hu and Morrison (2002) examined the segment of VFR travellers in the United States in the context of marketing perspectives. Focusing on socio-demographic and trip behavioural differences between VFR travellers and non-VFR travellers, Hu and Morrison (2002) found that several factors distinguish these groups. Similarly, examining travellers in the East North Central census region of the USA, Braunlich and Nadkarni (1995) found that VFR travellers were older than their leisure counterparts and had similar household incomes compared to pleasure travellers but less than business travellers. They concluded that VFR travellers occupied a great part of the leisure travel market and showed a meaningful level of commercial accommodation use (Braunlich & Nadkarni, 1995). Applying Moscardo *et al.*'s VFR model to the Florida market, Pennington-Gray (2003) identified three VFR sub-segments: *travellers whose main purpose was to visit and stay with friends and relatives (AFR), travellers whose main purpose was to visit friends and relatives and stay in commercial accommodation (NAFR) and travellers whose main purpose was not visiting friends and relatives but who stayed with friends and relatives (OAFR)*. Her study found that the AFR segment was the youngest, tended to be single, had lower income and stayed the longest time. The NAFR segment was the oldest, had higher incomes and education and stayed the shortest time. The OAFR segment was composed of younger couples living in all-adult homes with various levels of income and staying almost one week on average.

While we have a hint of US VFR travel patterns, 'VFR travel remains well-known but not known well' (Backer, 2007: 2). In an effort to address this need to 'know well', US VFR travellers will be examined in comparison with business and other leisure purpose travellers. Then in an effort to assess if the economic recession has changed VFR patterns, survey data from 2006 and 2011 will be compared to ascertain changes in patterns that might be developing.

Methods

For purposes of conducting the VFR exploration, a set of proprietary data were obtained. DKSA's (D.K. Shifflet and Associates) TRAVEL PERFORMANCE/Monitor[SM] is a comprehensive study measuring the travel behaviour of US residents. DKSA contacts 50,000 distinct US households monthly and has done so since 1991. DKSA is able to provide current behaviour and long-term trended analyses on a wide range of travel.

DKSA data are collected using an online methodology employing KnowledgePanel®, an address-based sample panel offered by Knowledge Networks. The sample is drawn as a national probability sample and returns are balanced to ensure representation of the US population according to the most recent US Census. Key factors used for balancing are origin state, age, income, education, gender, ethnicity/race and return rates. The Knowledge Networks sample is used to create benchmark weights which are applied to surveys returned from other managed panels used by DKSA.

Both travelling and non-travelling households are surveyed each month, enabling DKSA to generate the best estimate of travel incidence (volume) within the total US population. Among those who have travelled (overnight in the past three months, and daytrips in the past month) details of their trip(s) are recorded for each month. This overlapping, repeating monthly approach boosts the observed number of trips for each travel month and controls for seasonality and telescoping biases. 'Travel' is defined as either an overnight trip, defined as going *someplace, staying overnight and then returning home*, or as a day trip, defined as *a place away from home and back in the same* day. Respondents report travel behaviour for each stay of each trip, an approach that enhances reporting for specific travel events, activities and spending.

A wide variety of general travel information is collected including travel to destinations at a city level, hotel stayed in, purpose of stay and activities, expenditures, mode of transportation, party composition, length of stay, travel agent and group tour usage, satisfaction and value ratings, and demographics, including origin markets.

Several open-ended questions are asked to ensure that the responses are not influenced by a pre-listed set of response categories. Each respondent identifies the actual destination visited with an open-end response. This is particularly significant for obtaining accurate data for smaller cities and counties and representing total travel. Time and expense are increased to accurately capture these responses but quality requires it.

Extensive coding lists are updated regularly to ensure that all data is recorded accurately. DKSA's quality control committee conducts bi-monthly meetings to review survey results and examine methods to maintain and improve quality control. For purposes of this analysis, trip purpose, socio-demographics (age, household size), number of trips, length of stay, trip distance and expenditures were employed as variables for comparison. In addition, because of possible changes due to the economic recession, data from the years 2006 and 2011 were examined and compared.

Results

Overall, it appears that the US VFR market has remained relatively constant across the years in terms of level of involvement. For the 2006 survey, there were 23.3% business travellers, 51.1% general leisure travellers and 25.7% VFR travellers based on purpose of visit data. Similarly, the 2011 survey indicated there were 20.9% business, 53.4% general leisure and 25.7% VFR travellers reported by their main trip purpose respectively. In the following sections, VFR travellers' profile and comparisons between 2006 and 2011 survey results are presented.

Profile of the VFR travellers

The sample of this analysis is based on the categorisation of VFR by main purpose. VFR travellers are defined as those who report their main trip purpose as visiting friends and relatives. Because this choice is made, it may underestimate the total amount of VFR travel that could be identified if, for example, VFR as an activity was selected as the basis for a definition. Those who reported combined trip purpose, that is, both for business and leisure or business and VFR, were not included in this analysis. Compared to business and general leisure travellers, VFR travellers are about 47 years old on average and live in a smaller household in terms of family size (2.6 persons) (Table 9.1). It also appears that the VFR market is heavily populated with

Table 9.1 ANOVA and Crosstabulation Test results for Demographics: Trip purpose, age, household size, sex (2011 survey)

Variables	Group	N	Mean	Standard deviation	F-Value	P-Value
Age	Business	34780	44.77	13.49		
	Leisure	88877	46.98	15.26	270.05	<.001
	VFR	42855	46.75	16.15		
Size of household	Business	34784	2.83	1.38		
	Leisure	88883	2.70	1.32	414.57	<.001
	VFR	42853	2.56	1.30		

Sex	Men	Women	Chi^2	P-Value
Business	61.4%	38.6%		
Leisure	43.8%	56.2%	3979.45	<.001
VFR	40.6%	59.4%		

Table 9.2 Analysis of variance results for general trip behaviour (2011 survey)

Variables	Group	N	Mean	Standard deviation	F-Value	P-Value
No. of visits in 3 years	Business	27382	6.66	10.74		
	Leisure	54754	4.64	8.14	1212.30	<.001
	VFR	28457	7.90	10.36		
Stay days	Business	34793	2.42	2.91		
	Leisure	88891	1.96	2.67	700.94	<.001
	VFR	42857	2.57	3.44		
Trip distance	Business	34485	966.67	1423.19		
	Leisure	87548	765.95	1253.99	425.80	<.001
	VFR	42402	716.25	1125.99		

women travellers. In line with general leisure travellers, more women travelled for VFR purposes than men (59% versus 41%, respectively).

For trip behaviour characteristics, VFR travellers seem more active than their business and general leisure counterparts, reporting 7.9 visits on average in the last three years. This was significantly higher than business and leisure (Table 9.2). On their trip, each stay for a VFR traveller lasted 2.57 days on average. This was also longer than their business and leisure equivalents. However, compared with business and leisure travellers, they tended to travel a shorter distance, reporting about 716 miles (around 1152 kilometres) on average for a round trip.

Trip expenditure

The analysis results (Table 9.3) show that VFR travellers spent less than their business and leisure counterparts. On average they reported spending US$95.90 per person per day on their VFR trip. In every expenditure category they spent less than the other two groups. Also, they seem to spend the least on accommodation, probably relying on their host's hospitality for a place to stay (Table 9.3).

Comparisons between two periods: 2006 vs. 2011 surveys

As Table 9.4 indicates, there are noticeable changes in the US VFR market regarding travellers' demographics. A comparison of the two years indicates that interesting changes occurred in the periods investigated. First, the age of the US VFR travellers in 2006 survey was 52.7 years old, while in 2011 data showed VFR travellers to be much younger, 46.8 years old on average. Similarly, the gender composition of the VFR market showed a sharp contrast. In 2006 the VFR traveller was 73.1% female and

Table 9.3 Analysis of variance results for expenditures (2011 survey)

Variables	Group	N	Mean	Standard deviation	F-Value	P-Value
Total*	Business	32111	175.50	214.91		
	Leisure	811.43	118.10	163.28	2161.55	<.001
	VFR	41879	95.90	139.64		
Transportation	Business	32111	96.68	140.37		
	Leisure	81143	38.34	90.28	4298.46	<.001
	VFR	41879	39.54	77.04		
Food	Business	32111	35.39	39.96		
	Leisure	81143	27.26	38.26	1124.41	<.001
	VFR	41879	22.04	35.95		
Entertainment	Business	32111	11.53	28.23		
	Leisure	81143	17.75	34.48	1030.79	<.001
	VFR	41879	10.08	24.39		
Shopping	Business	32111	17.99	50.15		
	Leisure	81143	25.12	55.35	381.19	<.001
	VFR	41879	17.82	44.08		
Other	Business	32111	14.89	47.71		
	Leisure	81143	9.62	36.32	477.353	<.001
	VFR	41879	6.39	28.66		
Accommodation	Business	32111	75.48	76.26		
	Leisure	81143	23.20	40.72	20921.353	<.001
	VFR	41879	6.69	23.44		

*Total expenditure excludes the expenses for accommodation.

26.9% male; in 2011, 40.6% were male and 59.4% were female travellers. In terms of household size, a comparison of the 2006 and 2011 surveys shows a significantly larger size (2006, 2.32 vs. 2011, 2.56). This change could be related to age shift noted above; younger household heads tend to have children at home.

There were significant differences for trip expenditures between 2006 and 2011 (Table 9.5). Compared to 2006, respondents surveyed in 2011 travelled less, stayed for a shorter time but travelled farther. On average VFR travellers in the 2006 survey reported 11.8 visits, a stay length of 2.85 days and travelled 523.55 miles (842.57 kilometres) for a round trip; VFR travellers in 2011 reported 7.9 visits in the last three years, 2.55 days for the length of stay, and 716.2 miles for an average round trip.

Table 9.4 Demographics (Student t-test and Chi-square results): Age, household size, gender (2006 and 2011 surveys)

Variables	N		Mean		Standard deviation		t-Value	P-Value
	2006	2011	2006	2011	2006	2011		
Age	36464	42855	52.70	46.75	14.72	16.15	53.88	<.001
Household size	36449	42853	2.32	2.56	1.22	1.30	−26.302	<.001

Sex	Men	Women	Chi²	P-Value
2006	26.9%	73.1%	1645.78	<.001
2011	40.6%	59.4%		

Table 9.5 Student t-test results for general trip behaviour (2006 and 2011 surveys)

Variables	N		Mean		Standard deviation		t-Value	P-Value
	2006	2011	2006	2011	2006	2011		
No. of visits in 3 years	7842	28457	11.08	7.90	17.68	10.36	20.24	<.001
Stay days	36285	42857	2.85	2.55	3.93	3.43	11.31	<.001
Trip distance	36099	42402	523.55	716.25	782.58	1125.99	−27.37	<.001

The results in Table 9.6 indicate that VFR travellers in 2011 reported slightly higher expenditure levels compared to their 2006 counterparts. On average, one person spent about $100 per day on their VFR trip. Compared with 2006 VFR travellers' expenditure pattern, the 2011 analysis indicated that the respondents spent more on transportation ($39.54), food ($22.04) and slightly more on other expenses ($6.39) compared with respondents in 2006. Interestingly, VFR travellers in the 2011 survey reported significantly less spent on accommodation ($6.69). However, there were no significant changes in expenditures on entertainment and shopping between the two surveys.

Conclusion

The information developed in this analysis has described the basic structure of the VFR travel market in the USA using an important data source that allowed for a relatively unique investigation for one point in time and then over time. The literature over the last 20 years has discussed at least two key approaches to examining VFR travel: trip purpose and activity. In more recent years, however, a few researchers argue that VFR

Table 9.6 Student t-test results for expenditure (2006 VFR vs. 2011 VFR)

Variables*	N		Mean		Standard deviation		t-Value	P-Value
	2006	2011	2006	2011	2006	2011		
Transportation	34466	41879	32.17	39.54	44.35	77.04	−15.74	<.001
Food	34466	41879	20.68	22.04	23.36	35.95	−6.066	<.001
Entertainment	34466	41879	9.87	10.08	21.70	24.39	−1.27	.202
Shopping	34466	41879	18.05	17.82	35.29	44.08	.75	.448
Other	34466	41879	5.27	6.39	14.26	28.66	−6.61	<.001
Accommodation	34466	41879	7.29	6.69	20.02	23.44	3.74	<.001
Total Exp.**	34505	41892	91.19	100.34	97.97	147.66	−9.85	<.001

*All expenditure variables are based on person per day spent on each category.
**Total expenditure may be slightly different from the sum of all items.

must include the accommodation VFR. While the main focus of the current study is on trip purpose, VFR subsequent investigation should explore both the activity and accommodation facets of this behaviour to ascertain if the patterns of change persist or are different. This would be an important step. As the literature reviewed in this chapter points out, main purpose is probably an underestimation of the large scale of this travel pursuit. The results presented here are unique because it has not been developed in other literature that is available. The approach is also important because it makes an effort to address a key question related to VFR travel although it probably applies to all other travel purposes as well – has the 2008 economic recession in the US impacted travel behaviour? A comprehensive examination of large-scale survey information was conducted for VFR travel from 2006 and 2011 in an effort to address this question. In general, every comparison that has been made across these two time periods pointed towards statistically significant changes in each variable examined. The data resources used in this investigation were large, so the 'law of large numbers' could moderate the interpretation of significance. Yet there were changes that appeared – age, sex and trip length – that raise important questions about traveller characteristics and behaviour.

The data suggests that change has occurred. Does the change represent a fundamental shift in VFR travel behaviour or is it only temporary? Is a move back to the old patterns foreseeable or is this a shift that would impact marketing, planning and forecasting models? These are important questions to be answered. Researchers from around the world have observed that VFR travel does not receive much attention for a variety of reasons even though a persistent 25% VFR proportion for the US in reported travel purpose and significant expenditures is noted here. The changes noted in this analysis point towards a need to bring more attention to this important segment.

References

Advertising Age (2009) How this ad recession compares. *Advertising Age* 80 (27), 18.

Asiedu, A. B. (2008) Participants' characteristics and economic benefits of visiting friends and relatives (VFR) tourism – an international survey of the literature with implications for Ghana. *International Journal of Tourism Research* 10, 609–621.

Backer, E. (2007) VFR travel: An examination of the expenditures of VFR travellers and their hosts. *Current Issues in Tourism* 10 (4), 366–377.

Backer, E. (2011) VFR travellers of the future. In I. Yeoman, C. Hsu, K. Smith and S. Watson (eds) *Tourism and Demography* (pp. 74–84). Oxford: Goodfellow Publishers.

Backer, E. (2012). VFR travel: It *is* underestimated. *Tourism Management* 33, 74–79.

Braunlich, C.G. and Nadkarni, N. (1995) The importance of the VFR market to the hotel industry. *The Journal of Tourism Studies* 6 (1), 38–47.

Hay, B. (1996) An insight into the European experience: A case study on domestic VFR tourism within the UK. In H. Yaman (ed.) *VFR Tourism: Issues and Implications. Proceedings from the Conference held at Victoria University of Technology* (pp. 52–66).

Hu, B. and Morrison, A. (2002) Tripography: Can destination use patterns enhance understanding of the VFR market? *Journal of Vacation Marketing* 8 (3) 201–220.

International Trade Administration (ITA) (2002) Survey of international air travellers (in-flight survey) programme. Office of Tourism Industries, US Department of Commerce.

Jackson, R.T. (1990) VFR tourism: Is it underestimated? *Journal of Tourism Studies* 1 (2), 10–17.

King, B.E. and Gamage, M.A. (1994) Measuring the value of the ethnic connection: Expatriate travellers from Australia to Sri Lanka. *Journal of Travel Research* 33 (2), 46–50.

Lee, G., Morrison, A., Lehto, X., Webb, J. and Reid, J. (2005) VFR: Is it really marginal? A financial consideration of French overseas travellers. *Journal of Vacation Marketing* 11 (4), 340–356.

Lehto, X., Morrison, A. and O'Leary, J. (2001) Does the visiting friends and relatives' typology make a difference? A study of the international VFR market to the United States. *Journal of Tourism Research* 40, 201–212.

Lockyer, T. and Ryan, C. (2007) Visiting friends and relatives: Distinguishing between the two groups. *Tourism Recreation Research* 32 (1), 59–68.

McKercher, B. (1996) Host involvement in VFR travel. *Annals of Tourism Research* 23 (3), 701–703.

Morrison, A., Hseih, S. and O'Leary, J. (1995) Segmenting the visiting friends and relatives market by holiday activity participation. *The Journal of Tourism Studies* 6 (1), 48–63.

Moscardo, G., Pearce, P., Morrison, A., Green, D. and O'Leary, J. (2000) Developing a typology for understanding visiting friends and relatives markets. *Journal of Travel Research* 38, 251–259.

Navarro, R. and Turco, D. (1994) Segmentation of the visiting friends and relatives travel market. *Visions in Leisure and Business* 13 (1), 4–16.

Pearce, P.L. and Moscardo, G. (2005) Domestic and visiting friends and relatives tourism. In D. Buhalis and C. Costa (eds) *Tourism Business Frontiers: Consumers, Products and Industry* (pp. 48–55). Oxford: Elsevier.

Pearce, D. (2012) *Frameworks for Tourism Research*. Oxfordshire: CABI.
Pennington-Gray, L. (2003) Understanding the domestic VFR drive market in Florida. *Journal of Vacation Marketing* 9 (4), 354–367.
Ritchie, J.V., Molinar, C.M. and Frechtling D.C. (2009) Impacts of the world recession and economic crisis on tourism: North America. *Journal of Travel Research* 49, 39–451.
Seaton, A.V. and Palmer, C. (1997) Understanding VFR tourism behavior: The first five years of the United Kingdom tourism survey. *Tourism Management* 18 (6), 345–355.
Seaton, A.V. and Tagg, S. (1995) Disaggregating friends and relatives in VFR tourism research: The Northern Ireland evidence 1991–1993. *Journal of Tourism Studies* 6 (1), 6–18.
Uriely, N. (2010) 'Home' and 'away' in VFR tourism. *Annals of Tourism Research* 37 (3), 857–860.

10 VFR Travel in Sub-Saharan Africa: The Case of South Africa

Christian M. Rogerson

Introduction

Despite widespread acknowledgement that VFR travel is a large component of the global tourism economy, until recently VFR travel was, to a large extent, a 'hidden' aspect of international tourism (Palovic *et al.*, 2014). Indeed, Backer (2010) styles VFR travel as tourism's 'poor cousin'. Behind this standpoint are a combination of factors including consistent underestimates of the size of the VFR market (Jackson, 1990), a widely-held belief that VFR travellers inject negligible income into local economies (Backer, 2010) and a consequence of the view by many observers of 'the VFR market as mundane and lacking in the glamour of travel to exotic places' (Morrison & O'Leary, 1995: 5). This said, in recent years the volume of research interest has shown a marked upturn. Indeed, Capistrano (2013: 87) maintains studies of VFR travel now 'have become a significant area of analysis' within international tourism and hospitality scholarship.

VFR Travel and Africa

In a useful content analysis of the scholarly outputs on VFR travel which was conducted by Griffin (2013) for the period 1990 to 2010 it was confirmed this form of travel is garnering an increasing amount of attention. Nevertheless, Griffin's review still offers the caution that 'VFR is a relatively nascent topic in the tourism literature' (Griffin, 2013: 782). Importantly, the analysis points to the existence of marked geographical unevenness in international research endeavours around VFR travel with 'North America and Australia and New Zealand being the predominant areas of interest' (Griffin, 2013: 790). Arguably, in terms of existing international scholarship around VFR travel, the most under-represented area concerns the Global South (Asiedu, 2005, 2008; Chen *et al.*, 2013; Poel *et al.*, 2006; Rule *et al.*, 2003). Here, the region of sub-Saharan Africa is one of the most neglected in respect of VFR research as confirmed by its lack of representation among the presentations on VFR travel at the Surrey Tourism Research Centre's think tank on reconceptualising the topic of VFR travel (Palovic et al., 2014). Moreover, whilst a number of recent overviews of tourism scholarship point towards an expansion of tourism research investigations, most attention in Africa is upon themes relating to international leisure tourism (Rogerson & Rogerson, 2011; Rogerson & Visser, 2011; Dieke, 2013).

Among the least well-understood dimensions of the African tourism economy is VFR travel. In one World Bank investigation on tourism in Africa, Christie et al. (2013: 55) note 'data on tourist visiting friends and relatives is not collected by all countries but is likely to comprise about 20 percent of (international) arrivals' in Africa. Nevertheless, in terms of air travel passengers on African airlines it is estimated that 30% are travelling for VFR purposes (Christie et al., 2013: 56). Further evidence of the importance of VFR travel within international travel within Africa is offered by Ezeuduji (2013) who demonstrates that for Nigerian tourist visits to South Africa VFR purpose of travel is highly significant. Beyond the international dimensions of VFR travel in sub-Saharan Africa it is recognised that policy makers must accord attention to the domestic tourism market and 'specifically the growing visiting friends and relatives component of African tourism flows, an area that calls for greater research attention' (Fourie & Santana-Gallego, 2013: 362).

It is against the backdrop of this knowledge deficit in tourism research about sub-Saharan Africa that this chapter provides an examination of the South African experience and record of VFR travel. Two sections of material are provided. The next section highlights the critical need for students of VFR travel in the Global South to embed an understanding of VFR travel within migration research. This argument is demonstrated by unpacking the dimensions and patterns of VFR travel in South Africa.

Understanding VFR in the Global South: The Migration Nexus

In Northern scholarship on VFR travel much work surrounds how to classify such travel and boost its commercial ramifications (Pearce, 2012: 128). In establishing a categorisation of the VFR market Backer (2012: 75) draws distinctions between three groups. The first are 'pure' VFRs who are travellers who stay with friends and relatives and state VFR as the main purpose of a trip. Second, are the CVFRs or commercial accommodation VFRs who stay in commercial forms of lodging but who have travelled to particular destinations with a VFR purpose. Last, there are EVFRs who are styled as 'exploiting' VFRs as they are staying with friends and relatives, albeit the visit to them is not the prime purpose of a visit. Overall, for academic analysis of VFR travel Pearce (2012: 1028) identifies 'two trajectories needed to understand the concept; on the one hand travellers may visit friends and relatives or they may be hosts to such visitors'. These central issues are reflected in a growing body of research about VFR travel in various countries of the Global North (e.g. Asiedu, 2008; Backer, 2007, 2010; Griffin, 2013; McLeod & Busser, 2014; Shani & Uriely, 2012; Uriely, 2010; Young *et al.*, 2007).

In seeking to understand the character and patterns of VFR travel in the Global South, however, it can be argued that the nexus between migration and VFR activity must be acknowledged as the starting point for analysis. The strength of this relationship is also recognised in Northern research. Williams and Hall (2002: 3) stress that VFR travel is 'an outgrowth of migration' and that it 'epitomises the circular links that exist between tourism and migration' (Williams & Hall, 2002: 40). In addition, Boyne *et al.* (2002: 241) articulate that 'VFR tourism enjoys a distinctive relationship with migration in that some form of migration is (in most cases, even if it involves an inter-generational time lag) a pre-requisite for VFR tourism'. In seeking to reconceptualise and 'refresh' international research on VFR travel Palovic *et al.* (2014) re-iterate it 'is an expression of the intricate relationship between tourism and migration'. In an examination of what are described as emerging world tourism regions Cohen and Cohen (2015) make clear that historically spatial movements in these areas would be typically low in scale, slow and confronting a range of barriers, geographical, political and technological. Under such circumstances VFR was one of the major practices of the lower strata with visits between friends and relatives frequent, particularly on festive occasions, but typified by short distances of travel (Cohen & Cohen, 2015). Overall, much of the practice of VFR in the Global South can be conceptualised as part of the 'informal sector' of travel and tourism (Gladstone, 2005).

The distinguishing traits of VFR travel within the Global South must be understood in part as a consequence of a differential trajectory of urbanisation there as compared to that which was experienced in the Global North. Dick and Reuschke (2012) point out that both in the Global North and South historically the evolution of circulatory patterns of migration has been related to processes of urbanisation. This said, whereas in the Global North 'in the second half of the 19th century circular migration and urbanisation were byproducts of industrialisation in the Global South the opposite is true' (Dick & Reuschke, 2012: 181). Urbanisation processes taking place in the Global South differ markedly from the so-termed 'first urbanisation wave' as experienced in now advanced economies. Most importantly, the first wave of urbanisation was accompanied by and aligned to industrialisation processes and the growth of what would be described as formal work opportunities. By contrast, in the Global South the phenomenon of urbanisation without industrialisation has formed the key structural foundation for persisting circular migration flows which drive a large share of the VFR travel phenomenon. In addition, the conventional urbanisation paradigm based on empirical observations from Europe, North America and Japan assumes that by the second generation at the latest a transition from rural to urban lifestyle will be completed. As emphasised by Schmidt-Kallert (2012: 173) this is a 'typical Eurocentric abstraction which cannot be supported by empirical evidence'.

With the expansion of 'precarious urbanisation' and the mushrooming of informal work in cities across much of Asia and Africa VFR travel has expanded considerably in scale in the wake of the maintenance of circulatory migration flows between urban and rural areas which involves the splitting and dispersion of family and social networks (Dick & Reuschke, 2012). Consequently, the growth of rhythmic home trips by circulatory rural to urban migrants becomes commonplace, particularly during public holidays. Beyond domestic VFR travel, the rise of international labour migration from less to more developed regions has also catalysed an expansion of formal (and informal) sector VFR movements (Cohen & Cohen, 2015). Formal sector manifestations of international VFR travel which are inseparable from migration would include family visits to expatriate communities, including students studying abroad (Asiedu, 2008; King & Gamage, 1994).

Table 10.1 captures a cross-section of reasons to explain why individuals continue to be engaged in circular migration in the Global South. Four essential sets of structural factors are recognised which must be understood as conditioning factors for a substantial share of VFR mobilities in the Global South. These relate to economic transformations, spatial structures, improvements in transportation and communication technology, and societal modernisation. In an important contribution Dick and Reuschke (2012) draw attention to the fact that in many countries of Asia and sub-Saharan Africa the phenomenon of 'precarious tertiarisation', involving the absorption in urban areas of circular migrants in various forms of informal sector work, represents the economic background for persistent circular migration. From this perspective VFR travel which is associated with circular migration forms a necessary component for individual and household survival. Indeed, with major spatial inequalities – interregional and urban-rural – existing in life opportunities across much of the Global South distinctive patterns of mobility are set in train (Cohen & Cohen, 2015). Most importantly, against the backcloth of urbanisation without (industrial) growth and the expansion of urban informalisation the maintenance of a foothold in rural areas is often a vital strategy for household survival (Steinbrink, 2009).

In much of the Global South the growth of forms of non-permanent or circular migration and of associated multi-locational households has

Table 10.1 Reasons for circular migration and VFR travel in the Global South

Structural factors	Key issues
Economic transformation	• A tradition of seasonal, agriculture-based mobility in the pre-colonial period • Circular migration to mines in colonial times often coercive • In the post-colonial period, precarious tertiarisation linked to urbanisation without industrialisation • Expansion in demand for women workers in domestic service and other activities
Spatial structures (inequalities)	• Urban primacy • Strong urban-rural inequalities • Informalisation of urban settlements
Transport and communication technologies	• Infrastructural improvement, especially roads, in peripheral and rural areas enabling greater mobilities • Growth of mobile telephony
Societal modernisation	• Increased female autonomy and acceptance of women's mobility • Dual breadwinner households linked to economic survival

Source: Adapted from Dick and Reuschke (2012: 180).

accelerated in recent decades (Dick & Reuschke, 2012). Lohnert and Steinbrink (2005) identify that a significant and growing number of households in the Global South organise their livelihoods in the context of networks that bridge the rural-urban divide. This results in the proliferation of terms such as 'multiple home households', 'split households' and 'multilocal or translocal households'. As a whole, such 'terms represent a notion of two or more spatially dispersed residential units, united in joint decision-making under an imaginary roof of a single household' (Greiner, 2013: 204). Although national census data fail to capture this phenomenon of circular migration several detailed research investigations attest to its rising significance particularly in sub-Saharan Africa, most importantly across Southern Africa (Greiner, 2013; Lohnert & Steinbrink, 2005; Steinbrink, 2009, 2010). Multilocational households live separately, usually in urban and rural areas, with their livelihood strategy taking advantage of opportunities in both, usually urban and rural areas, with their livelihood strategy taking advantage of opportunities in both areas. Across the Global South it is maintained that 'multilocational householding can be conceived as a strategy to enhance income accumulation and risk resilience' (Dick & Reuschke, 2012: 188). Nevertheless, the combining of urban and rural livelihoods is not just about enhancing economic resilience as the rural part of the household can fulfil vital social and reproductive functions through child rearing, schooling of children as well as care and support for the elderly (Schmidt-Kallert, 2009).

VFR Travel in South Africa

In contemporary South Africa VFR travel occurs with both international and domestic manifestations. Data on VFR travel in South Africa is available from official sources, including those of South African Tourism (2013) and Statistics South Africa (2013). In addition, further information can be accessed from the (unpublished) database of Global Insight which allows the construction of a spatially differentiated picture on VFR travel. Although the actual estimates from these different sources reflect variations in methodology they confirm several critical themes. Over the past decade VFR travel has been a substantial and growing component of South Africa's international as well as the domestic tourism economy. VFR travel exceeds the number of leisure or business travellers and, despite lower expenditures per trip, must be considered as exerting potentially significant impacts for VFR destinations. Critically, VFR travel in South Africa is the segment of travel which is massively dominated by black African travellers (Rule *et al.*, 2003). In all investigations about VFR travel in the country, the black population represents approximately 78% of VFR travellers.

Table 10.2 depicts a profile of the growth of VFR travel in South Africa over the period 2001–2010. It discloses a near doubling in the volume of travel for VFR purposes during this period and an expanded share of VFR travel in all travel which is recorded over that decade. For South Africa VFR travel accounts approximately for two-thirds of all trips. In particular, in common with many parts of the world, it is shown that VFR travel is the most popular form of domestic tourism in South Africa (Rogerson & Lisa, 2005; Rule *et al.*, 2003). According to official data VFR travel constitutes

Table 10.2 VFR travel in South Africa, 2001–2010

Year	National total of trips	Total of VFR trips	% Share of VFR trips
2001	23 147 702	13 261 969	57.3
2002	27 984 928	16 988 161	60.7
2003	31 732 042	20 291 514	63.9
2004	32 692 699	21 685 761	66.3
2005	32 740 684	22 074 621	67.4
2006	33 236 276	22 382 741	67.3
2007	33 288 798	21 870 521	65.7
2008	33 867 066	21 883 627	64.6
2009	36 710 607	23 612 550	64.3
2010	37 372 891	23 566 791	63.1

Source: Author – adapted from Global Insight data.

72% of all domestic trips in South Africa with seasonal peaks occurring at Easter and Christmas. The average length of VFR trip is recorded as 4.8 nights with an average spend per trip of R642 per trip (June 2014 exchange 1US$ = R10). It is significant that, as compared to other purposes of travel, average expenditure per trip for VFR travel is considerably less than that recorded for either business (R2290) or holiday (R1742) purposes (South African Tourism, 2013). For the groups of mostly black travellers who are engaged in travelling between urban and rural 'homes' the shared minibus taxi represents the most important mode of transportation. The minimal role of what Backer (2012) calls CVFRs (VFR travellers who stay in commercial accommodation) is revealed as a distinctive facet of domestic VFR travel in South Africa. Indeed, according to a survey which was undertaken by Statistics South Africa (2013) only 3.9% of surveyed VFR travellers used commercial forms of lodging.

In South Africa the geography of the VFR market exhibits a close (but not perfect) relationship to the national distribution of population. Figure 10.1 shows the number of VFR trips according to each local

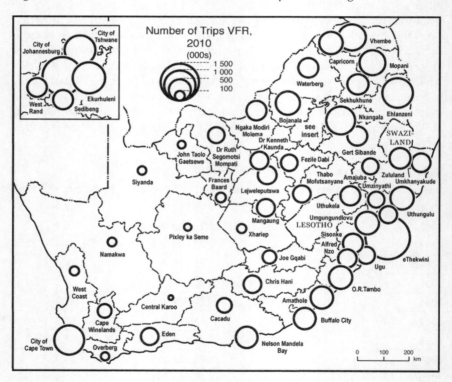

Figure 10.1 The spatial distribution of VFR trips in South Africa, 2010
Source: Author – adapted from Global Insight data.

municipality in the country for 2010. It reveals a number of significant findings. First, that South Africa's largest cities are the major destinations for VFR travel and therefore that VFR travel is an important constituent of the expanding urban tourism economies of cities such as Johannesburg, Cape Town, Durban or Pretoria. It is shown that in terms of local municipalities the four largest VFR destinations are Ethekwini (Durban), the City of Johannesburg, the adjoining municipality of Ekurhuleni and the City of Tshwane (Pretoria). Together these four municipalities are destinations which account for 24% of all VFR travel in South Africa. Second, Figure 10.2 reveals a large number of mainly rural municipalities which are significant destinations for VFR travel in South Africa. District municipalities such as Capricorn, Vhembe, Ehlanzeni, Mopani, O.R. Tambo, Uthungulu, Amatole or uMgungundlovu are large receiving destinations for VFR travel. These particular district municipalities encompass the major parts of what formerly were known as the Homelands or Bantustan areas that were created under apartheid.

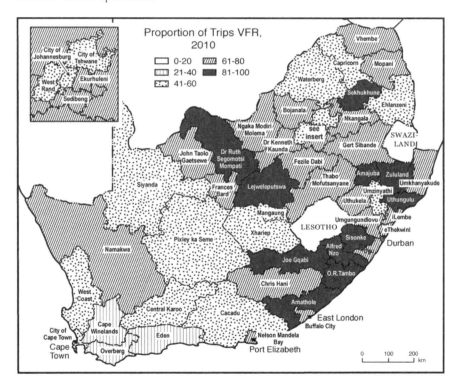

Figure 10.2 The relative share of VFR trips in all trips for each municipality in South Africa, 2010
Source: Author – adapted from Global Insight data.

The Homeland areas were traditionally the source regions of migrant labour for the cities of South Africa. Indeed, such areas were the sending regions for 'cheap labour' and were created by a coercive labour regime that separated geographically the areas of labour force maintenance and renewal (Wolpe, 1972). The former 'Native Reserves' and subsequently the Homelands therefore became the essential foundations for South Africa's exploitative labour system that was forged in colonial times and honed under apartheid. The making of these cheap labour reservoirs and the role of migrant labour in the political economy of South Africa is explored in detail in works by Wolpe (1972), Magubane (1975) and Legassick (1977). The historical emergence and growth of VFR travel in South Africa therefore is essentially the other side of the making of a cheap migrant labour economy, part and parcel of the political economy of capitalist development.

Cheap labour power in South Africa hinged upon maintenance of the oscillatory movements of (mainly male) black labourers. The system was strengthened further by the articulation and workings of South Africa's closed city programmes of influx control which were designed to contain permanent black urbanisation in the country's so-termed white metropolitan areas. In terms of South Africa's trajectory of capitalist development this migratory labour arrangement was the 'backbone' of the apartheid political economy, keeping wages artificially low, as it allowed for the externalisation of 'reproduction costs for the labour power needed in the urban-industrial centres of the country' (Steinbrink, 2010: 38). Another factor that reinforced the potential for the Homelands to be sources of circulatory migrants and destinations for VFR travel was the uprooting and forced removal of established communities and their 'dumping' in remote and often barren rural slums. This massive exercise in social engineering was one of the cornerstones of calculated apartheid planning for 'separate' ethnically based Bantustans (Rogerson, 1989, 1995).

With the transition to democracy in 1994, many observers assumed with the demise of the apartheid controls that circular migration between urban and rural areas would decline as people would be able to settle permanently close to their urban places of work. However, the evidence suggests this has not occurred and that circular migration continues to be an important dimension of the urbanisation dynamics of contemporary South Africa (Todes et al., 2010). It was widely expected with political transformation and the abolition of influx control that migration patterns would normalise with permanent settlement superseding circular migration. However, in common with trends observed in other parts of the Global South, circular migration has remained a central phenomenon in South Africa. As Steinbrink (2010) shows, circular migration persists, albeit in a different form, as households have changed the way of organising migration. After the collapse of apartheid the informal organisation of translocal livelihoods replaced the state-enforced migrant labour system, resulting in the continuation of circulatory movements. It was observed that circular migrants, including a growing stream of female migrants, were absorbed in a range of low income, insecure or casual forms of urban work (Todes *et al.*, 2010). This reflects the process of precarious tertiarisation as referred to by Dick and Reutschke (2012).

The continuation and even expansion of circular migration can no longer be understood in terms of direct state intervention and coercive labour regimes but must be analysed in relation to individual and household agency. Many poor South African households choose to 'organise their livelihoods across vast distances between rural and urban areas' (Steinbrink, 2010: 39). This triggers the formation of translocal households which transcend rural-urban boundaries and are maintained across considerable distance (Greiner, 2012). In contemporary South Africa Steinbrink (2009: 248) points out that 'the majority of the population in the rural areas of former homelands and also large parts of the population living within or on the fringes of urban centres are embedded in translocal contexts'. The frequency of return VFR trips to the rural home varies but most commonly is once a month. Similar findings are disclosed from several recent research investigations on migration and urbanisation in South Africa (Clark *et al.*, 2007; Lohnert & Steinbrink, 2005; Steinbrink, 2009; Todes *et al.*, 2010). In the rural village of Nomhala in Transkei, a former apartheid-fostered Bantustan, 70% of households were primarily reliant on social welfare and remittances from urban migrants which confirms that under the general political and economic conditions within post-apartheid South Africa 'migration is still a vital aspect in the livelihood strategies of people' (Lohnert & Steinbrink, 2005: 99). Arguably, these migratory flows establish the essential conditions and framework for VFR travel.

As a whole, therefore, across South Africa 'circular migration predominantly connects rural and urban areas and tends to involve poor households' (Dick & Reuschke, 2012: 190). It is evidenced that most migrants maintain intensive contact with relatives in rural areas with 74% of the migrants from Nomhala to Cape Town visiting the home village at least once in the previous 12 month period with visit duration varying in length from three days to as much as several months (Steinbrink, 2009). Return visits occur mainly at school holiday periods, for celebrations and ceremonies (funerals, weddings, circumcision) and for traditional healing. Migrant associations, which function as support networks in urban areas, reinforce urban-rural connectivities and encourage return trips to rural areas by urban migrants (Steinbrink, 2009, 2010). Thus, with a large segment of the population in rural areas of former Bantustans as well as a majority of the marginalised population residing within or on fringe of cities integrated into translocal contexts of living, the phenomenon of VFR travel in South Africa is reinforced among the country's poor (Lohnert &

Steinbrink, 2005: 102). This means that, as Hoogendoorn (2011) shows, low income earners in the Global South also are second home owners, a fact which is little acknowledged in Northern second home scholarship. In South Africa the 'second home' of low income earners is part of household survival and reproduction rather than used for purposes of recreation (Hoogendoorn, 2011: 46).

Figure 10.2 maps out the proportion of VFR trips as a share of all travel trips for each local municipal area in South Africa. The geographical distribution and local impacts of VFR travel in South Africa reflect a complex set of issues which relate to urban-rural mobilities, the maintenance of a rural 'home' by many black urban dwellers as well as a small layer of white domestic VFR travel. Notwithstanding the large-scale nature of VFR travel, the policy environment in South Africa mainly overlooks this aspect of the tourism economy may potentially impact upon local economies. A number of important points can be observed. First, although the actual volume of VFR trips in South Africa's major metropolitan centres is substantial, in relative terms the importance of VFR travel is diminished. The cities of Cape Town, Durban, Pretoria and Johannesburg, all major nodes for VFR travel, have diversified urban tourism economies (Rogerson & Visser, 2007). Leisure travel is significant for both Cape Town and Durban and business travel is of great importance for Johannesburg, South Africa's finance capital, and Pretoria, the centre for national government. Second, in several parts of South Africa VFR travel constitutes only a small element in total recorded trips. In particular throughout much of the Western Cape the proportion of VFR travel in total travel is much less than the national average of 63% in 2010. For the Cape Winelands, Overberg and Eden municipalities, all attractive leisure destinations, VFR travel is only a minor component of local tourism economies.

Third, the most striking feature of Figure 10.2 is the almost exclusive dominance of visitor trips in many parts of South Africa by VFR travel. For most of the eastern parts of the country VFR travel constitutes over 70% of all visits. In certain areas, however, the dominance of VFR travel exceeds over 80%. In district municipalities such as Sekhukhune, Zululand, Amajuba, Joe Gqabi, O.R. Tambo or Alfred Nzo there are few other forms of tourism mobilities apart from VFR travel. These are areas where labour migration persists and translocal livelihoods are articulated across large distances. Previously such areas were part of a migrant labour system that was anchored upon formal state coercion. The formal system has now been replaced by an informal system that is organised around household risk and survival with migrants oscillating between urban and rural spaces. VFR travel is at the heart of this new landscape of circular migration in South Africa and for the most part it would be considered as 'ordinary tourism' or part of an informal sector of travel (Cohen & Cohen, 2015; Gladstone, 2005).

Conclusions

It has been argued that urbanisation and migration processes in much of the Global South have taken a different trajectory to those of Europe, North America or other advanced economies. The most distinguishing trait of migration in the Global South is that circular forms of migration have persisted in a context of precarious tertiarisation and informal work, the consequence of the growth of urbanisation which is disconnected from industrialisation processes. An understanding of this migration context is an essential starting point for unpacking the nature and patterns of VFR travel in many parts of the Global South. The interesting case of South Africa was under scrutiny in this chapter. The roots of large-scale VFR travel in the country must be interpreted as part of the making of a coercive labour regime organised around cheap migrant labour power in colonial times and subsequently under apartheid. The ending of apartheid has not produced the anticipated demise of circular migration. Instead, as Steinbrink (2009, 2010) argues, the growth and maintenance of translocal households reflects a change from a formal to an informal system of circular mobilities that in turn relates to the existence of two separate but interconnected homes.

In the wider international context of VFR travel these findings underscore the heterogeneity of VFR mobilities. More specifically, they highlight a need to revisit and expand the typology of VFR travellers as developed by Backer (2012) in order to incorporate appropriately the specificities of mobilities in the Global South. In particular, what is required is an acknowledgement of the existence of a distinct 'Southern' category of VFR traveller that is associated with household survival or reproduction.

Acknowledgements

Thanks are due to Wendy Job, University of Johannesburg, for the accompanying maps and to the National Research Foundation, Pretoria, for research funding. This chapter is dedicated to Rosie Alberton, one of my best all-time friends, who sadly passed away during the write-up phase of this research.

References

Asiedu, A. (2005) Some benefits of migrants' return visits to Ghana. *Population, Space and Place* 11 (1), 1–11.
Asiedu, A. (2008) Participants' characteristics and economic benefits of visiting friends and relatives (VFR) tourism – An international survey of the literature with implications for Ghana. *International Journal of Tourism Research* 10, 609–621.
Backer, E. (2007) VFR travel: An examination of the expenditures of VFR travellers and their hosts. *Current Issues in Tourism* 10, 366–377.

Backer, E. (2010) VFR travel: An assessment of VFR versus non-VFR travellers. Unpublished PhD thesis, Southern Cross University, Lismore, NSW, Australia.

Backer, E. (2012) VFR travel: It *is* underestimated. *Tourism Management* 33, 74–79.

Boyne, S., Carswell, F. and Hall, D. (2002) Reconceptualising VFR tourism. In C.M. Hall and A.M. Williams (eds) *Tourism and Migration: New Relationships Between Production and Consumption* (pp. 241–256). Dordrecht: Kluwer.

Capistrano, R.C.G. (2013) Visiting friends and relatives travel, host-guest interactions and qualitative research: Methodological and ethical implications. *Asia-Pacific Journal of Innovation in Hospitality and Tourism* 2 (1), 87–100.

Chen, Y-X, Wu, B., Li, L-B and Dong, Z. (2013) Study on visiting friends and relatives behaviour of immigrants in Shanghai. *Procedia – Social and Behavioral Sciences* 96, 522–527.

Christie, I., Fernandes, E., Messerli, H. and Twining-Ward, L. (2013) *Tourism in Africa: Harnessing Tourism for Growth and Improved Livelihoods.* Washington DC: The World Bank.

Clark, S.J., Collinson, M.A., Kahn, K., Drullinger, K. and Tollman, S.M. (2007) Returning home to die: Circular labour migration and mortality in South Africa. *Scandinavian Journal of Public Health* 35 (Suppl. 69), 35–44.

Cohen, E. and Cohen, S.A. (2015) A mobilities approach to tourism from emerging world regions. *Current Issues in Tourism* 18 (1), 11–43.

Dick, E. and Reuschke, D. (2012) Multilocational households in the global south and north: Relevance, features and spatial implications. *Die Erde* 143 (3), 177–194.

Dieke, P.U.C. (2013) Tourism in Sub-Saharan Africa: Production-consumption nexus. *Current Issues in Tourism* 16, 623–26.

Ezeuduji, I. (2013) Nigerian tourists to South Africa: Challenges, expectations and demands. *Acta Commercii* 13 (1), 1–9.

Fourie, J. and Santana-Gallego, M. (2013) The determinants of African tourism. *Development Southern Africa* 30, 347–366.

Gladstone, D. (2005) *From Pilgrimage to Package Tour: Travel and Tourism in the Third World.* Abingdon: Taylor and Francis.

Greiner, C. (2012) Can households be multilocal?: Conceptual and methodological considerations based on a Namibian case study. *Die Erde* 143 (3), 195–212.

Griffin, T. (2013) A content analysis of articles on visiting friends and relatives tourism, 1990–2010. *Journal of Hospitality Marketing & Management* 22, 781–802.

Hoogendoorn, G. (2011) Low-income earners as second home tourists in South Africa. *Tourism Review International* 15 (1/2), 37–50.

Jackson, R.T. (1990) VFR tourism: Is it underestimated? *Journal of Tourism Studies* 1 (2), 10–17.

King, B.E.M. and Gamage, M.A. (1994) Measuring the value of the ethnic connection: Expatriate travellers from Australia to Sri Lanka. *Journal of Travel Research* 33 (2), 46–50.

Legassick, M. (1977) Gold, agriculture and secondary industry in South Africa, 1885–1970: From periphery to sub-metropole as a forced labour system. In R. Palmer and N. Parsons (eds) *The Roots of Rural Poverty in Central and Southern Africa* (pp. 175–200). Berkeley: University of California Press.

Lohnert, B. and Steinbrink, M. (2005) Rural and urban livelihoods: A translocal perspective in a South African context. *South African Geographical Journal* 87 (2), 95–105.

Magubane, B. (1975) The 'native reserves' (Bantustans) and the role of the migrant labor system in the political economy of South Africa. In H.I. Safa and B.M. du Toit (eds) *Migration and Development* (pp. 225–267). The Hague: Mouton.

McLeod, B. and Busser, J.A. (2014) Second homeowners hosting friends and relatives. *Annals of Leisure Research* 17 (1), 86–96.

Morrison, A.M. and O'Leary, J.T. (1995) The VFR market: Desperately seeking respect. *Journal of Tourism Studies* 6 (1), 2–5.

Palovic, Z., Kam, S., Janta, H., Cohen, S. and Williams, A. (2014) Surrey think tank – Reconceptualising visiting friends and relatives travel. *Journal of Destination Marketing & Management* 2, 266–268.

Pearce, P.L. (2012) The experience of visiting home and familiar places. *Annals of Tourism Research* 39, 1024–1047.

Poel, P., Masurel, E. and Nijkamp, P. (2006) The importance of friends and relations in tourist behavior: A case study on heterogenity in Surinam. In M. Giaoutzi and P. Nijkamp (eds) *Tourism and Regional Development: New Pathways* (pp. 219–238). Burlington VT: Ashgate.

Rogerson, C.M. (1989) The disaster of apartheid forced removals. In J. Clarke, P. Curson, S.L. Kayastha and P. Nag (eds) *Population and Disaster* (pp. 256–264). Oxford: Basil Blackwell.

Rogerson, C.M. (1995) Forgotten places, abandoned places: Migration research issues in South Africa. In J. Baker and T. Aina (eds) *The Migration Experience in Africa* (pp. 109–121). Uppsala: Nordic Africa Institute.

Rogerson, C.M. and Lisa, Z. (2005) 'Sho't left': Promoting domestic tourism in South Africa. *Urban Forum* 16, 88–111.

Rogerson, C.M. and Rogerson, J.M. (2011) Tourism research within the Southern African development community: Production and consumption in academic journals, 2000–2010. *Tourism Review International* 15 (1/2), 213–222.

Rogerson, C.M. and Visser, G. (eds) (2007) *Urban Tourism in the Developing World: The South African Experience*. New Brunswick, NJ and London: Transaction Press.

Rogerson, C.M. and Visser, G. (2011) African tourism geographies: Existing paths and new directions. *Tijdschrift voor Economische en Sociale Geografie* 102 (3), 251–259.

Rule, S., Viljoen, J., Zama, S., Struwig, J., Langa, Z. and Bouare, O. (2003) Visiting friends and relatives (VFR): South Africa's most popular form of domestic tourism. *Africa Insight* 33 (1/2), 99–107.

Schmidt-Kallert, E. (2009) A new paradigm of urban transition: Tracing the livelihood strategies of multilocational households. *Die Erde* 140 (3), 319–336.

Schmidt-Kallert, E. (2012) Non-permanent migration and multilocality in the global south. *Die Erde* 143 (2), 173–176.

Shani, A. (2013) The VFR experience: 'Home' away from home? *Current Issues in Tourism* 16, 1–15.

Shani, A. and Uriely, N. (2012) VFR tourism: The host experience. *Annals of Tourism Research* 39, 421–440.

South African Tourism (2013) *2012 Annual Tourism Report*. Johannesburg: South African Tourism.

Statistics South Africa (2013) *Domestic Tourism Survey 2012. Reference Period: January to December 2011*. Pretoria: Statistics South Africa, Statistical Release P.0352.1.

Steinbrink, M. (2009) Urbanisation, poverty and translocality: Insights from South Africa. *African Population Studies* 23 (Supplement), 220–252.

Steinbrink, M. (2010) Football and circular migration systems in South Africa. *Africa Spectrum* 45 (2), 35–60.

Todes, A., Kok, P., Wentzel, M., Van Zyl, J. and Cross, C. (2010) Contemporary South African urbanization dynamics. *Urban Forum* 21, 331–348.

Uriely, N. (2010) 'Home' and 'away' in VFR tourism. *Annals of Tourism Research* 37, 854–857.

Williams, A.M. and Hall, C.M. (2002) Tourism, migration, circulation and mobility: The contingencies of time and place. In C.M. Hall and A.M. Williams (eds) *Tourism and Migration: New Relationships between Production and Consumption* (pp. 1–52). Dordrecht: Kluwer.

Wolpe, H. (1972) Capitalism and cheap labour power in South Africa: From segregation to apartheid. *Economy and Society* 1, 253–285.

Young, C.A., Corsun, D.L. and Baloglu, S. (2007) A taxonomy of hosts visiting friends and relatives. *Annals of Tourism Research* 34, 497–516.

11 The VFR Phenomenon in Italy

Antonino Mario Oliveri

Introduction

VFR travel has been underestimated for decades by academics and tourism practitioners for reasons that have been widely discussed since the first fundamental contributions on the topic (Jackson, 1990; King & Gamage, 1994; Morrison & O'Leary and the other contributions included in the special issue of *The Journal of Tourism Studies* on the VFR market, 1995; Seaton & Palmer, 1997). Nevertheless, VFR travel accounts for a large share of tourist flows and contributes to tourist demand and expenditures. The more general aspects of the phenomenon are discussed in other chapters of this book. Though scientific literature on the subject has recently broadened to the point of warranting the first reviews (Ramachandran, 2006; Griffin, 2013; Capistrano, 2013), VFR continues to win little interest from the numerous national and/or local tourist marketing organisations. Italy is no exception (Etzo *et al.*, 2013), although there are reliable and easily accessible secondary sources offering detailed information resulting from research carried out at national or local levels. This chapter is an endeavour to summarise the main features of VFR in Italy in recent years, what is of necessity a selection from the remarkable wealth of available resources. In particular, the data presented here relate exclusively to VFR travel by Italians (domestic tourism). The first section introduces the official secondary sources which can be accessed in various formats for analysing VFR. The second section and corresponding subsections detail the characteristics of small-scale research and the main results derived. The conclusions point out the strengths and weaknesses of the approach.

VFR in Italy: An Overview Derived from Official Statistics on Tourist Demand

In Italy, tourist demand is currently 'officially' investigated by two periodical surveys:

(1) The Bank of Italy border survey on Foreign Tourism. Each year a sample of international travellers is personally interviewed at borders, at the end of their trip. The research aims mainly at estimating tourist

expenditure. Target populations consist of Italians coming back from a trip abroad and foreign travellers exiting Italy. This sample survey employs a two-stage sampling design. The Primary Sampling Units (PSUs) consist of time intervals (road borders) or origin/destination pairs (other borders) at 82 border points. The Secondary Sampling Units (SSUs) are travellers, selected at regular intervals (Alivernini *et al.*, 2013: 44–45). Yearly, some 140,000 international travellers (both foreigners in Italy and Italians abroad) who have crossed Italian road, rail, air or naval borders are interviewed. In this chapter, only Italian domestic tourism is investigated; consequently, no further analyses are performed on Bank of Italy data.

(2) Italian National Institute of Statistics (ISTAT) performs quarterly Computer Assisted Telephone Interviewing (CATI) through sample-based surveying on 'Trips and Holidays of Italians' (ISTAT, 2014a). Italian residents are approached at home and the sample is drawn according to a probabilistic one-stage, stratified cluster design. The strata are constructed by regions and size of municipalities; clusters are households corresponding to telephone numbers (Bagatta & Perez, 2003). Yearly, some 14,000 Italian households are surveyed.

Both studies enable the adequate quantification of VFR trips. The Bank of Italy survey includes a question about the reasons for the trip. Another section of the question sheet queries the type of accommodation used. The ISTAT survey distinguishes travelling for business reasons from travelling for a vacation. The latter category targets information regarding the main reason for travel and the principal accommodation. Unlike the surveys from other countries involving similar research to the above, the Italian official sources provide information both on motivational VFR and accommodation-based VFR. By cross-tabulating motivation and accommodation, it is possible to quantify VFRs according to the definitional model by Backer (2012), via their classification into 'pure' VFRs (PVFRs), 'commercial' VFRs (CVFRs) and 'exploitative' VFRs (EVFRs).

The recent report by ISTAT (2014b) on the provisional results of the 2013 Italian holiday and travel survey reveals a dramatic drop in the number of trips conducted by Italian residents (-19.8% year on year). As to VFR, in the case of short holidays (i.e. lasting one to three days) 37% of the trips undertaken in 2013 involved overnight accommodation in the homes of relatives or friends. Hotel accommodation accounted for 39.9%. Other types of accommodation were used far less. Percentages change for longer holidays (four or more nights): 30.4% associated with staying with friends or relatives and 31.6% for hotels.

This highlights the relevance of VFR accommodation in the context of an economic crisis which has had a profound impact on the nation. VFR very nearly represents the most frequent type of travel in the country, with an absolute increase in 2013 of 1% (compared to 2012 data) for short holidays, 2.8% for longer holidays and 5.1% for business trips (for which in any case the ratio of those lodging with friends and relatives remains a minority: 12.3% in 2013). With respect to motivational VFR, the ISTAT report reveals that visiting friends and relatives was the second-highest holiday travel motivation in 2013, preceded only by the very broad 'leisure and recreation' category, which also includes spa and health treatments (only if not prescribed by a doctor). As highlighted by Backer (2012), the frequent overlapping of motivational categories should be given proper consideration, since many travellers also visit friends and relatives during a leisure trip, thus recording the 'leisure and recreation' motivation at the expense of VFR. In 2013, visiting friends and relatives was the main motivation behind 41.3% of short holidays and 23.7% of longer holidays. The 'leisure and recreation' motivation respectively accounted for 54.4% and 74.4%.

As mentioned above, the classification of VFR travel can be performed by cross-tabulating the data pertaining to principal motivation with that of accommodation, so as to correctly estimate VFR. Notwithstanding the fact that preliminary results for 2013 have already been distributed, the microdata file has not yet been made available by ISTAT, which has however authorised access to the data for previous years. Of the total of 68,699,188 estimated holiday trips undertaken in 2012, those with visiting friends and relatives as the principal motivation accounted for 25.8%. Trips that involved accommodation with friends and relatives accounted for 31.6%. By cross-tabulating the two variables, the pattern shown in Table 11.1 is obtained, which closely observes the definitional model by Backer (2012). The data given in Table 11.1 are affected by a limited number of missing data regarding motivations (0.1% of all holiday trips). It appears that the three VFR trip categories identified by Backer together constitute 35.42% of the total, well above the percentages attributable only to VFR accommodation or motivation and, naturally, less than the sum of the two.

Not all those who travel to visit friends and relatives choose to lodge with them. In this case, accommodation facilities are not necessarily of a commercial nature. Some VFR people could stay in accommodation facilities which they own or are part of a timeshare arrangement (houses, boats). This information is collected from ISTAT, under the residual category 'other type of private accommodation'. In accordance with Backer (2012), the aggregate shown in the top right cell of Table 11.1 should be defined as CVFRs. However, it can be broken down into two quantities: proper commercial VFRs (CVFRs), involving people lodging at structures where fees are incurred, and non-commercial VFRs (NCVFRs), involving private accommodation at no charge. The ISTAT 2012 data permit an estimation of 2.2% for commercial and 1.6% for non-commercial VFRs.

Table 11.1 Classification of VFRs for holiday trips of Italian residents, year 2012 (valid total percentages)

Purpose of visit	Accommodation		Totals
	Friends and relatives (VFR)	Non-friends and relatives (Non-VFR)	
VFR	15,100,216 (21.99%)	2,606,700 (3.80%)	17,706,916 (25.79%)
Non-VFR	6,608,782 (9.63%)	44,344,240 (64.58%)	50,953,022 (74.21%)
Subtotals	21,708,998 (31.62%)	46,950,940 (68.38%)	68,659,938 (100.00%)

Source: ISTAT, 'Trips and Holidays: Trips' research. In different shades of grey, from light to dark: PVFRs, CVFRs + NCVFRs, EVFRs, Non-VFRs.

The choice by motivational VFRs not to stay with friends or family depends on many factors. Unfortunately these cannot be derived from the ISTAT survey. Apart from the possible incapacity of hosts to accommodate any guests, which would close the issue, in other cases it is reasonably plausible to assume that motivational VFRs decide not to stay with friends and relatives in order to maintain privacy, situational control and sociability, which are essential for feeling 'at home' (Uriely, 2010). It is in fact quite clear that staying with relatives/friends reduces freedom of action, introduces feelings of gratitude and may oblige guests, sometimes reluctantly, to respect rules/programmes defined by the host. This of course also undermines the equal relationship, a fundamental component of sociability. In light of these considerations, the choice of staying elsewhere is understandable for NCVFRs, who can easily recreate the 'at home' sensation while on vacation, using their own resources; staying on their own is of greater importance if it is a choice made by individuals who prefer to spend money rather than have their autonomy and freedom of movement restricted. It is not difficult to imagine that these kinds of travellers may also be significantly differentiated along broader socio-demographic characteristics, holiday style and travel motivation categories. Unfortunately, there are no data available to test this hypothesis on an empirical basis, and, consequently, the issue can only be left to be explored in the future.

The ISTAS data do however allow testing of certain hypotheses advanced in literature with respect to the characteristics of VFR trips.

Hypothesis 1: VFR travel is distributed more evenly over the year compared to non-VFR travel, meaning that it is less prone to seasonality (Seaton & Palmer, 1997; Ramachandran, 2006). In fact, people visit friends or relatives for various reasons and happenings that are distributed throughout the year, rather than necessarily concentrated in peak periods. While plausible in general terms, this hypothesis is probably not valid for all VFR subgroups. In fact, for EVFRs with non-VFR motivations, it seems reasonable to expect behaviours would be more in line with those of non-VFRs. For NCVFRs, it could be argued that owners of accommodation are more likely to be emotionally tied to a particular destination, or have moved for work purposes and are returning to their place of origin, where they still own their house. For them a destination where friends or relatives reside may therefore constitute a holiday destination during traditional peak periods, without the danger of having to compete for accommodation or other services (like catering) with other travellers, as these amenities can be enjoyed in total autonomy.

Hypothesis 2: VFR travel is distributed more evenly over space, to destinations that do not necessarily involve heavy tourist traffic (Seaton & Palmer, 1997). Generally speaking, people are more willing to visit touristic than non-touristic towns. Nevertheless, there is no theoretical reason to think of friends or relatives living more frequently in touristic towns.

Hypothesis 3: VFR is more prevalent for short holidays. Numerous studies have pointed out this feature of VFR travel patterns, which relates to 'a desire for rest and relaxation followed by the pursuit of some specific interest' (Murphy *et al.*, 2010: vii). The average VFR trip's length was 2.86 nights, while it was 3.52 for all trips in Great Britain in 2012 (VisitEngland *et al.*, 2013).

Table 11.2 helps to explain Hypothesis 1. Summer constitutes the traditional high season for holidays in Italy. Table 11.2 shows a peak for

Table 11.2 Time series of trips, by month and kind of travel, year 2012 (column percentages)

Months	PVFRs	EVFRs	CVFRs	NCVFRs	Non-VFRs	Totals
DEC 2011	3.3	1.2	0.0	1.3	.9	1.5
JAN 2012	9.8	4.1	1.2	7.3	2.9	4.8
FEB 2012	7.0	3.6	6.5	.4	2.5	3.8
MAR 2012	7.3	1.1	5.8	1.4	4.2	4.6
APR 2012	7.3	11.2	9.5	9.5	8.3	8.4
MAY 2012	7.6	4.3	8.3	1.0	5.8	6.0
JUN 2012	8.0	7.7	19.9	8.8	14.0	11.9
JUL 2012	8.3	20.9	4.1	18.2	19.6	16.7
AUG 2012	12.6	30.4	6.5	44.8	24.4	22.2
SEP 2012	3.0	4.9	17.1	3.7	6.9	5.9
OCT 2012	6.3	2.1	4.9	2.1	3.7	4.1
NOV 2012	5.6	4.3	5.3	.6	3.0	3.8
DEC 2012	13.8	4.1	10.8	.8	3.7	6.3
Totals	100.0	100.0	100.0	100.0	100.0	100.0

Source: Analysis of ISTAT data, 'Trips and Holidays: Trips' research, year 2012.

NCVFR, EVFR and non-VFR departures between July and August, while the peak departure periods for CVFRs correspond to June and September. PVFR is more evenly distributed throughout the year, with more frequent departures in August and December-January. It seems that the ISTAT 2012 data do not fully support hypothesis 1.[1]

In respect to Hypothesis 2, VFR destinations could be distinguished according to whether they are places of emigration or immigration for work purposes. Recent decades have seen substantial emigration in Italy of labour resources from the regions of Southern Italy to the more economically developed Northern regions that offer greater employment opportunities. This phenomenon has not stopped. The regions of Southern Italy are traditionally places subject to emigration. The VFR trips to the North involve the reunification of people with friends and relatives who have moved for employment reasons; to the South, these mainly involve the return to territories of origin by those who have moved elsewhere for work.

The ISTAT data show that VFR travels are distributed uniformly in Italy, ranging from 4.0% to 7.0% between the North, Central and Southern Italy, with the exception of trips to Tuscany and Veneto (respectively 8.0% and 7.4%). An analysis of VFR subgroups revealed some interesting patterns. PVFR travellers prefer Lazio (9.4%) and Lombardy (11.7%), whose capital cities are, not coincidentally, the two biggest cities in Italy, namely Rome and Milan. In fact, flows to Lombardy are focused primarily, but not exclusively, on the province of Milan (38.4%). Flows entering Lazio are mainly directed towards the province of Rome (58.9%). EVFR trips involve relatively high percentages entering Abruzzo (13.0%) and Sardinia (8.6%), with slightly lower rates (7.0%) for Lombardy, Lazio and Tuscany. CVFR trips are clearly higher for Lombardy (10.7%), Lazio (13.7%) and Campania (11.7%). Non-VFRs are more frequently directed towards Veneto (with the famous city of Venice), Emilia Romagna and Tuscany (with Florence). NCVFRs are mainly directed towards Lazio (17.7%), Campania (23.0%) and Calabria (23.5%). The latter two regions are subject to high emigration. As shown in Table 11.3, the calculation of the relative Shannon's entropy H index[2] on the frequency distributions for each travel category is greater than 0.80 for all VFR trips and categories, except for NCVFR for which the

Table 11.3 Relative Shannon's entropy index by types of trips, year 2012

Italian regions (destinations)	Types of trips					
	PVFRs	EVFRs	CVFRs	NCVFRs	NVFRs	All trips
Shannon's entropy H index	0.91	0.89	0.82	0.71	0.91	0.93

Source: Analysis of ISTAT data, 'Trips and Holidays: Trips' research, year 2012.

value of 0.71 is still very high. The point is that the H index is even higher for NVFRs (0.915). This means that, focusing on the regional scale, there is no evidence that for Italy VFR leads to a more heterogeneous distribution of tourist flows across the nation. This result is consistent with the evidence that the different categories of VFR travellers are more or less clearly directed towards specific destinations in comparison to other travellers, which contradicts Hypothesis 2.

Regarding Hypothesis 3, the average duration of VFR travel was found to differ significantly to what was hypothesised on the basis of results obtained in different tourist markets. In particular, Seaton and Palmer (1997) concluded that, between 1989 and 1993, VFR in the UK involved short holidays (one to three days), especially for domestic travel. Subsequently, similar results were obtained in Australia (Murphy *et al.*, 2010) and, more recently, in Great Britain (VisitEngland *et al.*, 2013). In contrast, Hänsel and Metzner (2011) reported higher average lengths of stay for VFR travel compared with holiday trips.

Limiting the analysis of the ISTAT 2012 data to domestic travel only, it can be found that the average duration of VFR travel in Italy is more than three days and subject to high variability. Since in general the mean is influenced by few extreme values, outliers were eliminated and the trimmed mean was calculated. This did not significantly alter the situation. As reported in Table 11.4, a clear exception concerns CVFR trips, which are different to the others as to warrant more complex, multiple-comparison operations. It seems that visiting friends and relatives when accommodation costs are involved means limiting trips to the minimum duration necessary (for example, the days needed to participate in family events).

Average stay durations were compared to assess the significance of differences between them. The distribution of the variable 'duration of trip' in the sample is skewed for all the trips together as well as for the VFR-related types. This was confirmed by the Kolmogorov-Smirnov test, which

Table 11.4 Average duration of overnight accommodation, by VFR group, year 2012

Group	Average duration (overnight accommodation)	Standard deviation (overnight accommodation)	5% trimmed mean
PVFR	5.46	8.76	4.09
EVFR	8.99	13.51	6.80
CVFR	2.91	3.78	2.23
NCVFR	8.86	9.55	7.89
Non-VFR	6.60	8.53	5.33

Source: ISTAT, 2012.

suggested that the assumption of normality is never fulfilled. Consequently, the comparison of average holiday durations was performed by means of the non-parametric Kruskal and Wallis test in place of the traditional parametric Analysis of Variance (AnOVa) approach. The Kruskal-Wallis test proved significant (p-value = 0.00), indicating that difference between groups is not attributable to chance.

Analysing VFR at the Local Scale: Research in Sicily 2005–2012

Unfortunately, official national statistics are generally unsatisfactory when research questions are related to local tourism. Estimates derived from national sample surveys cannot be easily associated with sub-regional areas because of the small number of interviews conducted in each city. Supply side statistics are also unsatisfactory. In Italy, ISTAT regularly gathers data on arrivals and overnight stays at accommodation establishments. These data are collected and disseminated at the municipal level. However, the number of arrivals in accommodation structures is not a correct measure of the number of tourists arriving at a destination for several reasons: firstly, because the customers of hospitality establishments may or may not be tourists; secondly, because the same tourist frequently moves around the territory and lodges at more than one location (Parroco et al., 2012), thus causing replications of arrivals in territories as large as regions and therefore inflating the estimated number of tourists. On the other hand, the number of tourists is underestimated because those staying in unofficial accommodations are not accounted for in official statistics. This creates unobserved tourism in some countries. At certain periods of the year unobserved tourism is so widespread as to render arrivals-based estimates of the number of tourists unrealistic.

Staying with friends and relatives is becoming more and more popular, and contributes strongly to unobserved tourism. In this case, it involves recording deficiencies and could thus be more accurately defined as statistically unnoticed tourism (Oliveri & Vaccina, 2013) as opposed to hidden tourism, the latter dependent on the generation of hidden income and tax evasion. It was with the aim of addressing the estimation of unnoticed tourism and the analysis of tourist mobility within Sicily that a research team from Palermo and Catania Universities conducted research between 2004 and 2010, which also involved the detection of VFR travel. Sicily is the biggest island in the Mediterranean Sea and a renowned tourist destination. The detailed results of this research are outlined by Oliveri and De Cantis (2013). Here, the elements most directly related to VFR are discussed. What is more, in 2012 the European Union funded, as part of their programme 'ERDF: European Regional Development Fund 2007–2013', research on the attractiveness of the tourist districts recently established in Sicily. Members of the group who had led the 2004–2010 research could participate in this new research, which proved to be useful for analysing VFR travel.

The Aeolian Islands research

From July to September, 2004, a tourist sample survey was carried out in the Aeolian Islands Archipelago, a renowned Mediterranean seaside destination which also constitutes a tourist system where all access points are easily detectable. From a statistical point of view, this facilitates the identification of the frame population of tourists. Tourists were approached at Lipari (the capital) harbour. Some 2000 CAPI interviews were obtained and a complex probabilistic sampling design was performed: two-stage cluster on Saturdays and weekdays, one stage cluster on Sundays. Sampling issues are addressed more in depth in Mendola and Milito (2013). In order to exclude non-tourists, the questionnaire included filter questions. The main body of the questionnaire included questions on travel and holiday, accommodation, consumption and expenditure. The aims of this research proved useful for the detection of VFR, albeit only with respect to accommodation. According to the operationalisation at the time, tourists were classified as unobserved if 'they had stayed in their own home, a rented home, a home that was free of charge; had spent their holiday in a boat' (Giambalvo, 2005: 234; translation from Italian).

In the end, 57.0% of respondents were classified as unobserved tourists. Tourists who had mainly lodged in homes free of charge totalled 5.3%.

The Aeolian Islands research lends itself to the empirical testing of a hypothesis that can be drawn by research results mentioned in the most part of VFR literature.

Hypothesis 4: VFR travellers spend less money at the destination compared to other categories. Although research has been undertaken on this topic, there are some reasons for extending the investigation. In fact, several scholars point out that VFR involves hosts as well as guests, since both arrange activities and enjoy tourist assets (Backer, 2007; Hänsel & Metzner, 2011; Young et al., 2007). The estimates of expenditure should therefore correspond to the host-guest union and not only to guests as is usually the case.[3] However, this point was not addressed by the Aeolian Islands research.

The average expenditure per capita per night for accommodation-based VFR was about US$53, which was only higher than non-VFR travellers who stayed in owned/time-shared homes (just over US$45). If, however, costs associated with housing are excluded, VFR expenditure gets closer to that of other categories of travellers, especially those who go camping or rent a house/room (respectively, approximately US$63 and US$65 per capita per night).

After grouping trips into the categories of VFR/non-VFR, the average expenditure per night per person for VFRs (net of housing costs) was somewhat lower than for non-VFRs: US$53 for VFRs, US$72 for non-VFRs. In order to compare averages, the Kolmogorov-Smirnov test was first applied, the results of which suggested rejection of the hypothesis of normality. Consequently, the non-parametric Mann-Whitney test was run, which proved significant (p-value = 0.00), indicating that differences between the two groups could not be attributed to chance. Notwithstanding the fact that expenditure data are not usually very reliable and are subject to high non-response rates, for which the Aeolian Islands research is no exception, it seems that it observed a lower expenditure by VFRs over non-VFRs, with the exception of second homes owners.

Research in Cefalù

Between July and September 2005, research was performed in the city of Cefalù, a popular tourist destination located on the northern coast of Sicily, with the same main objective of estimating the number of tourists, as well as the portion attributable to unobserved ones. Unlike the Aeolian Islands, Cefalù is an extended seaside resort town located on the mainland with access by sea and by land, and this prompted a change to the survey design compared with its predecessor. The target population was tourists and excursionists and eventually about 2500 people were interviewed at the locations and times where they were most likely to be found, with intervals determined by systematic sampling adjustment (Mendola & Milito, 2013).

Like the Aeolian Islands, the share of underground tourism in Cefalù proved to be very high, with the quantity of beds available being actually much higher than the official count. A parallel survey conducted on the web on 1 September 2006, showed a total of 1151 unofficial beds compared to 6588 official beds: 175 online unobserved accommodation beds per 1000 official ones. This survey was repeated in August 2013 and the results were even more striking: this time the unofficial beds totalled 6518 in comparison with 5665 official beds: 1151 unofficial beds per 1000 official ones. These data are very useful to highlight the role of the Internet in the digital emergence of a significant portion of underground tourism. Apart from the role of the internet, these data allow us to highlight the extent of underground tourism in Sicilian tourist destinations, especially during the high season. How much of this unobserved supply actually accommodates paying tourists or tourists visiting friends or family is of course not known.

As with the Aeolian Islands, accommodation arrangements in Cefalù were also queried, thus permitting identification of accommodation-based

VFR. As the fundamental objective of this research was to estimate underground tourism, motivational aspects were not of particular interest. Unobserved tourists comprised 52.5% of the total number of tourists interviewed. Those staying in free house/room accommodation with friends or family amounted to 17.3% of the total, far more than the situation in the Aeolian Islands. Since travellers were approached during the holiday, expenditure data were not based on expenses actually incurred, but rather those anticipated. The VFRs' expected cost per person per day, excluding housing, was about US$89, this time not below those staying in other accommodation. The expected average cost (per day, per capita) for non-VFR tourists amounted to US$72 and the Mann-Whitney test was significant for the limit of the 5% level (p-value = 0.047). Hence, in contrast with the results from the Aeolian Islands research, research carried out in Cefalù did not reveal lower expenditure for the VFR travellers group.[4]

Research carried out in Cefalù also lends itself to the empirical testing of another research hypothesis.

Hypothesis 5: Seaton and Palmer (1997), Asiedu (2008) and Hänsel and Metzner (2011) suggest that VFR is particularly prevalent among younger people. However, research results have been contradictory on this point. For example Kim *et al.* (2014) argue that while VFR travellers were especially aged 56 years and older in the USA in 2006, in recent years the share of younger VFR travellers has increased. The same authors (2) cite Hu and Morrison (2002) who 'argued that VFR travellers are more evenly allocated among different age groups than non-VFR travellers'. Table 11.5 shows that research in Cefalù contradicts Seaton and Palmer's conclusions, while it supports Hu and Morrison's ones. In fact, the conditional distributions for the kind of travellers by age group look similar. The Goodman and Kruskal's tau index (type of traveller as the dependent variable) is close to zero (Tau = 0.004; p-value = 0.112).

Table 11.5 Distribution of the number of trips by age and category of respondents (row %)

| Age group | Category of traveller | | Totals |
	Accommodation-based VFR	Non-accommodation-based VFR	
<25-year-olds	23 (16.9)	113 (83.1)	136 (100.0)
25–44-year-olds	159 (18.6)	697 (81.4)	856 (100.0)
45–64-year-olds	89 (15.2)	498 (84.8)	587 (100.0)
>65-year-olds	13 (27.1)	35 (72.9)	48 (100.0)
Totals	284 (17.5)	1343 (82.5)	1627 (100.0)

Source: Sample survey on unobserved tourism in Cefalù, year 2005.

The investigation on intra-destination mobility in Sicily

Between Summer 2009 and Spring 2010, a border sample survey was carried out in Sicily at the main exit points from the island: ports and airports and the ferry stations along the Straits of Messina. This time, the main research objective was to analyse intra-destination tourist mobility, i.e. within Sicily (which is commonly considered a single tourist destination). The issue of unobserved tourism remained in the background. The investigation also targeted additional objectives, including the analysis of motivations, behaviours and satisfaction. For this reason, both accommodation and the main reason for the trip were queried. This made it possible to analyse both accommodation and motivational VFR. With respect to accommodation, free housing with friends and relatives was inserted into the broader category of 'free accommodation', which also included the somewhat residual categories of accommodation in the means of transport or outdoors, in nature. While the category of friends and relatives cannot be separated from the other types of free accommodation, it can be reasonably assumed that the latter have very little influence.

The survey was carried out by the construction of a two-stage probabilistic time location sample (Kalton, 1991). In the first stage, certain venue-day-time units (VDTs) were randomly extracted with unequal probabilities; in the second stage, tourists were selected on a systematic basis (De Cantis & Ferrante, 2013). In the end, some 4000 CAPI interviews were conducted. After weighting, they provided information on many more trips. As reported in Table 11.6, VFRs summed together comprise 48.5% of the total. Also in this case, the aggregate of those who are not guests in free housing (non-accommodation-based VFRs), but are in any case motivational VFRs, can be broken down into those staying in fee structures and those staying in own structures. The total of 117,208 subjects is thus divided into 55,195 CVFRs (3.2%), and 62,013 NCVFRs (3.6%).

The survey also investigated the destination image in terms of expected problems prior to the execution of the trip, dedicating a specific section of

Table 11.6 Classification of VFRs for holiday trips in Sicily (total percentages)

Purpose of visit	Accommodation		Totals
	Free accommodation	Other accommodation (non-VFR)	
VFR	405,339 (23.6%)	117,208 (6.8%)	522,547 (30.4%)
Non-VFR	311,276 (18.1%)	886,793 (51.5%)	1,198,069 (69.6%)
Totals	716,615 (41.6%)	1,004,001 (58.4%)	1,720,616 (100.0%)

The cells of progressively darker shades of grey represent, respectively, PVFRs; CVFRs + NCVFRs; EVFRs; non-VFRs. Source: Border sample survey in Sicily, years 2009–2010.

the questionnaire to this aspect. Expected problems were then compared to the problems actually encountered during the holiday in Sicily, in order to assess tourist satisfaction. The greater familiarity with the destination which should characterise VFR travellers (Larsen *et al.*, 2007; Uriely, 2010) should also influence the image of the destination, at least in terms of expected hazards. Investigation of this aspect is of particular interest for Sicily as a tourist destination because of its image, which is strongly influenced by association with the Mafia. Under these conditions, the feeling of insecurity that in some way characterises the tourist experience could be heightened for Sicilian destinations, but dampened for VFR travellers who are familiar with their destination. This leads to the following hypotheses.

Hypothesis 6: Are VFRs less likely than other tourists to expect they will encounter problems while travelling?

Hypothesis 7: Do VFRs feel safer than other tourists?

Hypothesis 8: Do VFRs expect fewer problems with the accommodation than other tourists?

Hypothesis 9: Do VFRs have fewer problems with security than others?

Hypothesis 10: Do VFRs have fewer problems with accommodation than other tourists?

Percentages are given in Table 11.7. For all the variables considered for hypotheses 6–10 testing (in bold), the differences between VFRs and

Table 11.7 Trips by category of respondents and dangers/problems anticipated or experienced (percentages of yes-answers)

	VFRs	Non-VFRs
Expected problems		
– **in general**	18.6	17.8
– regarding infrastructure	15.4	13.9
– **regarding safety**	3.6	6.8
– **regarding accommodation**	0.7	1.7
– regarding interrelations (hospitality, helpfulness)	0.2	0.6
Actually had problems		
– in general	45.0	55.4
– regarding infrastructure	53.3	38.3
– **regarding safety**	8.6	8.5
– **regarding accommodation**	0.6	3.5
– regarding relations	0.6	1.0

non-VFRs, although present, are not very high. The high sample size ensures that chi-square-based tests return results significantly different to zero. However, indices always have very low values. For example, the Goodman and Kruskal's lambda index, which was used in order to quantify the dependency relationships between nominal variables (with the variable 'pertinence group' as an explanatory variable), was always very close to zero. Therefore, it does not seem that assumptions 6–10 are supported by empirical evidence.

Research on the attractiveness of the tourist districts in Sicily

A new border sample survey was conducted at ports and airports in Sicily between June 2012 and February 2013, aimed at tourists who were leaving the island at the end of their vacation. A probabilistic time-location sampling design was performed: in the first stage one week was selected within each climate season; then tourists were surveyed at each data gathering location for the duration of the entire day. The CAPI procedure was performed and 3219 valid interviews were finally obtained. The main objective of the study was to analyse the levels of attractiveness of the 25 tourist districts recently established by the Sicilian Regional Administration with the aim of promoting the management of tourist services from a systemic perspective (Cusimano *et al.*, 2014). The study of attractiveness proved very useful for revealing the characteristics of motivational VFR. With the aim of performing subsequent segmentation of tourists (and to assess how attractive individual districts are for each tourism cluster), the main motivation of the trip was investigated. Motivational VFRs comprised 20.8% of the total.

The 2012 research permitted testing of a number of theoretical assumptions discussed above, together with additional hypotheses.

Hypothesis 5: VFR trips are more popular among younger age groups.
Hypothesis 11: with respect to life cycle, VFR is considered more prominent among young singles or young couples with children who are less than 15 years old. Research carried out in 1986 in New Zealand demonstrated that VFR travels were especially undertaken by young singles (under 25 years old), full nest 1 families (families with pre-school children), full nest 2 families (families with school-age children), solitary survivors (retired) (Lawson, 1991). In their report on the first results of the United Kingdom Tourism Surveys, Seaton and Palmer (1997) arrived at similar results: the majority of VFR travels was undertaken by young singles (up to 34 years old) and young couples or singles (up to 34 years old), but with children under the age of 15, pertaining to life cycle stages defined as I and III. More recently, Backer (2011) has argued that VFR travel is likely to grow in the future with specific reference to singles and older families.

In the 2012 research in Sicily, the composition and characteristics of the holiday group were determined in considerable detail. Nevertheless, age groups were defined as '<25-year-olds' and '25–44-year-olds'. The upper limit of 44 years is clearly above Seaton and Palmer's 35 years. Unlike these authors, the term 'marriage' was substituted by 'couple' which accounts for more cases. Children were grouped into 0–6-year-olds, 6–12-year-olds and more-than-12-year-olds. In contrast to the UK study, the upper limit of 12 was therefore adopted in place of 15.

Hypothesis 12: VFR trips are associated with typical information search patterns. Research has shown that VFRs are less interested in traditional tourism marketing and rely on the advice from their friends/ relatives to source travel information. Morrison, Hsieh and O'Leary (1995), as well as Bieger *et al.* (2005) highlight the importance of informal, personal and non-commercial channels for VFR travel. These authors discuss also the growing role of the internet, which allows users to strengthen personal ties and form new ones within social networks (Mokhtarian *et al.*, 2006). After getting acquainted on the internet, people often decide to meet face to face, therefore organising additional (internet-induced) VFR travel.

Hypotheses 5, 11 and 12 were tested simultaneously through a log-linear model, which allowed multivariate analysis for categorical variables (Agresti, 2007).

The variables included in the model are:

A = Motivational VFR (no/yes);
B = Age below 45 years old (no/yes);
C = Information search (Informal/Internet/Formal);
D = Stages I–III life cycle (no/yes).

The AB/AC/AD/BC/BD hierarchical model fitted data well (Likelihood ratio = 17.543; df = 11, p-value = 0.093). The model is expressed with simplified notation. For example, the AB term indicates the interaction (the relationship) between variables A and B, as well as the inclusion in the model of the main effects of both variables. The model includes the parameters related to hypotheses 5, 11 and 12. It also includes parameters regarding the obvious relationship between age and life cycle stage, as well as between age and information search behaviour. This relationship is not discussed here, as it goes beyond the aims of this chapter. Estimates converged after only seven iterations and are reported in Table 11.8.

Estimates show that the relationship between motivational VFR and life cycle stages, as well as the relationship between motivational VFR and information search are significant. These results can be interpreted by referring to the anti-logarithms of estimates, which consist of odds ratios.

Table 11.8 AB/AC/AD/BC/BD log-linear model: Estimates and p-values

Parameter	Estimate	Std. error	Z	Sig.
Constant	1.353	0.275	4.925	0.000
[B]	0.756	0.233	3.241	0.001
[A]	1.898	0.260	7.313	0.000
[D]	–1.206	0.178	–6.785	0.000
[C]	1.435	0.290	4.952	0.000
[C]	1.639	0.265	6.182	0.000
[A] * [B]	0.146	0.186	0.784	0.433
[B] * [C=1]	0.527	0.232	2.274	0.023
[B] * [C=2]	0.612	0.190	3.219	0.001
[B] * [D]	1.471	0.160	9.206	0.000
[A] * [D]	0.739	0.120	6.162	0.000
[A] * [C=1]	–1.957	0.236	–8.282	0.000
[A] * [C=2]	–0.980	0.227	–4.315	0.000

Source: Authors' analysis of data from the 2012 research on the attractiveness of Sicilian tourist districts.

Given as 1 the ratio between non-motivational VFRs and motivational VFRs in the group of those belonging to stages I and III, this ratio becomes $e^{0.739} = 2.09$ for those who are not in these stages. Consequently, non-VFRs are more numerous (compared to VFRs) among those that do not belong to stages I and III. Passing from those who use formal channels to those who use informal channels, non-VFRs are less numerous (compared to VFRs): $e^{-1.957} = 0.14$. The same is observed when passing from those who use formal channels to those who use the Internet: $e^{-0.980} = 0.37$. It can be concluded that hypotheses 11 and 12 are supported while hypothesis 5 is not. This last outcome essentially confirms results from the survey conducted in Cefalù.

Conclusions

The general category of VFR travel does not constitute a single homogeneous block. The classification of travellers with respect to motivation as well as accommodation categories allows the distinction of VFR travellers into four categories: PVFRs, EVFRs, CVFRs, NCVFRs. The last of these categories enriches and gives further detail to the definitional model by Backer (2012). This chapter has presented some data on the magnitude of VFR in the Italian tourist market. The sample surveys by ISTAT, as well as the 2009–2010 border survey in Sicily, proved to be suitable for classifying VFR on the basis of both the accommodation and motivational criteria. The share of VFR travel always proved to be quite high. The 2009–2010 investigation in Sicily returned an estimate of 48.5%, which is much higher than 35.4% estimated in 2012 by ISTAT for the whole of Italy.

Other small-scale research carried out in Sicily demonstrated that the accommodation-based VFR rate was higher in Cefalù than in the Aeolian Islands but far smaller than in all of Sicily. However, it is worth noting that there are far more populated cities in Sicily than the Aeolian Islands and Cefalù, to which the law formulated by Seaton and Palmer (1997) probably applies:

> The total of VFR tourism to a region and the proportionate concentration of VFR tourism in a region relative to its total tourism and holiday tourism varies in direct proportion to the size and density of the region's population. (349)

Of all the hypotheses formulated on the basis of specific VFR literature, only two were clearly supported (hypotheses 11 and 12), concerning the stage of travellers' life cycles and information search patterns. Hypothesis testing of lower expenditure by VFRs showed conflicting results. The set of data now available on the VFR phenomenon in Italy is substantial, even though data are rarely exploited. For the sake of brevity, in this work it was possible to present just some results with sole reference to trips (not to nights) and to domestic VFR.

Acknowledgements

The author wishes to thank the Italian National Institute of Statistics (ISTAT) for providing access to microdata from the survey 'Holidays and Trips: Trips, Individuals'.

Notes

(1) The validity of these considerations is clearly limited by the fact that they are only based on data for the year 2012.

(2) The relative Shannon's H entropy index measures the lack of uniformity within a frequency distribution. It is calculated by the following formula: $H = \dfrac{-\sum_{i=1}^{k} f_i * \log(f_i)}{\log(k)}$, $0 \le H \le 1$. The index takes the value 0 when all frequencies are concentrated on a single category of the distribution (zero heterogeneity), and 1 if they are equally distributed across all categories (maximum heterogeneity). K is the number of categories of the distribution, and f_i are proportions.

(3) Moreover, there is no reason to believe that CVFRs, staying in paid accommodation exactly like non-VFR travellers, would spend less. However, since only

accommodation VFR was studied, research at the Aeolian Islands did not involve analysis of the expenditure of CVFRs.

(4)   The reliability of these results is however affected by only 25% of answers on spending.

References

Agresti, A. (2007) *An Introduction to Categorical Data Analysis*. Hoboken, NJ: Wiley & Sons.

Alivernini, A., Breda, E., Cannari, L. and Franco, D. (eds) (2013) Il turismo internazionale in Italia: dati e risultati. *Proceedings of the Bank of Italy Conference Held in Rome, Italy, 22 June 2012*. See http://www.bancaditalia.it/pubblicazioni/seminari_convegni/conv-12;internal&action=_setlanguage.action?LANGUAGE=en (accessed 13 April 2014).

Asiedu, A. (2008) Participants' characteristics and economic benefits of visiting friends and relatives (VFR) tourism – An international survey on the literature with implications for Ghana. *International Journal of Tourism Research* 10 (6), 609–621.

Backer, E. (2007) VFR travel: An examination of the expenditures of VFR travellers and their hosts. *Current Issues in Tourism* 10 (4), 366–377.

Backer, E. (2011) VFR travellers of the future. In I. Yeoman, C.H.C. Hsu, K.A. Smith, and S. Watson (eds) *Tourism and Demography* (pp. 73–84). Maidenhead: McGraw-Hill Education.

Backer, E. (2012) VFR travel: It *is* underestimated. *Tourism Management* 33 (1), 74–79.

Bagatta, G. and Perez M. (eds) (2003) *Metodologia e organizzazione dell'indagine multiscopo sulla domanda turistica 'Viaggi e vacanze'*. Rome: ISTAT.

Bieger, T., Beritelli, P. and Laesser, C. (2005) Information behaviour of the VFR market: The case of Switzerland. In A.J. Frew (ed.) *Information and Communication Technologies in Tourism 2005. Proceedings of the International Conference in Innsbruck, Austria, 26–28 January 2005* (pp. 405–416). Wien: Springer.

Capistrano, R.C.G. (2013) Visiting friends and relatives travel, host-guest interactions and qualitative research: Methodological and ethical implications. *Asia-Pacific Journal of Innovation in Hospitality and Tourism* 2 (1), 87–100.

Cusimano, G., Parroco, A.M. and Purpura A. (2014) *I distretti turistici: strumenti di sviluppo dei territori. L'esperienza nella regione Sicilia*. Milano: Franco Angeli.

De Cantis, S. and Ferrante, M. (2013) The sampling design of the survey on incoming tourism in Sicily: a TLS approach. In A.M. Oliveri and S. De Cantis (eds) *Analysing Local Tourism*. (pp. 171–186). Maidenhead: McGraw-Hill Education.

Etzo, I., Massidda, C. and Piras, R. (2013) Migration and outbound tourism: Evidence from Italy. MPRA Paper No. 54173. See http://mpra.ub.uni-muenchen.de/54173/ (accessed 18 April 2014).

Giambalvo, O. (2005) La stima del totale dei turisti non ufficiali nelle Isole Eolie. In A.M. Parroco and F. Vaccina (eds) *Isole Eolie. Quanto turismo?!* (pp. 233–245). Padua: Cleup.

Griffin, T. (2013) Research note: A content analysis of articles on visiting friends and relatives tourism, 1990–2010. *Journal of Hospitality Marketing & Management* 22 (7), 781–802.

Hänsel, M. and Metzner, T. (2011) Visiting friends & relatives (VFR): Ambiguity of an underestimated form of tourism. In A. Papathanassis (ed.) *The Long Tail of Tourism: Holiday Niches and Their Impact on Mainstream Tourism* (pp. 35–44). Wiesbaden: Gabler-Verlag.

Hu, B. and Morrison, A. (2002) Tripography: Can destination use patterns enhance understanding of the VFR market? *Journal of Vacation Marketing* 8 (3), 201–220.

ISTAT (2014a) Multipurpose survey on households: trips, holidays and daily life. See http://siqual.istat.it/SIQual/visualizza.do?id=0098401&refresh=true&language =EN (accessed 13 April 2014).

ISTAT (2014b) Anno 2013: Viaggi e vacanze in Italia e all'estero. See http://www.istat. it/it/archivio/112343 (accessed 18 April 2014).

Jackson, R. (1990) VFR tourism: Is it underestimated? *The Journal of Tourism Studies* 1 (2), 10–17.

Kalton, G. (1991) Sampling flows of mobile human populations. *Survey Methodology* 17 (2), 183–194.

Kim, J.E., O'Leary, J.T., Lee, J. and Nadkarni N. (2014) Travel in the United States: Changes in the VFR phenomena. *GWTTRA Presentations for 'Unmasking the Voice of the Consumer', Denver, April 16–18, 2014*. See http://www.gwttra.com/PDFs/Denver%20 Papers/Changes%20in%20VFR.pdf (accessed 8 June 2014).

King, B.E.M. and Ari Gamage M. (1994) Measuring the value of the ethnic connection: Expatriate travelers from Australia to Sri Lanka. *Journal of Travel Research* 33 (2), 46–50.

Larsen, J., Urry, J. and Axhausen K.W. (2007) Networks and tourism: Mobile social life. *Annals of Tourism Research* 34 (1), 244–262.

Lawson, R. (1991) Patterns of tourist expenditure and types of vacation across the family life cycle. *Journal of Travel Research* 29 (4), 12–18.

Mendola, D. and Milito, A.M. (2013) Sampling in local tourism quantification: Critical issues and field experience. In A.M. Oliveri and S. De Cantis (eds) *Analysing Local Tourism* (pp. 53–64). Maidenhead: McGraw-Hill Education.

Mokhtarian, P.L., Salomon, I. and Handy, S.L. (2006) The impacts of ICT on leisure activities and travel: A conceptual exploration. *Transportation* 33 (3), 263–289.

Morrison, A.M. and O'Leary, J.T. (1995) The VFR market: Desperately seeking respect. *Journal of Tourism Studies* 6 (1), 2–5.

Morrison, A.M., Hsieh, S. and O'Leary, J.T. (1995) Segmenting the friends and relatives market by holiday activity participation. *Journal of Tourism Studies* 6 (1), 48–63.

Murphy, P., Niininen, O. and Sanders D. (2010) *Short-break holidays: A competitive destination strategy.* Gold Coast: CRC for Sustainable Tourism.

Oliveri, A.M. and De Cantis, S. (eds) (2013). *Analysing Local Tourism.* Maidenhead: McGraw-Hill Education.

Oliveri, A.M. and Vaccina, A. (2013) Unobserved tourism and observable on-line tourism accommodation supply. In A.M. Oliveri and S. De Cantis (eds) *Analysing Local Tourism* (pp. 127–144). Maidenhead: McGraw-Hill Education.

Parroco, A.M., Vaccina, F., De Cantis, S. and Ferrante, M. (2012) Multi destination trips: A survey on incoming tourism in Sicily. *Economics: The Open-Access, Open-Assessment E-Journal* 6, 2012–44. See http://www.economics-ejournal.org/economics/ discussionpapers/2012-21 (accessed 18 April 2014).

Ramachandran, S. (2006) Visiting friends and relatives (VFR) market: A conceptual framework. *TEAM Journal of Hospitality & Tourism* 3 (1), 1–10.

Seaton, A. and Palmer, C. (1997) Understanding VFR tourism behaviour: The first five years of the United Kingdom tourism survey. *Tourism Management* 18 (6), 345–355.

Uriely, N. (2010) 'Home' and 'Away' in VFR Tourism. *Annals of Tourism Research* 37 (3), 854–857.

VisitEngland, VisitScotland and Visit Wales (2013) The GB tourist – Statistics 2012. See http://www.visitengland.org/bounce.aspx?PG=/Images/GB%20Tourist%20 2012%20-%2030-08-2013%20-%20FV_tcm30-38527.pdf (accessed 8 June 2014).

Young, A.C., Corsun, D.L. and Baloglu S. (2007) A taxonomy of hosts: Visiting friends and relatives. *Annals of Tourism Research* 34 (2), 497–516.

12 Examining Visiting Friends and Relatives (VFR) Demand in the Emirate of Abu Dhabi, United Arab Emirates

Hamed M. Al Suwaidi, Shabbar Jaffry and Alexandros Apostolakis

Introduction

The development of a new tourism destination and its long-term survival depend on the utilisation of all those features that constitute its comparative advantage over rival tourism destinations. Inter alia, this activity is usually translated into a detailed scrutiny of current and potential tourism demand for that destination. The evidence from the literature indicates that tourism demand analysis usually entails an analysis of consumer preferences, demand segmentation, consumption patterns and touristic motivation. Unsurprisingly, the issue of touristic motivation (purpose of visit) is of greater importance to newly emerging tourism destinations (Ali-Knight, 2011; Lohman, 2004; Young et al., 2007). This is because emerging destinations first need to identify their demand niche.

One newly emerging tourist destination that is seeking to identify its source of comparative advantage is the Abu Dhabi (AD) Emirate in the United Arab Emirates (UAE). Tourism in the UAE generally has been growing at a considerable pace (Hazime, 2011). Within the UAE, tourism development in the Abu Dhabi Emirate in particular has received a lot of attention as a result of focused government action towards economic differentiation and the informed decision to divert sources of revenue (Business Management Middle East, 2012; Ponzini, 2011). This chapter aims to provide evidence that would substantiate the existence of a separate and financially viable segment of tourism demand in Abu Dhabi, United Arab Emirates. The thesis of this chapter is that the Abu Dhabi Emirate is uniquely placed to support a VFR tourism demand market, due to the existence of a sizeable expatriate community, comprised mainly of

Europeans, as well as a strong Middle Eastern segment of demand that travels to the emirate for cultural and religious purposes.

The AD Emirate has invested strategically into tourism in the last 10 years or so in an effort to minimise the economy's heavy dependence on oil and energy. Abu Dhabi is the capital city of the seven United Arab Emirates. With almost 1.5 million residents it is the largest and most prosperous emirate in the United Arab Emirates state (the other six emirates are: Dubai, Sharjah, Ajman, Umm Al Qaiwain, Ras Al Khaimah and Fujairah). Recently, the administration in Abu Dhabi has publicised its intentions to break away from its monoculture economy, which is heavily reliant on oil reserves, by tapping more systematically into the tourism and hospitality industries, following the example of neighbouring Dubai. The leadership of Abu Dhabi intends to build on Dubai's successful practices without repeating the same mistakes (tourism on a mass scale, prostitution and gambling, exclusion of indigenous population from the property market).

However, the efforts of the AD tourism authorities are facing two particular challenges. Until recently, policy makers and planners in AD have had very little exposure to tourism and tourism activity, with all the relevant expertise and experience coming from neighbouring Dubai. However, rather unusually for a Middle East tourism destination, the AD Emirate has been blessed with a strong segment of tourists visiting the area for VFR purposes (Dubai Economic Council, 2009; Nyarko, 2010). This is due to the fact that there is a substantial (mainly European) expatriate community in the emirate as well as a strong Middle Eastern demand to visit the emirate for cultural and religious purposes. Both international markets have strong links with residents in the emirate and are motivated to visit the area.

From a research perspective, the abovementioned situation provides an incentive to study in greater depth the VFR travel tourism demand segment in the AD Emirate. The present chapter draws upon a recent survey-based study of tourism demand in Abu Dhabi. In particular, this chapter seeks to capture patterns of tourist expenditure experienced by visitors in Abu Dhabi.

More specifically, this chapter targets those travellers to AD whose purpose of travel is to visit friends and relatives and also to reside with them during their stay. These comprise an aggregation of the 'pure' and 'exploitative' VFR travellers as identified by Backer (2012), which was discussed in Chapter 5. Hence, the focus of the chapter is to identify particular behavioural traits and other features that distinguish or separate VFRs (based on purpose of visit, i.e. PVFRs and EVFRs combined) from the rest of the tourism demand at the destination. Whilst some chapters in this book, such as Chapter 5 and the previous chapter, discussed VFR based on the three VFR types in the VFR definitional model, this chapter will focus on the aggregation of two VFR types (PVFRs and EVFRs) and identify notable differences between those VFR travellers and overall tourism demand in Abu Dhabi. This will be accomplished by examining their respective socio-demographic profiles and their expenditure patterns within the destination. By substantiating VFR travellers to AD as a distinguishable category of tourism demand, it will be possible for policy makers and planners to target their marketing strategies more effectively and efficiently.

Multivariate Analysis

Based on the aforementioned discussion, the analysis next considers respondent expenditure patterns. Tables 12.2 and 12.3 summarise the respective discussion (Table 12.2 deals with the overall tourist expenditure, whereas Table 12.3 considers VFR traveller expenditure patterns). The dependent variable in these two cases refers to overall daily tourism expenditure while in AD. The dependent variable is broken down into three categories (low, medium and high levels of individual expenditure patterns). Tables 12.4 and 12.5 summarise the findings from the marginal effects analysis considering the two demand groups (overall and VFR in AD). Since the chapter's objective is to identify the variables that affect individual expenditure patterns whilst in AD, and individual expenditure patterns are defined in terms of changes in expenditure patterns that cross several thresholds, the analysis will be considering a multivariate econometric model that allows the dependent variable to be of a discrete nature. As a result, in this empirical examination we make use of the multinomial logistic regression model (MNL), which is mostly used in cases where the dependent variable is discrete and consists of more than two categories.

In order to explain the MNL model that will be used in this investigation, the discussion must first consider the particular outcomes $1, 2,...m$ the dependent variable Yi will assume. In our case the dependent variable assumes three outcomes (categories). These are the low (up to 5000AED), medium (5001AED–17,500AED) and high levels (more than 17,500AED) of individual expenditure patterns (1AED = \$0.28, or €0.20, or £0.16). For the purposes of this investigation, the low spending category is going to be considered as the base for all the econometric estimations. In addition to that, the analysis also defines a set of independent variables, summarised in the matrix **X**. In the case of the MNL model, the discussion estimates a set of coefficients $\beta(2),..., \beta(N)$ that corresponds to each outcome category. Outcome 1 and the set of associated coefficients $\beta(1)$ is used as the base for the empirical investigations. Thus, when outcome Y = 1, then effectively $\beta(1) = 0$. Following that:

$$\Pr(Y=1) = \frac{1}{1+e^{X\beta^{(2)}} + \ldots + e^{X\beta^{m}}}$$

$$\Pr(Y=2) = \frac{e^{X\beta^{(2)}}}{1+e^{X\beta^{(2)}} + \ldots + e^{X\beta^{m}}}$$

....

$$\Pr(Y=m) = \frac{e^{X\beta^{(3)}}}{1+e^{X\beta^{(2)}} + \ldots + e^{X\beta^{(m)}}}$$

Empirical Results

Descriptive analysis

Driven by Seaton and Tagg's (1995) hypothesis regarding different typologies of VFR travellers, the analysis first considers the hypothesis regarding any differences between VFR travellers by purpose of visit and overall tourism demand in AD. Seaton and Tagg (1995) argued that it is not only the distinction between overall tourism demand and VFR tourism demand that should concern managers and policy makers. VFR visitors may also be further distinguished into smaller groups of demand based on their socio-demographic (i.e. age and gender) and attitudinal characteristics (i.e. type of holiday activity). This exercise will contribute to the current discussion in two ways.

- On the one hand, the examination of whether or not there are any marked (statistically significant) differences between the two populations could provide further justification of the whole research undertaking. Given the paucity of research in the field, this empirical investigation will assist in providing further insight on the travel and tourism sector in Abu Dhabi and help policy makers target their marketing strategies more closely.
- On the other hand, it could confirm the validity of claims in the literature regarding the need to differentiate the VFR segment of tourism demand (Backer, 2012; Lehto et al., 2001; Morrison & O'Leary, 1995; Young et al., 2007). In this way, the study would respond to claims by Seaton and Palmer (1997) that further conceptualisation and generalisation is needed. It is noted that relying on percentages alone does not really unmask the true distinguishing features between populations.

As is customary in these cases, the discussion identifies a set of two hypotheses to test. Thus, the null hypothesis is that these two populations are identical over respective characteristics, whereas the alternative hypothesis (H1) assumes that these two populations differ in terms of their respective attributes or characteristics. Hence:

Null (H(0)): P(ALL) = P(VFR) and
Alternative (H(1)): P(ALL) ≠ P(VFR).

The empirical results are summarised in Table 12.1. These indicate that VFR travellers exhibit statistically significant differences as compared to the overall sample (hence, providing evidence to *reject the null* hypothesis)

Table 12.1 Comparison of VFR purpose of visit travellers (PVFR + EVFR) and other travellers (CVFR + non-VFR) in Abu Dhabi

	All tourists (%) (A)	VFR (%) (B)	Ho: P(A) = P(B) H1: P(A) ≠ P(B)	Decision rule accept/reject HO
Length of stay				
Up to 3 days	41.6	18.2	−11.107	Reject
Up to a week	43.4	59.1	7.210	Reject
Up to 2 weeks	11.8	18.2	4.384	Reject
More than 2 weeks	3.4	4.5	1.349	Accept
Place of residence				
Europe	43.4	22.7	−9.710	Reject
North America	7.4	4.5	−1.571	Accept
South America	1.4	0.5	5.725	Reject
Asia	34.8	57.1	10.461	Reject
Australia	5.0	4.5	−0.211	Accept
Africa	7.8	10.6	1.751	Accept
Gender				
Male	70.4	57.6	−6.277	Reject
Female	29.6	42.4	6.277	Reject
Job in hospitality				
Yes	9.2	10.6	0.629	Accept
No	90.6	89.4	−0.380	Accept
Marital status				
Single (not married)	20.2	21.2	0.571	Accept
Divorced	6.8	7.6	0.720	Accept

(Continued)

Table 12.1 (Continued)

	All tourists (%) (A)	VFR (%) (B)	Ho: P(A) = P(B) H1: P(A) ≠ P(B)	Decision rule accept/reject HO
Widowed	2.2	3	1.207	Accept
Separated	5.0	4.5	−0.531	Accept
Co-habiting	3.8	10.6	8.307	Reject
Married	60.6	52	−4.195	Reject
Re-married	1.4	0.5	−1.878	Accept
Age group				
Under 20	0.8	1.5	−3.116	Reject
21–30 years of age	14.6	33.3	11.069	Reject
31–40 years of age	32.8	36.4	2.378	Reject
41–50 years of age	34.2	24.2	−4.903	Reject
51–64 years of age	15.4	3	−8.468	Reject
65+ years of age	2.4	1.5	−1.528	Accept
Education				
Compulsory schooling	6.2	18.2	9.805	Reject
Vocational	8.6	4.5	−3.506	Reject
Degree (BA, BSc)	43.6	54.5	5.012	Reject
Postgraduate (MA, PhD)	38.4	21.2	−8.263	Reject
Other	3.0	1.5	−2.120	Reject
Income				
Low	21.5	15.8	−2.440	Reject
Medium	34.7	48.1	4.674	Reject
High	43.8	36.1	−2.282	Reject

in terms of their length of stay (LoS) at the destination, their gender, their age structure, educational attainment and income distribution. On the other hand, the results suggest that the two populations exhibit similar characteristics (*accept the null* hypothesis) in terms of their marital status (in most of the cases), their professional relationship with the hospitality sector and partly their place of residence. Some of these results make intuitive sense, but for others one needs to turn to the literature for justification and confirmation. For brevity and space limitation reasons the analysis will only consider the cases where the two samples exhibit statistically significant differences.

First, it seems that LoS is one of the most effective ways to distinguish VFR travellers from the rest of tourism demand. The issue of length of stay was also analysed in the previous chapter, revealing interesting differences in trip duration between the different VFR types in Sicily. Length of stay was also discussed in Chapter 3, revealing differences even between VRs and VFs. According to the empirical results presented in Table 12.1, length of stay appears to be a reliable factor to distinguish the behaviour of VFR tourists from the rest of the tourism demand in the destination. This observation is interesting given Lehto et al.'s (2001) and Garcia and Raya's (2008) admittance regarding the short stay nature of VFR travel. However, the empirical results from this investigation seem to align with the conclusions reached by De Menezes et al. (2008) in the sense VFR visitors tend to stay longer as opposed to the rest of visitors in their respective area of investigation.

Similarly, the examination of the gender variable indicates that male and female VFR travellers in AD share some notable differences with the rest of their male and female counterparts. The fact that all but the senior group of VFR travellers in AD appear to exhibit statistically significant differences from the rest of tourism demand in the destination is also a quite provoking piece of information that goes contrary to popular belief (Chen et al., 2013) that VFR activity is mainly the prevalence of middle aged and mature visitors. The evidence from the empirical analysis so far indicates that the VFR phenomenon is even more widely spread across visitors. According to a study by Backer and King (2014) on the VFR phenomenon in Australia, individuals travelling for VFR purposes occupied a much wider demographic base than was originally thought to be the case.

The same applies, even more profoundly, as far as the effect of income variable is considered. The empirical evidence indicates that VFR travellers in AD are statistically different to other visitors. This piece of empirical evidence partly debunks the myth of the insignificant contribution of the VFR segment of tourism demand on host economies. The empirical results in Table 12.1 indicate that VFR travellers can be distinguished from the rest of tourism demand in the case study as far as their income and their financial contribution (either directly or indirectly) to the host economy is concerned. Identifying the precise extent of their contributions will be examined later in the chapter. Overall, this piece of evidence confirms the argument that VFR travellers are not a negligible category of tourism demand and there are valid reasons to be considered as a special segment of tourism demand.

In addition to the abovementioned observation, respondents' educational attainment also seems to exert a statistically significant effect as a discriminant factor between VFR visitors and the rest of visitors to AD. The results signify that VFR travellers differ in terms of their social capital accumulation as compared to the overall tourism demand in AD and hence justify the discussion regarding the identification of the said category as a separate segment of tourism demand in AD.

Econometric Results

In this section, the analysis extends the discussion on the basis of a multivariate analysis that deals with more than two variables simultaneously. The econometric model being used as the methodological tool for this discussion is the multinomial logit (MNL) model. As it was explained above, this is mainly because the dependent variable (expenditure patterns) is discrete, with more than two outcomes (low, medium and high expenditure patterns). The reference (or base) category in all estimations is the category 'low tourism expenditure'. In addition to that, the analysis will also consider marginal effects derived from the estimation of the econometric model. For consistency purposes, the analysis will consider the empirical results from Tables 12.2 and 12.3 organised in terms of sets of explanatory variables.

Table 12.2 Expenditure patterns (all visitors) – β coefficients

	Tourist expenditure (medium)	Tourist expenditure (high)
Constant	−2.080 (.005)***	−.737 (.078)*
Length of stay		
Up to 3 days	1.861 (.000)***	−2.460 (.000)***
Up to a week	2.367 (.000)***	−1.635 (.000)***
Up to 2 weeks	1.058 (.000)***	.304 (.266)
Place of residence		
Europe	−1.322 (.000)***	2.370 (.000)***
North America	−2.259 (.000)***	3.741 (.000)***
Asia	−1.563 (.000)***	1.878 (.000)***
Australia	−1.798 (.000)***	.376 (.579)
Africa	−1.724 (.000)***	2.561 (.000)***
Male	−.395 (.000)***	.040 (.728)
Job in Hospitality	−.781 (.000)***	1.995 (.000)***
Marital Status		
Single (not married)	1.504 (.000)***	−1.171 (.001)**
Divorced	1.030 (.000)***	−.978 (.013)**
Separated	1.908 (.000)***	−1.478 (.000)***
Co-habiting	1.602 (.000)***	−1.111 (.008)**

(Continued)

Table 12.2 (Continued)

	Tourist expenditure (medium)	Tourist expenditure (high)
Married	1.163 (.000)***	–.986 (.005)**
Re-married	1.122 (.000)***	–.799 (.569)
Age group		
21–30 years of age	–.167 (.752)	.948 (.340)
31–40 years of age	–.865 (.099)*	.084 (.320)
41–50 years of age	–1.174 (.026)**	.663 (.129)
51–64 years of age	–1.022 (.0537)	.173 (.565)
65+ years of age	–.153 (.788)	.280 (.569)
Education		
Compulsory schooling	.054 (.822)	.058 (.827)
Vocational	.302 (.169)	–1.611 (.000)***
Degree (BA, BSc)	.304 (.116)	.699 (.000)***
Postgraduate (MA, PhD)	.106 (.408)	.759 (.002)**
Income		
Medium	.699 (.034)**	.671 (.002)***
High	.851 (.005)**	.885 (.001)***
N	4500	
McFadden R2	.268	
LL function	–2668.251	

Length of stay

According to the empirical results in Tables 12.2 and 12.3, a short duration of stay (up to three days) has a negative impact on high expenditure levels for both VFR travellers and the overall tourism demand in AD. Indeed, the results indicate that VFR travellers in AD are less influenced by their duration of stay in the destination as compared to the overall tourism demand. In other words, VFR travellers' expenditure patterns appear to be much less responsive to length of stay, as compared to the overall tourism demand. In actual terms, VFR travellers staying in AD for up to three days are approximately 28.5% less likely to engage in considerable expenditure activity as compared to transit travellers. The corresponding figure for the overall tourism demand is 26.5%. This is an extremely interesting finding for two reasons. On the one hand, the abovementioned evidence confirms earlier findings from the descriptive analysis, where it was argued that LoS

Table 12.3 Expenditure patterns (VFR visitors) – β coefficients

	Tourist Expenditure (Medium)	*Tourist Expenditure (High)*
Constant	−.061 (.460)	−1.312 (.000)***
Length of stay		
Up to 3 days	.457 (.117)	−1.538 (.000)***
Up to a week	1.113 (.000)***	1.434 (.000)***
Up to 2 weeks	1.471 (.000)***	1.837 (.000)***
Place of residence		
Europe	−.544 (.200)	1.899 (.000)***
North America	−.744 (.053)*	1.969 (.000)***
Asia	.741 (.389)	1.291 (.000)***
Australia	−.487 (.271)	.487 (.115)
Africa	−1.189 (.001)***	1.974 (.000)***
Male	−.402 (.526)	1.184 (.000)***
Job in hospitality	1.853 (.000)***	1.440 (.000)***
Marital status		
Single (not married)	−.028 (.159)	−.004 (.947)
Divorced	1.732 (.000)***	.043 (.836)
Separated	.520 (.107)	.497 (.115)
Co-habiting	−1.108 (.000)***	−.284 (.141)
Married	1.135 (.000)***	.695 (.010)*
Re-married	−.941 (.003)***	−.589 (.260)
Age group		
21–30 years of age	−1.4712 (.000)***	−1.962 (.000)***
31–40 years of age	−.955 (.328)	−1.851 (.000)***
41–50 years of age	−1.253 (.000)***	1.772 (.000)***
51–64 years of age	.017 (.896)	.998 (.025)**
65+ years of age	1.710 (.002)***	.460 (.117)
Education		
Compulsory schooling	−.121 (.728)	−1.100 (.000)***
Vocational	−.600 (.109)	.915 (.006)**
Degree (BA, BSc)	.655 (.418)	.333 (.248)
Postgraduate (MA, PhD)	.039 (.158)	1.125 (.000)***

(Continued)

Table 12.3 (Continued)

	Tourist Expenditure (Medium)	Tourist Expenditure (High)
Income		
Medium	1.102 (.001)***	.931 (.023)**
High	1.239 (.000)***	1.125 (.001)***
N	594	
McFadden R2	.189	
LL function	−2189.329	

seems to be an efficient way to discriminate between VFR travellers and the rest of the tourism demand in the area. On the other hand, this piece of empirical evidence confirms the existing evidence in the literature regarding the economic significance of VFR travellers on the host economy and provides solid grounding to the argument that VFR travellers essentially subsidise low (or non-existent) levels of hospitality expenditure with other forms of expenditure in the host economy.

Place of residence

Similar to the conclusion reached through the descriptive analysis earlier on, respondent expenditure patterns do not signify any major differences between the two populations. Thus, with the sole exception of those visitors travelling from Australia (both VFR travellers and the overall sample), all other respondents indicated a positive impact on higher levels of tourism expenditure, as compared to the base category (respondents from South America). What is more, when considering the evidence in Tables 12.4 and 12.5 (marginal effects for overall and VFR segments respectively), one realises that in all but one case (travellers from North America) VFR travellers are more likely to overspend at the destination as compared to the overall tourism demand. Indicatively speaking, respondents travelling from Europe are 42% more likely to spend in AD as compared to the base category (visitors from North America), whereas the corresponding figure for the overall tourism demand at the destination is 25.5%.

A further interpretation of these results reveals an underlying pattern concerning place of residence and expenditure patterns. It is evident that travellers from Europe and Asia (both VFR and overall) tend to spend more heavily as compared to the base category and the rest of their counterparts. Thus, there are two phenomena taking place here simultaneously. On the one hand, VFR travellers from Europe and Asia outspend the overall tourism demand from these respective markets. On the other hand, travellers from Europe and Asia tend to outspend their counterparts in general. Given

Table 12.4 Expenditure patterns (all visitors) – marginal effects

	Tourist expenditure (medium)	*Tourist expenditure (high)*
Constant		
Length of stay		
Up to 3 days	.305 (.000)***	−.265 (.000)***
Up to a week	.438 (.000)***	−.188 (.000)***
Up to 2 weeks	.194 (.000)***	.036 (.287)
Place of residence		
Europe	−.238 (.000)***	.255 (.000)***
North America	−.391 (.000)***	.488 (.000)***
Asia	−.284 (.000)***	.206 (.000)***
Australia	−.329 (.000)***	.044 (.594)
Africa	−.317 (.000)***	.334 (.000)***
Male	−.085 (.000)***	.004 (.727)
Job in hospitality	−.158 (.000)***	.263 (.000)***
Marital status		
Single (not married)	.281 (.000)***	−.117 (.000)***
Divorced	.196 (.031)**	−.098 (.004)***
Separated	.330 (.000)***	−.138 (.000)***
Co-habiting	.284 (.000)***	−.108 (.001)***
Married	.218 (.000)***	−.111 (.005)***
Re-married	.431 (.000)***	−.255 (.000)***
Age group		
21–30 years of age	−.034 (.748)	.013 (.544)
31–40 years of age	−.169 (.074)*	.056 (.322)
41–50 years of age	−.233 (.014)**	.022 (.319)
51–64 years of age	−.203 (.036)**	.010 (.595)
65+ years of age	−.031 (.788)	.067 (.681)
Education		
Compulsory schooling	.011 (.825)	.006 (.828)
Vocational	.061 (.163)	−.147 (.000)***
Degree (BA, BSc)	.062 (.114)	.080 (.000)***
Postgraduate (MA, PhD)	.032 (.405)	.095 (.032)**
Income		
Medium	.021 (.001)***	.221 (.000)***
High	.102 (.000)***	.418 (.000)***

the facts, it seems that there are particular reasons as to why this is the case with respect to these particular markets. Apparently, in AD there is a thriving Asian community, and there is also a big expatriate community from Europe (particularly the UK, the Netherlands and Germany) living and working there. Hence, it seems that the cultural connection (existence of family ties or already established national communities) makes a notable contribution to overall tourism spending at the destination.

Marital status

The empirical evidence derived from the examination of marital status is less straightforward, as compared to the abovementioned discussion. Regarding those respondents in a relationship (co-habiting, married, re-married), the results indicate that their influence among the two populations is not uniform. Overall, those in a formal relationship tend to exhibit a positive and statistically significant influence on medium levels of individual expenditure. In the opposite case, only married VFR respondents indicated a positive relationship with medium expenditure patterns. The same applies in the case of those not in a relationship (single, divorced and separated). Only divorced VFR respondents tend to exhibit similar (positive and statistically significant) expenditure patterns to the overall sample as far as the medium individual expenditure patterns are concerned.

Regarding the other category of tourism expenditure (high levels of individual expenditure patterns), the results are equally mixed. Thus, as far as those in a formal relationship are concerned, their impact over the two sample populations and the two expenditure categories varies. Illustratively, married individuals seem to exert a statistically significant but negative influence on high levels of expenditure in AD overall, but their effect is exactly the opposite for VFR visitors at the same expenditure category (positive and statistically significant).

Age groups

The empirical results derived from Tables 12.2 and 12.3 provide further validity to the findings reported in Table 12.2 above. Hence, as far as the age variable is concerned, VFR respondents seem to differ quite substantially as compared to the overall sample of visitors to AD. More specifically, the empirical results from Tables 12.4 and 12.5 reveal that mature (41 to 64 years of age) and senior (65+ years of age) VFR travellers are more likely to be spending more during their visit in AD as compared to the counterparts from the overall sample. In actual terms, the results from Tables 12.4 and 12.5 reveal that mature VFR travellers are approximately 44% (those in the 41–50 age group) and 21% (those in the 51–64 age group) more likely to engage in heavy expenditure behaviour

Table 12.5 Expenditure patterns (VFR visitors) – marginal effects

	Tourist expenditure (medium)	Tourist expenditure (high)
Constant		
Length of stay		
Up to 3 days	.231 (.219)	−.285 (.000)***
Up to a week	.209 (.000)***	.329 (.000)***
Up to 2 weeks	.328 (.000)***	.491 (.000)***
Place of residence		
Europe	−.129 (.232)	.421 (.000)***
North America	−.128 (.076)*	.485 (.000)***
Asia	−.183 (.439)	.295 (.001)***
Australia	−.320 (.332)	.102 (.485)
Africa	−.293 (.002)**	.467 (.000)***
Male	−.009 (.549)	.311 (.005)**
Job in hospitality	−.317 (.000)***	.383 (.000)***
Marital status		
Single (not married)	−.042 (.185)	−.002 (.599)
Divorced	.418 (.000)***	.089 (.681)
Separated	.299 (.129)	.110 (.219)
Co-habiting	−.295 (.000)***	−.029 (.218)
Married	.327 (.001)***	.129 (.057)*
Re-married	−.171 (.000)***	−.084 (.301)
Age group		
21–30 years of age	−.339 (.000)***	−.322 (.000)***
31–40 years of age	−.200 (.455)	−.302 (.000)***
41–50 years of age	−.211 (.003)**	.438 (.002)**
51–64 years of age	.029 (.592)	.210 (.036)**
65+ years of age	.415 (.000)***	.031 (.567)
Education		
Compulsory schooling	−.031 (.492)	−.228 (.000)***
Vocational	−.219 (.539)	.190 (.005)**
Degree (BA, BSc)	.284 (.384)	.007 (.692)
Postgraduate (MA, PhD)	.040 (.290)	.206 (.007)**
Income		
Medium	.239 (.000)***	.099 (.009)**
High	.285 (.000)***	.198 (.000)***

as compared to their young (21-year-old and younger) counterparts. This finding confirms the point regarding the differentiation of VFR travellers and their consideration as a distinctive category of tourism demand. In addition to that, these results confirm the point identified in Table 12.1 regarding the rejection of the null hypothesis (e.g. that VFR travellers and the rest of the sample are similar in terms of the age structure of each respective group). The practical interpretation of these results suggests that policy and decision makers should actively engage with mature and senior VFR visitors and incorporate them more actively in future marketing and promotion campaigns in AD.

Educational qualifications

The evidence regarding the educational attainment's effect on individual levels of expenditure reveals that the impact is somewhat similar between the two respective groups, albeit with some considerable differentiation among those with strong educational qualifications. This piece of evidence partly confirms the empirical findings from earlier parts of the discussion. On the one hand, it appears that educational attainment has a statistically significant effect only as far as high levels of individual expenditure are concerned. On the other hand, the empirical results indicate that those with high levels of educational attainment (degree and postgraduate degree holders) in both groups are more likely to spend more as compared to their counterparts from the same groups but with lower educational qualifications. So, for example, VFR travellers with a postgraduate degree are 20.6% more likely to engage in heavy expenditure, as compared to their counterparts with no educational qualifications. The corresponding figure for the overall tourism demand with similar educational characteristics is 9.5%. On this basis, one could argue that VFR travellers, alongside other highly educated travellers, do represent a financially rewarding group that practitioners should consider in their marketing campaigns. One could utilise this piece of evidence to extend the argument that VFR visitors represent a segment of tourism demand that is financially worth targeting. In this respect, it makes financial sense to carve, frame and protect this segment of tourism demand in AD, considering its higher willingness to spend when on holidays in AD. All in all, the results indicate that highly educated VFR travellers seem to be spending more at the destination, both in general and when considered against other highly educated groups of visitors.

Income classification

The evidence regarding the impact of the income variable on individual expenditure levels reveals no major surprises. In fact, uniformly all income categories seem to exert a positive and statistically significant effect on expenditure levels (medium and high) for both groups of visitors in AD. Thus, similar to the educational qualifications' case, one could utilise this piece of evidence to extend the argument that, similar to the overall tourism demand, affluent VFR visitors exhibit a higher intention to spend during their stay in AD, as compared to VFR visitors that are not as well off.

Gender

The effect of gender on individual expenditure levels seems to differ between the two groups. On the one hand, males seem to spend less than females as far as medium levels of expenditure are concerned. On the other hand, when it comes specifically to VFR travellers, males tend to spend more than their female counterparts as far as high levels of expenditure in AD are concerned. Again, this piece of evidence signifies the existence of some degree of heterogeneity in behavioural patterns, as far as the VFR travellers' segment is considered.

Professional affiliation

Finally, the inclusion of this variable in the survey design was decided on the basis of better selection of individuals from the tourism and hospitality sectors. The research argument is that those related to the sector would be exhibiting somewhat different behaviour to the rest of the sample. In any case, the empirical results from Tables 12.3 and 12.4 indicate that when it comes to the high level expenditure category, this close professional association with the hospitality sector is beneficial both overall and as far as VFR travellers are concerned.

In the VFR travellers' case, the abovementioned point implies that tourism and hospitality professionals, even when they choose to stay with friends and relatives (as is the case here), tend to spend more than their counterparts with no professional association with tourism and hospitality. Whereas one would assume otherwise, indeed tourism and hospitality professionals do not cut back on their individual expenditure patterns when they decide to reside with friends and relatives. Instead, they seem to substitute accommodation expenditure with other forms of spending in the local economy. This is a quite interesting observation because it suggests that employment in the hospitality sector does not seem to exert any negative effect on the VFR segment's expenditure patterns. Instead, the empirical evidence indicates that professional affiliation operates additively to the impact that the VFR segment exerts on the local/host economy. Hence, it appears that in terms of the local multiplier effect it is not the nature of the accommodation sector that matters the most, but instead the development and potential of the whole local economy that would maximise the industry's economic contribution.

Policy Implications/Recommendations

This section of the analysis deals mainly with the second objective of this chapter, namely the consideration of possible proposals for recommendation. These policy implications and recommendations could inform planners (i.e. destination managers) and practitioners in their decision making process. The analysis of the empirical results generates a number of interesting observations. First and foremost, one has to acknowledge the fact that both the descriptive as well as the econometric analysis of the survey results confirm the existence of heterogeneity among respondents and their preference patterns. The results indicate fairly clearly that the current segmentation between VFR travellers and the rest of tourism demand is indeed valid, corroborating Kotler *et al.*'s (2014) assertion on demand segments being distinctive and tangible. Practically, this observation implies that there is indeed a case for local policy makers and planners to substantiate a separate policy initiative and marketing campaign on VFR travellers in AD. The results considered in the discussion above suggest that AD could benefit from such an initiative. At the same time the empirical results imply that further attention and effort has to be devoted in examining visitors' behavioural patterns while on holidays in AD.

In addition to the heterogeneity argument presented above, there is an additional set of practical implications derived from the empirical results. On the one hand, the results make reference to the particular significance of respondents' place of residence. The fact that Asian and European VFR visitors expressed a higher likelihood to spend significant amounts of money in the local economy implies that managers and practitioners should also capitalise on the immigrant population's cultural proximity to the native culture. The evidence from the literature (Vriens & Hofstede, 2000) supports this point, arguing that any new tourist product or business enterprise that is successfully positioned along consumers' benefits or values (demand side) faces a lower threat of competitive imitation from incumbents (e.g. new tourist destinations). After all, potential visitors tend to affiliate more closely with concepts with which they feel an association (Fullerton, 2003). Potential visitors, especially from expatriate European and Asian communities, may feel closer to indigenous culture and thus more likely to support the incumbent tourism industry. Hence, managers and practitioners should actively promote cultural proximity branding on markets, such as the VFR market, in order to take advantage of the divergence of the population living and working in AD.

Finally, based on the length of stay findings, the empirical results indicate that, despite popular belief, duration of stay is not as significant as once initially thought as far as tourism expenditure is concerned. The empirical results suggest that VFR travellers do not spend proportional to their stay, with transit VFR travellers (less than three days in AD) spending more than those staying for up to three days. Practically, this piece of evidence tends to aligns with the conclusion reached in earlier parts of the discussion. That is, tourism's economic contribution to the host economy is not directly dependent upon length of stay or upscale and lavish hospitality developments. Decision makers and practitioners should ideally be looking to enrich the local tourism product offered by the local economy in order to maximise tourism and VFR travellers' receipts. From this perspective, the policy implications arising from this examination fall in line with those offered by Lehto *et al.* (2001) and Young *et al.* (2007).

Conclusion

This chapter has focused on the examination of VFR travellers in Abu Dhabi Emirate, as a separate case of tourism demand at the destination. This apparent segmentation of tourism demand in Abu Dhabi follows the emirate's intention to focus more on tourism activity as a means to differentiate its sources of revenue and break away from the mono-culture nature of the native economy. On this basis, emirate officials and policy makers should develop an effective way to generate some sort of comparative advantage for the destination. Building on the existence of a strong VFR market (mainly due to European and Asian populations living and working in Abu Dhabi), this chapter has provided evidence regarding the different nature of the VFR market in AD. This chapter has also examined to what extent expenditure patterns between the VFR segments differ from the rest of the tourists in Abu Dhabi. The empirical results provide support for both hypotheses.

First, the descriptive results indicate that VFR travellers to Abu Dhabi illustrate considerable heterogeneity as far as their duration of stay, their gender, their age structure, their educational attainment and the income classification. Second, the empirical evidence from the econometric analysis suggests that the current segmentation between VFR travellers and the rest of tourism demand is indeed valid, corroborating Kotler *et al.*'s (2014) assertion that demand segments are distinctive and tangible. The empirical results also suggest that policy makers and planners should take advantage of the current scale of values (culture and religion) in order to attract more VFR travellers. This is mainly due to the large European and Asian communities currently established in Abu Dhabi. At the same time, the results suggest that in terms of tourism impact from VFR activity, planners and decision makers should focus more purposefully on the enrichment of the local tourism product on offer, as opposed to investing hugely on upscale hospitality development projects. In other words, the interpretation of the empirical results calls for greater attention to pull motivation factors (i.e. through religion and culture) as opposed to push motivation factors (i.e. desire to reside in a lavish hotel).

References

Ali-Knight J.M. (2001) The role of niche tourism products in destination developments. Unpublished PhD thesis, University of Napier.

Backer, E. (2012) VFR travel: It *is* underestimated. *Tourism Management* 33, 74–79.

Backer, E. and King, B. (2014) The demographic dividend of VFR travel: Evidence from Australia. *Global Tourism & Hospitality Conference: Charting the New Path – Innovations in Tourism and Hospitality.* 18–20 May, Hong Kong.

Business Management Middle East (2012) *The Rise of Tourism.* See http://www.busmanagementme.com/article/the-rise-of tourism/ (accessed 13 February 2014).

Chen, K., Liu, H. and Chang F. (2013) Essential customer service factors and the segmentation of older visitors within wellness tourism based on hot springs hotels. *International Journal of Hospitality Management* 35, 122–132.

De Menezes, A.G., Moniz, A. and Vieira, J.C. (2008) The determinants of length of stay of tourists in the Azores. *Tourism Economics* 14 (1), 205–222.

De Vries, M. and Hofstede, F.T. (2000) Linking attributes, benefits and consumer values. *Journal of Marketing Research* 12, 4–10.

Dolnicar, S. and Fluker, M. (2003) Behavioural market segments among surf tourists – Investigating past destination choice. Research paper, University of Wollongong, Faculty of Commerce.

Dubai Economic Council (2009) *Clusters and Dubai's Competitiveness Report.* Dubai Economics Council.

Fullerton, G. (2003) When does commitment lead to loyalty. *Journal of Service Research* 5 (4), 333–344.

Garcia M.E. and Raya, J.M. (2008) Length of stay for low cost tourism. *Tourism Management* 29 (6), 1064–1075.

Hazime, H. (2011) From city branding to e-brands in developing countries: An approach to Qatar and Abu Dhabi. *African Journal of Business Management* 5 (121), 4731–4745.

Kotler, P., Bowen, J. and Makens, J. (2014) *Marketing for Hospitality and Tourism* (6th edn). Boston: Upper Saddle River Pearson

Lehto, X., Morrison, A. and O'Leary, J. (2001) Does the visiting friends and relatives' typology make a difference? A study of the international VFR market to the United States. *Journal of Travel Research* 40, 201–212.

Lohman, M. (2004) New demand factors in tourism. Paper presented at the European Tourism Forum, Budapest, Hungary.

Morrison, A.M. and O'Leary, J.T. (1995) The VFR market: Desperately seeking respect. *Journal of Tourism Studies* 6 (1), 2–5.

Nyarko, Y. (2010) *The United Arab Emirates: Some Lessons in Economic Development.* Working Paper No. 2010/11, United Nations University.

Ponzini, D. (2011) Large scale development projects and star architecture in the absence of democratic politics: The case of Abu Dhabi, UAE. *Cities* 28, 251–289.

Seaton, A.V. and Palmer C. (1997) Understanding VFR tourism behaviour: The first five years of the United Kingdom Tourism Survey. *Tourism Management* 18, 345–355.

Seaton, A. and Tagg, S. (1995) Disaggregating friends and relatives in VFR tourism research: The Northern Ireland evidence 1991–1993. *Journal of Tourism Studies* 6 (1), 6–18.

Vriens, M., and Hofstede, F. T. (2000) Linking attributes, benefits, and consumer values. *Marketing Research* 12 (3), 5–10.

Young, C., Corsun, D. and Baloglou, S. (2007) A taxonomy of hosts: Visiting friends and relatives. *Annals of Tourism Research* 34 (2), 497–516.

13 Do Families Hold the Pacific Together? VFR, Voyaging and New Expressions of Diasporic Networks

Jenny Cave and C. Michael Hall

Introduction

The notion of family is integral to the identity of Pacific Island peoples (Macpherson, 2004). So much so that it can be argued that cross-border relationships and networks of families hold the social fabric of the Pacific together, perhaps even more effectively than governments. This chapter examines this issue in the context of the various factors that contribute to VFR travel and diasporic mobilities in the Pacific.

Oceanic peoples (Melanesian, Polynesian and Micronesian) are highly mobile voyaging peoples for whom connecting and colonising new territories have been the norm for thousands of years. Yet despite recognition of the importance of out-migration and diasporic networks for tourism, research into the substantial visiting friends and relatives (VFR) market in the region is relatively neglected (Hall & Duval, 2004). The relationships between different modes of personal connectivity from pre-colonial through to post-colonial periods, including voyaging, trade, church, employment, communication and transport technologies and media, constitute the organising framework for this chapter. Rather than being seen as separate entities, these factors are seen to both contribute to and be strongly influenced by VFR and their entanglement is regarded as increasing the significance and amount of VFR travel in the foreseeable future, as part of the emergence of transnational families (Rosenau, 2003; Trask, 2010).

As Figure 13.1 illustrates, the mobility of the Pacific peoples has been enabled by a range of factors that have increased their dispersal over time. Importantly, these factors have not only encouraged mobility but several factors, amongst them trade, the church, employment and information communication technologies (ICT), have served to reinforce diasporic

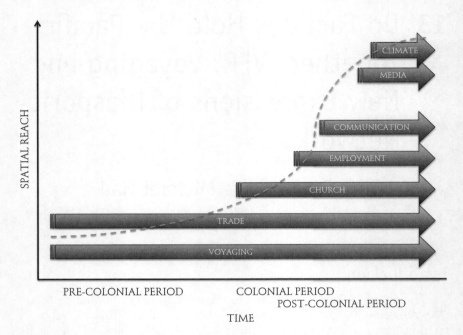

Figure 13.1 Factors contributing to VFR and diasporic mobilities in the Asia-Pacific

relations and hence the movement of people classified in tourism as VFR. This chapter therefore reinforces the understanding of VFR as one particular expression of diasporic populations. In the case of the Pacific, this is grounded in a context where the maintenance of family ties at a distance is integral to being, belonging and identity. To illustrate the Pacific situation, the chapter discusses the various layers of entanglement that contribute to contemporary VFR practice and process.

The Pre-colonial Period

Spanning one-third of the earth's surface, the Pacific Ocean encompasses the geographic region of the globe usually referred to as Oceania (Bier, 2012). Near Oceania includes the continental Melanesian islands of New Guinea, the Solomon Islands, Fiji and Tonga, bordered by the deep trench of the Andesite Line on the edge of the Pacific tectonic plate. Geologically, to the east of the line are the volcanic islands of the central Pacific, formed as tips of mountains above the ocean where the ratio of land mass to sea decreases substantially (Irwin, 2007). Although geographical contextualisation should not be interpreted as a form of environmental determinism, it is clear that the geography of the Pacific has historically provided both barriers and connections for the peoples of Near Oceania.

The key drivers of mobilities in the pre-colonial period are voyaging and trade, around epicentres of geographic and cultural influence. The Pacific Ocean necessitated ocean-going canoe technology, developed within the last 10,000 years, to be able to voyage across it (Howe, 2007). Although Australia and New Guinea were settled by modern human 50,000 years ago, the Pacific Islands were the most difficult to reach and so, in terms of human migration, are some of the most recently settled parts of the world. Five thousand years ago eastward-voyaging Austronesian peoples carried a portable economy of animals (chicken, rat, dog and pig) and plants as they moved across the Pacific as far as West Polynesia and northward into Micronesia (Irwin, 2007). There was an apparent pause for 1000 years at the Andesite Line (Irwin, 2007) until around 2000 BP, when eastward voyaging recommenced.

This is important historical and cultural context, as in contrast to westerners who view the Pacific as a vast ocean sprinkled with a few islands, Pacific peoples see the region as a readily accessed 'sea of islands'(Hau'ofa, 1997). Indigenous economies were based on the competitive production of local foods and ritualised consumables (betel, kava) which underpinned a system of valuables and currencies. Excess food production, beyond the complex exchange within the immediate extended family and social obligations, was transformed into hard wealth (stone and shell currencies; objects such as adzes, ornaments) and soft wealth items (textile valuables such as fibre bundles in Melanesia; fine mats and tapa in Polynesia). But Pacific wealth, familial and interfamilial exchange systems focus upon epicentres of traditional spheres of influence within Melanesia, Micronesia and Polynesia and are linked by long distance voyaging (Howe, 2007; Gibson & Nero, 2008b).

The Colonial Period

The key drivers of mobilities in the colonial period are voyaging and trade, still around epicentres of geographic and cultural influence. However new transport and labour technologies extend the reach of Pacific peoples beyond regional spheres of trade and exchange into new lands under the locus of colonial influence (Samson, 1998; Matsuda, 2004). New communication means, education, new languages and written technologies also transform and facilitate the transmission of ideas – for instance, the translation and printing of bibles and introduction of books, paper and writing utensils. Table 13.1 summarises the primary geopolitical and trade influences in the Oceanic region since the first-documented European exploration of the Pacific, seeking trade routes to the East in the 1500s.

The first European visitors to the Pacific were Portuguese (1525–95), whose ships were thought to be floating islands by early Tahitians. The Spaniard Quiros visited the Cook Islands in 1606. Dutch explorers visited

Table 13.1 Geopolitical influences

	Micronesia, Melanesia	Polynesia
1500s–1850s	Portuguese, Spanish, Dutch	British, French
1850s–WWI	British, German, USA	British, French, German, USA
WWI–WWII	Australia, British, Japan, USA	British, French, USA
Post-WWII–1990s	Australia, USA	Australia, France, New Zealand, USA
Contemporary	Australia, China, Japan, Taiwan, USA	Australia, China, France, Japan, New Zealand, Taiwan, USA

Tonga, New Zealand, Easter Island and Samoa in 1616–1772 but did not explore extensively, though they were influential in Micronesia and Melanesia until the 1850s. In the 18th century, the British and French colonised Polynesia and the Spanish and Dutch were imperial powers in Melanesia and Micronesia. Germany and the United States established bridgeheads in many regions in the 19th century, thus beginning the exchange of people in far flung places (Salmond, 2007) and creating a diaspora of people living beyond national borders and unable to return easily (Banner, 2009). However, the church plays a pivotal role in redirecting diasporan relationships and reinforcing social hierarchies (Porter, 2004).

After the 1850s the Portuguese, Spanish and Dutch withdrew from strategic positions in Melanesia and Micronesia but were replaced by German, British and USA missions. Inter-island cultural mobility expanded during the colonial era and by the mid-19th century, the labour trade extended from work on European and American ships to work in cane fields and sugar plantations in the Pacific and Queensland, Australia (Banivanua-Mar, 2007; Horne, 2007). Some also moved voluntarily to port towns such as Auckland (New Zealand) and Sydney (Australia) to access goods and wages which were sent home, but others were taken against their will in 'blackbirding' (Rediker *et al.*, 2003).

The Oceanic region was dominated until World War I by Britain, France, Germany and the USA. Following World War I, defeated Germany left the Pacific, but Japan and Australia extended their influence to fill the power vacuum in Melanesia and Micronesia until World War II. Post-World War II, until the 1990s, foreign policy and strategic colonial linkages across the region were influenced by Australia and the USA. Today, Britain has largely withdrawn from the Pacific, and France and New Zealand have concentrated their aid development in Polynesia. The network of friends and relatives within Pacific spheres of influence continues to engage, but primarily in regional and post-colonial alliances, thus continuing and expanding the ancient linkages.

European churches established bridgeheads in each of the island groups, profoundly influencing the culture, lifestyle and economies of the Pacific. Islander missionaries mainly moved west to east from the late 19th century prior to World War II, reversing the pre-colonial flows across the Pacific (Lee, 2009). The activities of the various churches also provided new networks of mobility as Pacific peoples become incorporated into the church structures and travelled to receive religious training. The increasing centrality of the church in the lives of many Pacific Islanders also meant that when they travelled for employment the church became an important link back to the home village, contributing to the flow of people and information in the Pacific diaspora, a role maintained to the present day.

The Post-colonial Period

The post-colonial period did not begin in the Pacific until the mid-20th century. Transport technologies such as steam- and diesel-powered ships and then aircraft played an enormously influential role in movements of goods and people over wider ranges of territory as well as conveying new images, representations and understandings of the Pacific to the wider world (see Lansdown, 2006, for an overview of the period). Telegraph, radio and telephone and other technologies enabled communication with family members offshore, to some extent mitigating their absence.

In the post-colonial period, trade and voyaging is extended even further. Circular migration becomes possible because of post-World War transport enabling long-haul travel and real-time communication. Internet-based communication technologies and globally accessible media further reinforce changes in human movement and connectivity. The scope and nature of inward and out-migration is able to shift in complexity, enhancing the movement and interactions of friends and relatives across increasingly borderless social worlds. Yet this mobility continues to engage cultural alliances and remain centred, for the first generation of migrants at least, on cultural spheres that had been initiated millennia ago.

Decolonisation in the Pacific began first in Samoa in the 1960s with independence and continued across the region over the next 20 years, prompting substantial out-migration, especially through post-colonial ties with New Zealand and the United States. However, Britain, Germany and Australia did not open pathways to their colonial countries. More French settlers moved to the prior colonies of France than in the other direction (Lee, 2009). Fijians and Indo-Fijians have moved rapidly and most recently in large numbers to North America, New Zealand and Australia, prompted by industry downturns and political instability as well as demand for skilled health workers, soldiers and technical trades in the Middle East (Lee, 2009).

As Pacific peoples continue to settle distant shores, new foods, technologies, valuables and currencies are incorporated into the traditional brother-sister dyad of exchange which echoes their common Austronesian roots of 5000 years ago (Salmond, 2007). Contemporary Trobriand Island males provide yams for their married sisters and husbands. These are used as food, seed and exchanged for male wealth items and cash. In turn, the sisters provide soft wealth textiles for gifts given at life stage and funeral ceremonies to demonstrate lineage and clan affiliations and ensure political stability between island neighbours (Weiner, 1976). Similar systems exist in Papua New Guinea but there conversion into cash and other goods is connected through pigs exchanged at regional levels (Strathern & Stewart, 1999). The same key relationships are evident in Polynesia. Regional exchanges of food and valuables (fine mats, tapa, canoes, parrot feathers) within Fiji, Tonga and Samoa are essential for connective relationships, regional stability and for trade (Kaeppler, 1978). Similarly, in Micronesia, dispersed matriarchal relationships permit Carolinian atoll dwellers to access high island forest and crop resources from the high islands of Yap (D'Arcy, 2001). Familial exchange systems extend now to new countries and include valuables such as Western goods (tinned foods, equipment and materials) scarce in homeland territories (Gibson & Nero, 2008b). Thus Pacific VFR flows are intrinsically material as well as social in character.

Returning home is characterised by gift giving and exchange that reinforces family ties and broader social networks (Alexeyeff, 2004). As noted by Thomas (1991), the material mobility of objects is deeply entangled with the diaspora in the Pacific. Diasporic relationships facilitate significant inward and outward flows of capital, including remittances, and material goods from family relations in migration destination countries back to family members in the home country and elsewhere within the transnational family network (James, 1997; Besnier, 2004; Lee, 2004). Simultaneously, VFR travel has become even more important as a result of the search for employment.

Migration

During the de-colonisation period of the 1960s, substantial out-migration from Polynesian and Micronesian islands was prompted by the emergence of small Pacific Island nation states, through diasporan ties, especially with New Zealand and the United States (Salmond, 2007). Today, all of the islands maintain some degree of relationship with past colonial powers (Gibson & Nero, 2008b). Yet, migration does not always follow the former coloniser and the flows of people across the Pacific are unevenly spread. For example, the majority of Kiribati emigrate to America, whereas Samoans, Tongans and Fijians move to Asia, New Zealand and Australia (Gibson & Nero, 2007). Political instability and demand for skilled health, military and technical workers has also encouraged mobility from Fiji (Lee, 2009). Historical colonial, church and military relationships mean that Micronesians and Polynesians voyage between Pacific Rim cities in the United States and New Zealand/Australia, their homelands and many other islands. Micronesians, except for Kiribati and Nauru, have assured migrant access to the United States (Ware, 2005). Kiribati and Nauru affiliate to New Zealand (Gibson *et al.*, 2011). As New Zealand citizens, Cook Islanders and Tokelauans are globally mobile. Tongans, Tuvaluans and Samoans have access to Australasia on an annual migrant quota system (Gibson *et al.*, 2011).

Eighty five percent of Oceania's peoples live in Melanesia (Papua New Guinea, Solomon Islands, Vanuatu and Fiji) yet they experience tight border controls and have little chance to migrate (Bedford & Hugo, 2008). Rapid population growth and inter-communal tension, compounded by lack of employment for youth and low education levels, have resulted in several coups and state failures and this populous region is considered both a future labour pool for Australasia and a security threat (Ware, 2005).

Net migration is another indicator of mobility. For instance, New Caledonia and Australia have seen inward migration increases of up to 5%, and Fiji has dropped by around 8% whereas Micronesia, Tonga and Samoa have seen net decreases (out-migration) in the order of 15–19% between 2005 and 2010 (UNPD, 2011). A study of migrant movements in the Pacific showed that around 60% of migrants had moved at least once in the eight years after they had settled and 62% of Pacific nationals had made one to four subsequent moves (Bedford, 2008), indicating a high degree of continued mobility. But the cycles of return and periodic absences deplete family structures and the local workforce, exacerbated by the costs of family education and sustaining homes in two locations (Rohorua *et al.*, 2009). Interruptions occur to inter-generational care continua (Kilkey & Merla, 2013) and knowledge transfers, as young people travel away for education, seek jobs in urban areas and remain where earning potentials are higher. Ironically, departees are precisely those who are most needed at home to maintain the basic subsistence activities of fishing, agriculture and animal husbandry and so significant gaps emerge (Rohorua *et al.*, 2009).

Overall, migration and tourism-related mobility and accessibility patterns have potential long-term implications for VFR travel. The various framing networks and linkages in tourism and migration systems that affect VFR are shown in Table 13.2. Pacific mobilities include short-term trips for employment, education, medical and family events (Hall, 2005), long-term displacements because of ecological or economic reasons (Tabucanon, 2013), returns after long absences (Bedford & Didham, 2001) and roots migration (by people who may never have been to their ancestral homelands) (Levitt, 2009) that follow family and opportunities in a continuous flow (Ley, 2010), creating a form of VFR travel (Janta *et al.*, 2013) which, in the Pacific, is more dependent upon family than friends (Taufatofua & Craig-Smith,

Table 13.2 Framing networks and linkages in tourism/migration systems

Types of linkages	State to state relations	Mass cultural connections	Family and personal networks	Migrant agency activities	Private/corporate sector
Tangible linkages	Trade and financial flows	International media diffusion	Informally channelled remittance flows	Job recruitment and promotional materials	Goods and services flows
	Bilateral economic and technical assistance		Correspondence from migrants	Officially channelled remittances	Investment and banking flows
	Tourist flows	Tourism and place promotion	VFR flows		Business travel and related expenditure
Regulatory linkages	Immigration and emigration policies	Norms governing out-migration	Family obligations	Rules and regulations governing migration process	Airline routes and scheduling
	Temporary worker policies	Societal acceptance of migrants	Community solidarity	Contracts with migrant workers	Legal framework e.g. company law, contracts, tax
	Tourist worker visas		Recipient networks		
Relational linkages	Complementarity of labour supply and demand	Cultural similarity	Relative social status of migrants and non-migrants	Complementarity of agency activities in sending country and receiving country	Clustering of SME firms and micro around companies
	Economic dependency	Compatibility of value systems			Value chain linkages

2009). Laskai (2013) has established that VFR plays an important role in the survival of language and culture and, because of the continuity of motivation to visit, can contribute towards the sustainability of tourism in the long run. Therefore the authors argue that it is families rather than governments that hold the Pacific together.

Yet for national governments, there are many short run benefits of migration for individuals, families and home countries, despite rising unemployment and recession in host countries. Governments have a major role to play in engendering or discouraging diasporan mobility and thus visits by friends and relatives, for example through barriers for out-migration as well as facilitation or barriers for inward mobility (Hugo, 2013).

Migration reduces unemployment (open and disguised), but also produces a loss of skilled resources which hinders development and requires replacement with inwards migration, an exception being the Cook Islands where there has been considerable return migration. In the long term, international migration may produce inequalities for gender, ages, income and quality of life (Connell & Brown, 2005). However, the poor or unskilled are less capable of migrating. Thus inequalities across the Pacific are growing between those who live in urban areas compared to many who remain in rural or urban centres in homeland islands. Hence, the visiting friends and relatives populations tend to be middle and skilled classes rather than the poor.

However, recent temporary seasonal labour schemes have been employed effectively in the Pacific region to extend access to international income earning more widely in the population of Pacific nations (UNESCAP, 2012). While in the past global South to North migration has predominated, today South-South migration is significant and equally important (Henning, 2012). Furthermore, the strength of a small island economy depends directly upon the GDP of its metropolitan patron (Bertram, 2004). On average across the Pacific Islands region, politically integrated units exhibit per capita incomes nine times higher than sovereign island states (Bertram & Karagedikli, 2004) and dependent territories have higher GNP per capita than the sovereign states, even controlling for a range of other factors such as economic structure, island status and aid transfers (Armstrong & Read, 2006).

International labour migration has been used as a way for Pacific nations to reshape their societies and economies, initially in Polynesia and then Micronesia. In the 21st century it is Melanesian countries that have become incorporated in the global flow of skilled migrant workers (Connell, 2010a, 2011). Out-migration has been seen as an opportunity to earn foreign exchange through remittances and transnational enterprise by many small states and is also a safety valve for the 'youth bulge' population explosions in the eastern and central Pacific. Residents of Vanuatu, the Solomon Islands and Papua and New Guinea have been restricted by border controls and experience minimal out-migration. Education levels are low, since 35% of the adult population have never been to school (Gibson & Nero, 2008b). Micronesians, except for Kiribati and Nauru, have assured migrant access to the United States. Population pressures and communal tensions are relieved by continuous out-migration as well as remittances (Ware, 2005).

There are differences too between the Polynesian island nations. As New Zealand citizens, Cook Islanders and Tokelauans are globally mobile, whereas Tongans, Tuvaluans, Samoans and Fijians have some limits placed on their external movements. There are also differences in their educational base. Most Tongan adult migrants come to New Zealand after up to 10 years of schooling, but in the past Tuvaluan and Samoan adults have often arrived as unskilled and labourers (Gibson & Nero, 2008a). This has particular importance in terms of calls from the communities for capacity building and assistance with enterprise potential in a migrant context where English literacy and numeric skills are essential. Specific pathways for eastward Asia-Pacific migration are directed to the oil-rich countries of the Gulf, to West Asia, South-East and North-East Asia and to the Russian Federation.

Pacific Island migrants tend to migrate permanently to settle in countries which have colonial and post-colonial histories with Pacific nations (Gershon, 2007) such as Australia, New Zealand and the USA (UNESCAP, 2012). Migrants tend to stay in the host country even though they express an intention of returning home and produce a substantial flow of remittances (Connell & Brown, 2005). The flow of people has diminished to New Zealand, Australia and the United States during the latter part of the past century as skilled migration was emphasised (Connell & Brown, 2005), economic conditions in host countries have deteriorated and migration regulations have been restructured, hastening return migration (Maron & Connell, 2008). Several island states however have an outflow, rather than inflow, of remittances that reflects both trade and the location of diaspora. For instance, migrants in the Marianas in Micronesia remit to the Philippines and to China. Kiribati and Tuvalu receive remittances from Nauru and remittances move from New Caledonia to Wallis and Futuna (Connell & Brown, 2005).

As a result of these flows, a 'migration culture' is now the norm in Polynesia (Christensen & Gough, 2012) and Micronesia (Nero, 2000), driven by external factors such as international demands for labour and internally by bourgeoning youth populations, rapid urbanisation, rural depopulation and shortages of agricultural land (Connell, 2010b). An equivalent number of Tongans now live in New Zealand as are located on the island archipelago as a whole. More extreme trends can be seen for Niue, Cook Islands and Tokelau (Spoonley, 2000) and are similar for six of the ten Polynesian island nations (Hayes, 2010). As a result, 'home' has become an ambivalent idea for second and third generations now resident in countries around the Pacific Rim (Connell & Brown, 2005).

Cash and non-cash remittances from migrant residents living overseas are the mainstay of the narrowly based small island economies, alongside externally supported state employment and international aid development programmes (Gibson *et al.*, 2011). Yet uncertainty surrounds the diversification of remittances and their continued role in economic exchange over successive generations. Furthermore, future geopolitical shifts across the region will affect where people live and the nature of transnational economic flows (International Migration Institute, 2012).

For much of the 20th century, labour was recruited internationally from the central and eastern Pacific for the extraction of timber and mining, commercial agriculture and fishing. Australia recruited substantial numbers of Melanesians for the sugar industry in the late 19th century. Today, however, there are few waged opportunities and very high numbers of youth and increasing urban drift, coupled with few opportunities for overseas migration (except for New Caledonia whose residents have access to France), leading to social unrest. This creates a major policy dilemma for those countries and their near neighbours such as Australia and New Zealand and a need for the development of regional migration and mobility strategies (Bedford, 2008).

Migrant flows into the Pacific islands have occurred for Chinese and Indian nationals. Indian migrants are prevalent within the Pacific, both in developed countries such as New Zealand and Australia and also in the less developed Pacific Islands such as Fiji where large numbers of migrant workers came to work in the sugar fields. Under British jurisdiction from 1950 to 1970, many semi-skilled Indian workers followed to work on construction projects in Fiji, the Solomons, Vanuatu, Tonga and Kiribati. When these nations became independent, many returned to India, except for those who had married locally (Khadria, 2007).

Communication and transport technologies

International migration across the Pacific has undoubtedly been assisted by international air travel in the 1960s and 1970s which facilitated and stimulated movements (Bedford, 2008), as has the introduction of 'no frills', low cost air carriers in the early 21st century (Gibson *et al.*, 2010; Gross & Luck, 2011; Taua'a, 2013). These have had significant implications for both VFR flows as well as short-term migration. The scale of VFR flows during the period since 1995 is illustrated in Table 13.3. (The table displays VFRs by purpose of visit, which does not capture all VFRs.)

Modern transportation technologies, coupled with stagnating rural economies and increased urbanisation, have increased the opportunity, logic for and incidence of migration in a region of the globe already accustomed

Table 13.3 Inbound arrivals by main purpose (Total and Other Personal Purpose) ('000) 1995–2010

Country		1995	2000	2005	2006	2007	2008	2009	2010
American Samoa	Total	34	44	25	25	..	..	..	..
	OPP	22	28	13	13	..	..	..	..
	%	64.70%	65.10%	52%	52%	..	..	..	..
Australia	Total	3,726	4,931	5,499	5,533	5,645	5,586	5,584	-
	OPP	898	1,423	1,443	1,428	1,509	1,592	1,734	-
	%	24.10%	28.60%	26.20%	25.80%	26.70%	26.70%	31.10%	-
Cook Islands	Total	49	73	88	92	97	95	101	104
	OPP	2	6	12	13	14	13	24	25
	%	4.10%	8.20%	13.60%	14.10%	14.40%	13.70%	23.80%	24.00%
Fiji	Total	318	294	545	549	540	585	542	632
	OPP	34	54	94	103	105	100	98	114
	%	10.70%	18.30%	17.20%	18.80%	19.40%	17.10%	18.10%	18.00%
French Polynesia	Total	172	..	208	222	218	196	160	154
	OPP	8	..	5	5	6	21	19	19
	%	4.70%		2.40%	2.30%	2.80%	10.70%	11.90%	12.30%
Guam	Total	..	1,269	1,185	1,184	1,181	1,092	..	..
	OPP	..	239	210	212	228	247	..	..
	%		18.80%	17.70%	17.90%	19.30%	22.60%		

New Caledonia	Total	86	114	101	100	103	104	99	99
	OPP	16	22	33	30	30	30	30	30
		18.60%	19.30%	32.70%	30%	29.10%	28.80%	30.30%	30.30%
New Zealand	Total	1,409	1,787	2,366	2,409	2,455	2,447	2,448	..
	OPP	427	623	855	886	914	951	985	..
		28.70%	34.90%	36.10%	36.80%	37.20%	38.90%	40.20%	
Samoa	Total	68	87	102	116	122	122	129	..
	OPP	38	46	58	61	66	59	67	..
	%	55.90%	52.30%	65.90%	52.30%	54.10%	48.40%	51.90%	
Solomon Islands	Total	..	5	..	12	14	16	18	..
	OPP	..	..	3	4	5	6	..	..
	%				33.30%	35.70%	37.50%		
Tonga	Total	29	35	..	..	..	..	..	..
	OPP	8	10	..	..	..	..	..	..
	%	27.60%	28.60%						
Vanuatu	Total	44	58	62	68	81	91	101	97
	OPP	7	7	6	6	7	11	6	7
	%	15.90%	12.10%	9.70%	8.80%	8.60%	12.10%	5.90%	7.20%

Source: Derived from UNWTO statistics.
Note: The Other Personal Purpose category consists mainly of VFR travel.

to high levels of short-term, long-term and return voyaging. In the past, migration was circular and associated with seasonal subsistence needs, over short distances. Long-distance, permanent migration was comparatively rare (Connell, 2011). However, today the pattern has reversed, with less emphasis on seasonal migration. Permanent rural-urban migration has tended to be from remote islands with few opportunities to earn income so that central urban islands have become the population core, diminishing the rural populations and delivery of essential services as well as housing and infrastructure (for example water and sanitation). This in turn prompts further migration to the islands' centre (Connell, 2011) but is somewhat offset in island groups where remittances flow from the centre to the periphery. Paradoxically, this maintains centres of traditional knowledge and practice (Connell, 2010b).

Technological advances in communication, transportation and connectivity are 'relative certainties' in the next 20 years for the Pacific (International Migration Institute, 2012). Approximately 60% of Pacific Islanders now have access to a mobile phone and this figure continues to increase (Cave, 2012). Gibson *et al.* (2010) have shown that access to phones and other ICT affects information about the availability of offshore short-term employment opportunities for Pacific Islanders. Although research on the relationships between ICT access and VFR are on-going it is already clear that improved communication connectivity may serve to reinforce family networks and relations. Vaka'uta (2012) reported a case study of a family of 76 individuals that indicated that cultural notions of the nurturing of Vā (the practice of nurturing/reaffirming relationships to maintain a sense of place, space and connectedness) are evident in the online 'activities' (types of exchanges) taking place between members of the same generation and across generations. Family members were networked through Facebook, Skype, email and mobile phone networks. Members were spread across Fiji, Samoa, Tonga, New Zealand, New Caledonia, Australia and USA. The fact that the most active online members were aged between 15 and 37 not only reflects a generation used to connecting in virtual places but perhaps also represents the next stage in an ongoing layering of enablers of mobility, networking and flow by which transnational family relations are maintained, and for whom co-presence is to be found in the VFR experience.

Conclusions

The period since 1990 has seen the entry of China and Taiwan as geopolitical forces across the Pacific region and the re-entry of Japan as an international development partner, seeking strategic trade positioning and access to natural resources from the waters of small, developing Pacific nations. Colonial influences thus have shifted from Western nations in a North-South geopolitical patterning to a reduced European presence, except for France, to concentration by Pacific Rim countries on the mineral, natural and human resources of Oceania and an upsurge of South-South relationships. All these have affected the various entanglements of voyaging people in the Pacific.

Pacific transnational families remain spatially dispersed yet organically linked by social obligation and hierarchies in multiple population nodes (Hayes, 1991). These form a web of international family operations that are circumscribed by culturally specific, interconnected webs of exchanges and kinship that circulate knowledge and resources (Marcus, 1981). Furthermore, Pacific diasporan peoples continually and unconsciously orient themselves epistemologically to homeland islands and have a clear and constant sense of identity as they move around the globe (Diaz & Kauanui, 2001). The Pacific may be seen in this chapter as 'a sea of families', circumscribed by culturally specific, interconnected webs of exchanges and kinship that circulate knowledge and resources (Gershon, 2007) within and across the Pacific Ocean.

For the transnational families of the Pacific, VFR is but one, albeit important, expression of a set of capital, cultural, material and social mobilities that are embedded within one another. Successive generations and new forms of networking and mobility continue to add to their extent and intricacy. This chapter has emphasised that understanding VFR, at least in the Near Oceania and Pacific context, should be seen within a much wider set of historical and contemporary influences that have shaped the Pacific diaspora both internally and externally. In such a situation VFR is a means to give physical expression to the maintenance of transnational family relations and to reinforce that in Pacific cultures identity is found not just in place but also in movement and relationality.

References

Alexeyeff, K. (2004) Love food: Exchange and sustenance in the Cook Islands diaspora. *The Australian Journal of Anthropology* 15 (1), 68–79.

Armstrong, H. and Read, R. (2006) Geographical 'handicaps' and small states: Some implications for the Pacific from a global perspective. *Asia Pacific Viewpoint* 47 (1), 79–92.

Banner, S. (2009) *Possessing the Pacific: Land, Settlers, and Indigenous People from Australia to Alaska*. Cambridge, MA: Harvard University Press.

Banivanua-Mar, T. (2007) *Violence and Colonial Dialogue: The Australian-Pacific Indentured Labor Trade*. Hawaii: University of Hawaii Press.

Bedford, R. (2008) Pasifika mobility: Pathways, circuits, and challenges in the 21st century. In A. Bisley (ed.) *Pacific Interactions* (pp. 85–134). Wellington: Victoria University of Wellington.

Bedford, R. and Didham, R. (2001) Who are the 'Pacific Peoples'? Ethnic identification and the New Zealand census. In C. Macpherson, P. Spoonley and M. Anae (eds) *Tangata O Te Moana Nui* (pp. 21–43). Palmerston North: Dunmore Press.

Bedford, R. and Hugo, G. (2008) *International Migration in a Sea of Islands: Challenges and Opportunities* (vol. 69). Hamilton, Population Studies Centre Discussion Paper, University of Waikato.

Bertram, G. (2004) On the convergence of small island economies with their metropolitan patrons. *World Development* 32 (2), 343–364.

Bertram, G. and Karagedikli, O. (2004) Core-periphery linkages and income in small Pacific Island economies. In J. Poot (ed.) *On the Edge of the Global Economy* (pp. 106–121). Cheltenham: Edgar Elgar.

Besnier, N. (2004) Consumption and cosmopolitanism: Practicing modernity at the second-hand marketplace in Nuku'alofa, Tonga. *Anthropological Quarterly* 77 (1), 7–45.

Bier, J. A. (2012) *Reference Map of Oceania: The Pacific Islands of Micronesia, Polynesia, and Melanesia* (2nd edn). Honolulu: University of Hawaii Press.

Cave, D. (2012) Digital islands: How the Pacific's ICT revolution is transforming the region. *November 2012*, 25. Retrieved from http://www.lowyinstitute.org/publications/digital-islands-how-pacifics-ict-revolution-transforming-region Lowy Institute for International Policy.

Christensen, A.E. and Gough, K.V. (2012) Island mobilities: Spatial and social mobility on Ontong Java, Solomon Islands. *Geografisk Tidsskrift-Danish Journal of Geography,* 112 (1), 52–62.

Connell, J. (2010a) From blackbirds to guestworkers in the South Pacific: Plus ça change. *The Economic and Labour Relations Review* 20 (2), 111–121.

Connell, J. (2010b) Pacific islands in the global economy: Paradoxes of migration and culture. *Singapore Journal of Tropical Geography* 31, 115–129.

Connell, J. (2011) *Small Island States and Islands: Economies, Ecosystems, Change and Migration* (vol. DR16). London: Government Office for Science.

Connell, J. and Brown, R.P.C. (2005) *Remittances in the Pacific: An Overview*. Asian Development Bank.

D'Arcy, P. (2001) Connected by the sea. *Journal of Pacific History* 36, 163–182.

Diaz, V.M. and Kauanui, J.K. (2001) Native Pacific cultural studies on the edge. *The Contemporary Pacific* 13 (2), 315–341.

Gershon, I. (2007) Viewing diasporas from the Pacific: What Pacific ethnographies offer Pacific diaspora studies. *The Contemporary Pacific* 19 (2), 474–502.

Gibson, J. and Nero, K. (2007) *Are Pacific Island Economies Growth Failures? Geo-Political Assessments and Perspectives*. Christchurch: University of Canterbury, Macmillan Brown Centre for Pacific Studies.

Gibson, J. and Nero, K. (2008a) *Pasifika in New Zealand, New Zealand in Pasifika*. Wellington: Institute of Policy Studies, Victoria University of Wellington.

Gibson, J. and Nero, K. (2008b) Why don't Pacific Island countries' economies grow faster? In A. Bisley (ed.) *Pacific Interactions: Pasifika in New Zealand and New Zealand in Pasifika* (pp. 191–244). Wellington: Institute of Policy Studies.

Gibson, J., Rohorua, H., McKenzie, D. and Stillman, S. (2010) Information flows and migration: Recent survey evidence from the South Pacific. *Asian and Pacific Migration Journal* 19 (3), 401–420.

Gibson, J., McKenzie, D. and Stillman, S. (2011) The impacts of international migration on remaining household members: Omnibus results from a migration lottery program. *Review of Economics and Statistics* 93 (4), 1297–1318.

Gross, S. and Luck, M. (2011) Flying for a buck or two: Low-cost carriers in Australia and New Zealand. *EJTIR* 11, 297–319.

Hall, C.M. (2005) Reconsidering the geography of tourism and contemporary mobility. *Geographical Research* 43 (2), 125–139.

Hall, C.M. and Duval, D. (2004) Transnational mobilities of Pacific Islanders resident in New Zealand. In T. Coles and D. Timothy (eds) *Tourism and Diaspora* (pp. 78–94). London: Routledge.

Hau'ofa, E. (1997) The ocean in us. In S. Mishra and E. Guy (eds) *Dreadlocks in Oceania* 1 (pp. 124–148). Suva: Department of Literature and Language, University of the South Pacific.

Hayes, G. (1991) Migration, metascience and development policy in Island Polynesia. *The Contemporary Pacific* 3 (1), 1–58.

Hayes, G. (2010) Maximizing development benefits and minimizing negative impact in the Pacific Islands sub-region. Paper presented at the Workshop on Strengthening National Capacities to Deal with International Migration, 22–23 April 2010, Bangkok. See www.unescapsdd.org.

Henning, S. (2012) *Migration levels and trends: Global assessment and policy implications.* Paper presented at the Tenth Coordination Meeting on International Migration, New York. See http://www.un.org/esa/population/meetings/tenthcoord2012/V.%20 Sabine%20Henning%20-%20Migration%20trends.pdf (accessed 12 December 2013).

Horne, G. (2007) *The White Pacific: US Imperialism and Black Slavery in the South Seas after the Civil War.* Honolulu: University of Hawaii Press.

Howe, K.R. (2007) The last frontier. In K.R. Howe (ed.) *Vaka Moana: Voyages of the Ancestors* (pp. 16–21). Honolulu: University of Hawaii Press.

Hugo, G. (2013) *What We Know about Circular Migration and Mobility.* Washington D.C.: Migration Policy Institute.

International Migration Institute (2012) *Global Migration Futures: Using Scenarios to Explore Future Migration in the Pacific. IMI Policy Briefing 12.* Oxford: University of Oxford.

Irwin, G. (2007) Voyaging and settlement. In K.R. Howe (ed.) *Vaka Moana: Voyages of the Ancestors* (pp. 55–91). Honolulu: University of Hawaii Press.

Janta, H., Cohen, S. and Williams, A. (2013) *Visiting Friends & Relatives: Reconceptualising the Everyday Mobilities Related to Migration.* Guildford: University of Surrey.

James, K. (1997) Reading the leaves: The role of Tongan women's traditional wealth and other 'contraflows' in the processes of modern migration and remittance. *Pacific Studies* 20 (1), 1–27.

Kaeppler, A. (1978) Exchange patterns in goods and spouses: Fiji, Tonga and Samoa. *Mankind* 11 (3), 246–252.

Khadria, B. (2007) Harnessing untapped development potential in the Asia-Pacific Island region through the mobility of skilled Indian workers. *International Journal on Multicultural Societies* 9 (2), 205–218.

Kilkey, M. and Merla, L. (2013) Situating transnational families' care-giving arrangements: The role of institutional contexts. *Global Networks* 14 (2), 210–229.

Lansdown, R. (ed.) (2006) *Strangers in the South Seas: The Idea of the Pacific in Western Thought – An Anthology.* Honolulu: University of Hawaii Press.

Laskai, I. (2013) Exploring the role and nature of 'Visiting Friends and Relatives' tourism in Niue (Unpublished Master of International Tourism Management Thesis). Auckland University of Technology.

Lee, H. (2004) 'Second generation' Tongan transnationalism: Hope for the future?. *Asia Pacific Viewpoint* 45 (2), 235–254.

Lee, H. (2009) Pacific migration and transnationalism: Historical perspectives. In H. Lee and S.T. Francis (eds) *Migration and Transnationalism: Pacific Perspectives* (pp. 7–42). Canberra: ANU E Press.

Levitt, P. (2009) Roots and routes: Understanding the lives of the second generation transnationally. *Journal of Ethnic and Migration Studies* 35 (7), 1225–1242.

Ley, D. (2010) *Millionaire Migrants: Trans-Pacific Life Lines* (pp. 225–250). Chichester: Wiley-Blackwell.

Marcus, G.E. (1981) Power on the extreme periphery: The perspective of Tongan elites in the modern world system. *Pacific Viewpoint* 22, 48–64.

Macpherson, C. (2004) From Pacific Islanders to Pacific people and beyond. In P. Spoonley and D.G. Pearson (eds) *Tangata Tangata: The Changing Ethnic Contours of New Zealand* (pp. 135–155). Southbank: Thomson Dunmore Press.

Maron, N. and Connell, J. (2008) Back to Nukunuku: Employment, identity and return migration in Tonga. *Asia Pacific Viewpoint* 49 (2), 168–184.

Matsuda, M.K. (2004) *Empire of Love: Histories of France and the Pacific*. Oxford: Oxford University Press.

Nero, K. (2000) The meaning of work. *The Contemporary Pacific* 12 (2), 319–348.

Porter, A. (2004) *Religion Versus Empire?: British Protestant Missionaries and Overseas Expansion, 1700–1914*. Manchester: Manchester University Press.

Rediker, M., Pybus, C. and Christopher, E. (2003) *Many Middle Passages: Forced Migration and the Making of the Modern World*. Berkeley: University of California Press.

Rohorua, H., Gibson, J., McKenzie, D. and Martinez, P. (2009) How do Pacific island households and communities cope with seasonally absent members? *Pacific Economic Bulletin* 24 (3), 19–38.

Rosenau, J. (2003) *Distant Proximities: Dynamics beyond Globalization*. Princeton: Princeton University Press.

Salmond, A. (2007) Two worlds. In K.R. Howe (ed.) *Vaka Moana: Voyages of the Ancestors* (pp. 248–269). Honolulu: University of Hawaii Press.

Samson, J. (1998) *Imperial Benevolence: Making British Authority in the Pacific Islands*. Honolulu: University of Hawaii Press.

Spoonley, P. (2000) *Reinventing Polynesia: The Cultural Politics of Transnational Pacific Communities. Working Paper No. 14*. Oxford: Transnational Communities Programme, University of Oxford.

Strathern, A. and Stewart, P. (1999) Objects, relationships and meanings: Historical switches in currencies in Mount Hagen, Papua New Guinea. In D. Akin and J. Robbins (eds) *Money and Modernity: State and Local Currencies in Melanesia* (pp. 164–191). Pittsburgh: University of Pittsburgh Press.

Tabucanon, G.M.P. (2013) An alternative home? ASEAN and Pacific environmental migration. *Cosmopolitan Civil Societies Journal* 5 (1), 19–38.

Taua'a, S. (2013) Tourism issues in the Pacific. In D. Hegarty (ed.) *Politics, Development and Security in Oceania* (pp. 153–165). Canberra: ANU E Press.

Taufatofua, R.G. and Craig-Smith, S. (2009) The socio-cultural impacts of visiting friends and relatives on host communities: A Samoan study. In J. Carlsen, M. Hughes, K. Holmes and R. Jones (eds) *CAUTHE 2009: See Change – Tourism & Hospitality in a Dynamic World* (pp. 1914–1922). Fremantle: Curtin University of Technology.

Thomas, N. (1991) *Entangled Objects: Exchange, Material Culture, and Colonialism in the Pacific*. Cambridge, MA: Harvard University Press.

Trask, B. S. (2010) *Globalization and Families*. New York: Springer.

UNESCAP (2012) Input of the United Nations Economic and Social Commission for Asia and the Pacific to the Tenth Coordination Meeting on International Migration. See http://www.un.org/esa/population/meetings/tenthcoord2012/P9.United%20Nations%20Economic%20and%20Social%20Commission%20for%20Asia%20and%20the%20Pacific.pdf (accessed 14 January 2014).

UNPD (2011) International migration: People. Table 1.9 database. *Statistical Yearbook for Asia and the Pacific* 1, 11–14. See http://www.unescap.org/stat/data/syb2011/index.asp (accessed 14 December 2012).

Vaka'uta, C.K.F. (2012) Cyberspace, place, identity & relationships: Are we digitizing the Vā? Panel presentation on Culture, Education and ICT – Cultural Dynamics of the 21st Century, International Conference on ICT & Oceanian Cultures, University of the South Pacific, Laucala Campus, Suva Fiji, 24 February 2012.

Ware, H. (2005) Demography, migration and conflict in the Pacific. *Journal of Peace Research* 42 (4), 435–454.

Weiner, A. (1976) *Women of Value, Men of Renown*. Austin: University of Texas Press.

Part 3

VFR Travel Futures

14 Local Impacts, Global Prospects: The Future of VFR Travel

Elisa Backer and Brian King

Introduction

In this final chapter, the editors present readers with thoughts about the future of VFR travel, rather than summarise the various preceding chapters. This chapter synthesises the previous discussions about the profiles and characteristics of VFR travellers by considering prospective future trends and research opportunities. The future of VFR is approached thematically and anticipates likely trends on the basis of examples drawn from the various settings that were explored in previous chapters. The link between VFR and events is introduced, in anticipation that this will be an important growth area. There is a brief discussion about citation trends as a means of understanding how research has been developing and will progress. The editors share some ideas about where VFR travel is heading and about industry and research opportunities. Though acknowledging that long-term speculations are possible, they note the statement by Abraham Lincoln that 'the best thing about the future is that it comes only one day at a time'. On the basis that the future of VFR begins today, the chapter adopts a short-to-medium-term outlook on the basis that this will be more meaningful for readers and for future scholarship about VFR travel.

Globalisation and Its Impacts

Evidence that the forces of globalisation continue to impact on the travel and tourism sector, including VFR travel, was provided by the news that international travel movements surpassed 1 billion in a single year (2012). The trend towards more long haul oriented travel has been strengthening global connectivities. The expansion is not only attributable to holiday and business travel, but also to traditional market sources in the developed countries. China recently displaced France as the world's most visited country and now tops the list of outbound and domestic tourism generating countries. Such changes are both a challenge and an opportunity for VFR researchers including VFR. The subjects of existing VFR travel research have been predominantly in the English speaking world. The extension of research written or translated in English into China and other emerging source markets and destinations demands cross-cultural understanding and sophistication. This challenge extends to the publishing world of tourism research which has been increasingly dominated by English, focused around a small number of 'global' publishing houses. The insights that are needed into the world of VFR travel research will need to tap into non-English sources exploring non-English settings. Even within the Western countries generally, and the English speaking countries in particular, more sophisticated research is needed that offers genuine insights into the applicable social structures. Greater dialogue between these different worlds is urgently needed, including the application of appropriate methodologies to understand networking amongst friends and relatives and the worlds that give rise to such networks.

A growing share of global tourism has been emanating to and from developing countries, shifting the historic concentration of tourism movements in the developed nations of Europe and North America. Since family and friendship networks differ markedly across cultures (e.g. people of Confucian background attach particular emphasis to the role of family and family hierarchies) future VFR travel patterns will unquestionably differ from those commonly encountered in the West. Given the strength of family networks in China and in India with their (combined) 2.6 billion people, there is merit in exploring the impacts of these structures on domestic travel, including VFR. There are also ramifications globally. China and India have substantial diasporas which have evolved over centuries and which play an important global role in business and the professions. Many Indian families are large and the population is relatively youthful. If the promise of economic growth arising from economic liberalisation in India is accompanied by falling birth rates, there could be a change in VFR travel patterns as more Indians travel overseas and research on domestic VFR travel becomes a topic of research interest in English language publishing. The demographics of China are very different and the so-called 'one child policy' remains a potent force. Some Chinese families travel in a pyramid – one child, two parents and four grandparents. Though mostly occurring in the domestic sphere, such travel patterns are worthy of examination.

Social Media

The advent of social media in both the developed and, more recently, in the developing world has prompted researchers to place a growing emphasis on understanding the social factors impacting on travel. This marks a shift from the earlier research emphasis on understanding travel motivations through the lens of psychology and the individual which was dominated by empirical and positivist approaches. By definition, the VFR phenomenon is socially driven because it involves a reunion dimension, either with friends or with relatives. Acquiring a deeper understanding of social motives should be particularly beneficial to societies such as those based on Confucian or Hindu principles, namely philosophies focusing less on individualism. Social media platforms facilitate instant communications between both family and friendship networks throughout the travel process, including the planning, travel and reflection stages. It is evident that more in-depth studies on VFR travel that consider social media driven communications will lead tourism scholars to a better understanding of the drivers of human mobility – not confined to leisure and business.

The increasing prevalence of social media will stimulate VFR travel. The formation of family or affinity networks and sharing of images about happy events (for example weddings and other celebrations) will stimulate participation. It is likely that more sophisticated research on social media and tourism will help to overcome some of the previous deficiencies of VFR travel-related research. As has been mentioned in chapters throughout this volume, the VFR travel phenomenon has been underestimated in part because official data have failed to capture the complex motives prompting such travel. Whilst all aspects of travel and tourism research are likely to be impacted by the study of social media, VFR comes from a more disadvantaged starting point and has arguably more to gain.

Commercial Accommodation

Various chapter authors in this book have noted that VFR travellers are active users of commercial accommodation. This has been an overlooked area of research, and the perception that VFRs do not use commercial accommodation has discouraged tourism providers from embracing VFR travel. There is a continuing view that VFRs overwhelmingly stay in the homes of hosting friends and relatives. The editors have identified three studies that have considered the use of commercial accommodation by VFR travellers, but more dedicated research is needed. The first was undertaken by Braunlich and Nadkarni (1995), followed by Lehto et al. (2001). A third study examined the profiles and characteristics of VFRs staying in commercial accommodation (Backer, 2010). Each of these authors has contributed to the present volume. More studies are needed about the use of commercial accommodation by VFR travellers to address industry misunderstandings.

The VFR travel phenomenon is evidently an important contributor to the commercial accommodation sector (Backer, 2010, 2012a; Braunlich & Nadkarni, 1995; Denman, 1988; Hay, 1996; Lehto et al., 2001; McKercher,

1994; Moscardo *et al.*, 2000; Seaton, 1996). VFR travellers are consumers of commercial accommodation (Beioley, 1997; Braunlich & Nadkarni, 1995; Navarro & Turco, 2004) as well as users of accommodation provided in the homes of friends and relatives. The paper by Braunlich and Nadkarni (1995) on 'The importance of the VFR market to the hotel industry' indicated that over one-fifth of VFR travellers in the East North Central region of the USA make use of commercial accommodation. The researchers also concluded that almost 9% of all nights spent in commercial accommodation were attributable to VFR travel. VFR travel is 'small but dependable' according to commercial accommodation operators who are more aware of the segment (Braunlich & Nadkarni, 1995: 38). VFR travel has greater potential as a market segment for commercial accommodation operators when seasonality factors are considered. It is less susceptible to seasonal variations than other forms of tourism (BBC World News, 2009; Hay, 1996; McKercher, 1994, 1995; Seaton & Palmer, 1997; Seaton & Tagg, 1995; Shani & Uriely, 2012). According to McKercher it is the 'one segment that is not affected by seasonality' (1995: 254) and can experience peaks during periods that are traditionally low season for other markets (Seaton & Palmer, 1997). VFR travel has also been acknowledged as holding up better during economic downturns, notably in rural areas (Backer, 2012b; BBC World News, 2009; King, 1996).

Seaton (1996) has identified that the commercial accommodation sector accounts for between 12% and 20% of total VFR expenditures. Morrison *et al.* (2000) also highlighted VFR usage patterns for commercial accommodation, noting that only 78% of VFR travellers to Spearfish, South Dakota stayed with friends and/or family. A significant number of the remaining VFR travellers (22%) are likely to have used commercial accommodation. In considering the role of university students in stimulating VFR trips, Bischoff and Koenig-Lewis concluded that 19% of all overnight visits involved commercial accommodation (Bischoff & Koenig-Lewis, 2007). Research undertaken in the Sunshine Coast (Queensland, Australia) concluded that 26% of VFRs stayed in commercial accommodation (Backer, 2010).

Many of the attributes of VFR travel depend on destination specific characteristics and these have been highlighted in the opening chapter of this volume. Subsequent chapters have highlighted some destination specific characteristics that were apparent in previous research, notably that VFRs are active users of commercial accommodation. In Chapter 5, it was found that almost 16% of VFRs in Australia used commercial accommodation rather than the homes of their friends and/or relatives. As discussed in Chapter 3, the phenomenon of VFRs who stay in commercial accommodation is 'an opportunity for local accommodation brokers'. It was noted that hosts and guests may both 'secretly wish that they or their guests took commercial accommodation'.

Improved documentation of the practice of VFR travellers staying in commercial accommodation can encourage the industry to embrace VFR travel more actively as a market segment. As was revealed in Chapter 2, many DMOs believe that VFR travel offers negligible benefit to their accommodation stakeholders and that on this basis it does not merit their attention or resources. The editors believe that VFRs will make increasing use of commercial accommodation into the future. Whilst the need to reconnect socially with friends and family will remain important, the factors underpinning the trip can be adjusted to ensure the trip is as positive as possible. The advent of the 'social economy' with emerging companies such as AirBnB and Lyft provide a range of accessible accommodation alternatives to the homes of friends and/or relatives. Such ventures are already providing competition for the established commercial accommodation sector and may be a worthy topic of investigation for VFR travel researchers. Staying with friends/relatives is stressful for some and may sometimes be impossible, notably where large families are visiting elderly relatives who reside in small units or aged care facilities. Research is needed to provide a better understanding of the profiles and characteristics of CVFRs.

Events

Events is an emerging sector of the global economy and one that is receiving increasing attention in tourism and hospitality schools. There is an important link with VFR travel. A growing number of event tourism papers have been published in the scholarly literature and are notable international journals (Getz, 2008). A literature review by Getz identified 423 research articles focused on festival studies (Getz, 2010). The relative neglect of VFR travel research (as discussed in Chapter 1) is evident when this is compared with the paltry outputs on VFR travel in tourism journals (Griffin, 2013). As discussed in the next section, it is also evidenced by low citation rates. The link between events and VFR travel offers an opportunity for future researchers as well as for industry. In a study of industry perceptions of events, it was revealed that the proportion of events attendees who were VFRs ranged from 17.5% to 80% (Backer, 2014). Some exploratory research conducted amongst local residents in Victoria, Australia concluded that there is a correlation between VFR travel and events. The following section will outline the study's findings with a view to prompting readers seriously at this link as a future research area.

According to the study, 85.4% of the resident respondents (n=44) reported receiving visits by between 1 and 16 friends and/or relatives from outside the region who stayed at least one night over the previous 12 months and attended tourism-related events within the region. Most respondents (95.1%) reported that their VFR travellers had attended family events such as weddings, significant birthdays and anniversaries. A further 84.1% of respondents reported travelling outside their home region to visit friends and/or relatives over the previous 12 months and staying at least overnight (either with the friend/relative or in commercial accommodation). Over half of these occasions (54.5%) involved attending a tourism event during a VFR-related trip. Though 29.5% of the respondents indicated that the presence of friends and/or relatives in the destination was not relevant to their attendance at the event, 13.6% described the VFR element as a 'minor' influence, 36.4% as a 'moderate' influence and 18.2% as a 'strong' influence. A further 2.3% stated that VFR was the sole influence and they attended the event exclusively because of the VFR link.

The foregoing summary of a small component of primary research undertaken in 2013 raises as many questions as answers. It does however point to a link between VFR and events, albeit based on a small sample in a single Australian locality. It is, however, unsurprising that the VFR events connection has been neglected as a field of study. In view of the growing interest in events, the connection appears to be worthy of further investigation. It would be particularly useful to understand the link between VFR and various types of event, as well as the extent to which events stimulate VFR. For example, were VFR trips motivated by a desire to attend community or family events, or were they just 'catch up' VFR experiences? The editors believe that these are worthwhile questions.

Citations

The paucity of relevant citations provides a quantitative indicator of the lack of respect that academics have afforded to the VFR travel phenomenon. Table 14.1 lists examples of various VFR-specific publications, highlighting the relatively low numbers of citations over an extended period. The table is not exhaustive and only represents the various publications listed in the first four pages of Google Scholar that relate to tourism (e.g. not publications in medical journals). On the basis of Table 14.1, the number of citations is modest, particularly when a number of papers were published two decades ago. Jackson's (1990) seminal article has for example only been referenced on 94 occasions and ranks third in the list. Only two publications have exceeded 100 citations – oth in leading journals and by authors who have contributed to this volume. Whilst the number of citations will undoubtedly increase into the future, the slow growth rate will continue to be a problem. If the average number of citations maintains its current trend, it is evident that VFR travel is still being neglected by researchers.

Table 14.1 Citations of VFR travel publications

Author	Year	Article	Journal	Citations
Jackson, Richard	(1990)	VFR tourism: Is it underestimated?	Journal of Tourism Studies	94
Paci, Enzo	(1994)	The major international VFR markets	Travel & Tourism Analyst	45
Braunlich, Carl Nadkarni, Nandini	(1995)	The importance of the VFR market to the hotel industry	Journal of Tourism Studies	53
McKercher, Bob	(1995)	An examination of host involvement in VFR travel	CAUTHE Conference Proceedings	10
Meis, Scott Joyal, Sophie Trites, Anne	(1995)	The US repeat and VFR visitor to Canada: Come again, eh!	Journal of Tourism Studies	50
Morrison, Alastair, Hsieh, Sheauhsing O'Leary, Joseph	(1995)	Segmenting the visiting friends and relatives market by holiday activity participation	Journal of Tourism Studies	60
Yuan, Tsao-Fang, Frigden, Joseph, Hsieh, Sheauhsing, & O'Leary, Joseph	(1995)	Visiting friends and relatives travel market: The Dutch case	Journal of Tourism Studies	51
McKercher, Bob	(1996)	Host involvement in VFR Travel	Annals of Tourism Studies	14
Seaton, Anthony Palmer, Christine	(1997)	Understanding VFR tourism behaviour: The first five years of the United Kingdom tourism survey	Tourism Management	140
Morrison, Alastair Woods, Barbara Pearce, Philip Moscardo, Gianna Sung, Heidi	(2000)	Marketing to the visiting friends and relatives segment: An international analysis	Journal of Vacation Marketing	23

(Continued)

Table 14.1 (Continued)

Author	Year	Article	Journal	Citations
Moscardo, Gianna, Pearce, Philip, Morrison, Alastair, Green, David, O'Leary, Joseph	(2000)	Developing a typology for understanding visiting friends and relatives markets	Journal of Travel Research	102
Lehto, Xinran Morrison, Alastair O'Leary, Joseph	(2001)	Does the visiting friends and relatives' typology make a difference? A study of the international VFR market to the United States	Journal of Travel Research	55
Hu, Bo Morrison, Alastair	(2002)	Tripography: Can destination use patterns enhance understanding of the VFR market?	Journal of Vacation Marketing	40
Pennington-Gray, Lori	(2003)	Understanding the domestic VFR drive market in Florida	Journal of Vacation Marketing	28
Lee, Gyehee, Morrison, Alastair Lehto, Xinran You Webb, Jonathan Reid, Jerome	(2005)	VFR: Is it really marginal? A financial consideration of French overseas travellers	Journal of Vacation Marketing	26
Pearce, Philip Moscardo, Gianna	(2006)	Domestic and visiting friends and relatives tourism	Tourism Business Frontiers (book)	9
Backer, Elisa	(2007)	VFR travel: An examination of the expenditures of VFR travellers and their hosts	Current Issues in Tourism	32

Backer, Elisa	(2008)	VFR travellers – Visiting the destination or visiting the hosts	*Asian Journal of Tourism and Hospitality Research*	20
Backer, Elisa	(2009)	VFR travel: An assessment of VFR versus non-VFR travellers	PhD thesis (SCU)	7
Backer, Elisa	(2010)	Opportunities for commercial accommodation in VFR travel	*International Journal of Tourism Research*	14
Backer, Elisa	(2012)	VFR Travel: it *is* underestimated	*Tourism Management*	28

However, if there is an acceleration in the rate of growth, it may indicate that there is belated recognition of the importance of VFR travel.

Conclusions

The history of VFR scholarship has extended over a quarter century, but there has been relatively slow growth and publications have been relatively few (Griffin, 2013). As outlined in Table 14.1, citations have also been sparse. A continuing challenge for those who advocate on behalf of VFR travel is that it can be sufficiently well explained and understood to win the respect of academics, thereby allowing it to be taught to the tourism marketers and managers of the future. As was discussed in Chapter 5, with VFR travel barely rating more than a cursory mention in core tourism texts and failing even to rate a place in the index of others, it is hardly surprising that VFR travel is regularly omitted from the higher education teaching syllabus for tourism units, resulting in its ongoing neglect. It is to be hoped that the appearance of a dedicated book will allow VFR travel to gain greater respect.

References

Backer, E. (2007) VFR travel – An examination of the expenditures of VFR travellers and their hosts. *Current Issues in Tourism* 10 (4), 366–377.

Backer, E. (2008) VFR travellers – Visiting the destination or visiting the hosts? *Asian Journal of Tourism and Hospitality Research* 2 (April), 60–70.

Backer, E. (2009) VFR travel: An assessment of VFR versus non-VFR travellers. Unpublished PhD thesis, Southern Cross University, Australia.

Backer, E. (2010) Opportunities for commercial accommodation in VFR. *International Journal of Tourism Research* 12 (4), 334–354.

Backer, E. (2012a) VFR travel: It *is* underestimated. *Tourism Management* 33 (1), 74–79.

Backer, E. (2012b) VFR travel: Why marketing to Aunt Betty matters. In H. Schänzel, I. Yeoman and E. Backer (eds) *Family Tourism: Multidisciplinary Perspectives* (pp. 81–92). Bristol: Channel View Publications.

Backer, E. (2014) Industry perceptions of events futures. In I. Yeoman, M. Robertson, U. McMahon-Beattie, E. Backer and K. Smith (eds) *The Future of Events and Festivals*. UK: Routledge.

BBC World News (2009) Family Traffic: Fast Track Programme. See http://news.bbc.co.uk/player/nol/newsid_8040000/newsid_8040900/8040921.stm?bw=bb&mp=wm&news=1&nol_storyid=8040921&bbcws=1# (accessed 13 August 2009).

Beioley, S. (1997) Insights. *Four Weddings, a Funeral and a Holiday – The Visiting Friends and Relatives Market* 8 (7), B1–B15.

Bischoff, E.E. and Koenig-Lewis, N. (2007) VFR tourism: The importance of university students as hosts. *International Journal of Tourism Research* 484 (June), 465–484.

Braunlich, C. and Nadkarni, N. (1995) The importance of the VFR market to the hotel industry. *The Journal of Tourism Studies* 6 (1), 38–47.

Denman, R. (1988) *A Response to the VFR Market: A Response to the English Tourist Board and Regional Tourist Boards.* London: British Tourist Authority.

Getz, D. (2008) Event tourism: Definition, evolution, and research. *Tourism Management* 29 (3), 403–428.

Getz, D. (2010) The nature and scope of festival studies. *International Journal of Event Management Research* 5 (1), 1–47.

Griffin, T. (2013) Research note: A content analysis of articles on visiting friends and relatives tourism, 1990–2010. *Journal of Hospitality Marketing & Management* (June 2013), 1–22.

Hay, B. (1996) An insight into the European experience: A case study on domestic VFR tourism within the UK. In H. Yaman (ed.) *VFR Tourism: Issues and Implications. Proceedings from the Conference held at Victoria University of Technology* (pp. 52–66).

Hu, B. and Morrison, A. (2002) Tripography: Can destination use patterns enhance understanding of the VFR market? *Journal of Vacation Marketing* 8 (3), 201–220.

Jackson, R. (1990) VFR tourism: Is it underestimated? *The Journal of Tourism Studies* 1 (2), 10–17.

King, B. (1996) VFR – A future research agenda. In H. Yaman (ed.) *VFR Tourism: Issues and Implications. Proceedings from the Conference held at Victoria University of Technology* (pp. 85–89).

Lee, G., Morrison, A.M. and Lehto, X. (2005) VFR: Is it really marginal? A financial consideration of French overseas travellers. *Journal of Vacation Marketing* 11 (4), 340–356.

Lehto, X.Y., Morrison, A.M. and O'Leary, J.T. (2001) Does the visiting friends and relatives' typology make a difference? A study of the international VFR market to the United States. *Journal of Travel Research* 40 (2), 201–212.

McKercher, B. (1994) *Report on a Study of Host Involvement in VFR Travel to Albury Wodonga*. Albury-Wodonga.

McKercher, B. (1995) An examination of host involvement in VFR travel. In R. Shaw (ed.) *Proceedings from the National Tourism and Hospitality Conference, 14–17 February 1995. Council for Australian University Tourism and Hospitality Education* (pp. 246–255). Canberra, ACT: Bureau of Tourism Research.

McKercher, B. (1996) Host involvement in VFR travel. *Annals of Tourism Research* 23 (3), 701–703. Charles Sturt University.

Meis, S., Joyal, S. and Trites, A. (1995) The U.S. repeat and VFR visitor to Canada: Come again eh! *The Journal of Tourism Studies* 6 (1), 27–37.

Morrison, A., Hsieh, S. and O'Leary, J. (1995) Segmenting the visiting friends and relatives market by holiday activity participation. *The Journal of Tourism Studies* 6 (1), 48–63.

Morrison, A., Woods, B., Pearce, P., Moscardo, G. and Sung, H. (2000) Marketing to the visiting friends and relatives segment: An international analysis. *Journal of Vacation Marketing* 6 (2), 102–118.

Moscardo, G., Pearce, P., Morrison, A., Green, D. and O'Leary, J.T. (2000) Developing a typology for understanding visiting friends and relatives markets. *Journal of Travel Research* 38 (3), 251–259.

Navarro, R. and Turco, D. (2004) Segmentation of the visiting friends and relatives travel market. *Visions in Leisure and Business* 13 (1), 4–16.

Paci, E. (1994) The major international VFR markets. *EIU Travel & Tourism Analyst* 6, 36–50.

Pearce, P. and Moscardo, G. (2006) Domestic and visiting friends and relatives tourism. In B. Dimitrios and C. Carlos (eds) *Tourism Business Frontiers: Consumers, Products and Industry* (pp. 48–55). Oxford: Elsevier.

Pennington-Gray, L. (2003) Understanding the domestic VFR drive market in Florida. *Journal of Vacation Marketing* 9 (4), 354–367.

Seaton, A. (1996) Making (even more) sense of the AFR category in tourism analysis. In H. Yaman (ed.) *VFR Tourism: Issues and Implications*. Melbourne: Victoria University of Technology.

Seaton, A. and Palmer, C. (1997) Understanding VFR tourism behaviour: The first five years of the United Kingdom tourism survey. *Tourism Management* 18 (6), 345–355.

Seaton, A.V. and Tagg, S. (1995) Disaggregating friends and relatives in VFR tourism research. *The Journal of Tourism Studies* 6 (1), 6–18.

Shani, A. and Uriely, N. (2012) VFR tourism. *Annals of Tourism Research* 39 (1), 421–440.

Yuan, T., Fridgen, J., Hsieh, S. and O'Leary, J. (1995) Visiting friends and relatives travel market: The Dutch case. *The Journal of Tourism Studies* 6 (1), 19–26.

Index